Religion and the New Technologies

Special Issue Editor
Noreen Herzfeld

MDPI • Basel • Beijing • Wuhan • Barcelona • Belgrade

MDPI

Special Issue Editor
Noreen Herzfeld
St. John's University
USA

Editorial Office
MDPI AG
St. Alban-Anlage 66
Basel, Switzerland

This edition is a reprint of the Special Issue published online in the open access journal *Religions* (ISSN 2077-1444) from in 2017 (available at: http://www.mdpi.com/journal/religions/special_issues/new_technologies).

For citation purposes, cite each article independently as indicated on the article page online and as indicated below:

Author 1, Author 2. Article title. *Journal Name*. **Year**. Article number/page range.

First Edition 2017

ISBN 978-3-03842-530-4 (Pbk)
ISBN 978-3-03842-531-1 (PDF)

Table of Contents

About the Special Issue Editor

Noreen Herzfeld, Nicholas and Bernice Reuter Professor of Science and Religion at St. John's University and the College of St. Benedict, holds degrees in Computer Science and Mathematics from The Pennsylvania State University and a Ph.D. in Theology from The Graduate Theological Union, Berkeley. Herzfeld is the author of In Our Image: Artificial Intelligence and the Human Spirit (2002), Technology and Religion: Remaining Human in a Co-Created World (2009), and The Limits of Perfection in Technology, Religion, and Science (2010), as well as numerous articles exploring the intersection between religion and modern technology.

religions

MDPI

Editorial
Introduction: Religion and the New Technologies

Noreen Herzfeld

College of St. Benedict and St. John's University, 207 Peter Engel Hall, St. John's University,
Collegeville, MN 56321, USA; NHerzfeld@CSBSJU.EDU

Received: 17 July 2017; Accepted: 19 July 2017; Published: 21 July 2017

In April 2000, *Wired* published a controversial article entitled "Why the Future Doesn't Need Us" by Joy (2000), co-founder and chief scientist at Sun Microsystems. In this article, Joy called for a moratorium on research in three technological fields—artificial intelligence, nanotechnology, and genetic engineering. He noted that, while we were poised to make rapid technological advances in each of these three areas, our understanding of the ethical questions these technologies would inevitably raise was lagging far behind. Fearing that a convergence of these technologies could be deadly, Joy writes, "We are being propelled into this new century with no plan, no control, no brakes. Have we already gone too far down the path to alter course? I don't believe so, but we aren't trying yet, and the last chance to assert control—the fail-safe point—is rapidly approaching."

The intervening years since Joy's warning have indeed brought significant advances in each of these technologies—Deep Learning, nanobots, CRISPER-Cas9, just to name a few. While a moratorium on their development was never in the cards, Joy was right about one thing. These technologies have huge implications for how human life will unfold, indeed, for what it might mean to be human in the coming decades. Each holds great promise—for new medical cures, for new materials, and for new insights into our world. They will bring great wealth to some and could ease the human condition for many.

However, as Joy warned, each of these technologies also brings the possibility of great peril. Science fiction writers have explored the worst-case scenarios. But we need not go to extremes to find reasons for concern. Artificial intelligence may not surpass human intelligence in the foreseeable future, but it is likely to soon displace many workers from their jobs. Nanotechnology may not end in the whole world converted to "grey goo," as engineer and futurist Eric Drexler once suggested, but we do not know what long term effects nanoparticles, and other technological innovations, could have on the environment. Genetic manipulation may not end in biological warfare, but it is likely to exacerbate the divide between those who can afford it and those who cannot. For good or ill, these technologies will change the way we work, live, think, and love. Thus, it makes sense to approach them from a religious perspective. How do these technologies change our understanding of ourselves, our place in the world, our relationships to one another, the way we face death, or our relationship to God?

These are not new questions. Since the first humans fashioned weapons and clothing and controlled fire, humans have been using technology to master our environment. French philosopher Jacques Ellul describes the purpose of technology as "to defend man" (Ellul 1964, p. 405). Through technology we seek shelter from the elements and from predation, cure from sickness, and ways to make our lives safer, longer, and more comfortable. But our technologies go beyond a defensive role. Early humans also mixed paint and fashioned brushes in order to express their awe of the natural world. Technology provides us with means for communication and creation. Through the three new technologies Joy mentions, we seek not only to make our lives safer and easier but also to create new intelligences or to use genes or atoms as the building blocks of a species or material that has never existed before. In so doing, we risk making fundamental changes to both the world around us and to our very nature as human beings. Are we, therefore, "playing God?" Is this a proper role for us? If it is, how do we exercise such tremendous power wisely, with humility and compassion?

Each of the authors in this volume grapple with one or more of these questions. Ted Peters examines this charge of "playing God" through the lens of CRISPR-Cas9, a technique that allows us to easily edit the genomic sequence, thus opening the door, not only to cures for a variety of genetically based illnesses, but also to the making of new creatures and the enhancing of our own genetic code. Who should regulate this technology? Should religious bodies have a say?

Brian Green points out that through much of history the Catholic (and, thus, Christian) church has paid little attention to technology. This is not to say that the development of technology, and its concomitant ethical issues has gone totally without notice in the Judeo-Christian tradition. Genesis 3–9 provides a digest of stories that examine both the good and the bad effects of several early technological developments—clothing, agriculture, the rise of cities, warfare, transportation. The cautionary tales of Cain and Abel, the Tower of Babel, and the Flood were designed to show the Israelites that when left to their own technological devices, without a covenant with God, things were likely to go from bad to worse. In the face of what could be ecocides climate change, Pope Francis echoes the Genesis lesson in his encyclical *Laudato Si*. Green examines this renewed interest in technology on the part of the Catholic church while Whitney Bauman expands on one of the pope's main points, that it is necessary for us to see ourselves as a bit less exceptional, to examine our human nature in the context of our embeddedness within our environment.

That we are and should remain a part of nature's biological continuum is not a universally accepted stance. Devotees of transhumanism, cryogenics, and artificial intelligence hope to transcend the limitations of our finite and fallible human bodies, either by uploading our minds to computers, or by making a new sort of progeny in intelligent machines. Cory Labrecque contrasts this intentional discarding of the body with the importance of the body that is central to Catholic teaching. Jeffrey Pugh asks whether such machines would truly be our "mind children" or whether something fundamental to our human nature would be lost in a silicon platform. Uploading the mind assumes that what is essential in our self is merely a pattern. Levy Checketts highlights a selection of writers who disagree and suggests that the variety of ways they conceive what is essential in our nature could provide fertile ground for rethinking our religious anthropologies. Brent Waters and Calvin Mercer note that the ultimate goal for many in the transhumanist movement is to fight our ultimate foe—death. Waters examines our desire to control the two endpoints of our lives, birth and death, while Mercer asks whether the movement to cryogenically preserve our bodies in hopes of either a bodily or mental resurrection in some more technologically advanced future is a perversion of the Christian hope in the Resurrection.

The dreams of transhumanism may look like science fiction and be easily relegated to a distant future. But the new technologies are changing our lives here and now. Computers have become ubiquitous. We spend increasing amounts of time staring at screens—shopping, reading, texting, and watching pornography or cat videos. In the meantime, the owners of the sites we visit are scooping up vast quantities of information about us, our habits, our friends and associates, our tastes, and our day to day activities. Michael Fuller raises several ethical questions created by the advent of techniques that allow computers to mine this data for relevant information and patterns, techniques we lump together under the term "big data," and looks to religion for ways to address these issues. Sara Lumbreras highlights a different breeding ground for new ethical issues in the increasing autonomy of our machines. Self-driving cars, drones, robotic care-givers, and autonomous weapons are only a few of the areas in which machines will be making complex decisions without human oversight. This has resulted in the development of the fledgling discipline of machine ethics. Should our machines make strictly utilitarian choices, or do we wish them to have a larger value set that mimics our own? What role should religion play in guiding our programming of these machines? If morality is programmable, such programming is not limited to autonomous machines. Tracy Trothen investigates the ethics of moral bioenhancement, the use of cognitive to influence human decision-making, again raising the question of what moral wisdom is and where it resides.

Do our technologies threaten religion itself? We used to believe in the power of God. Have we replaced that belief with a belief in the power of our own technologies? Several of our authors explore this question—Peters in terms of genetic manipulation, Green in reference to the environment, and Ionut Untea in reference to what produces the experience of awe in our lives today.

Bill Joy ends his warning regarding the potential of our new technologies by observing, "Whether we are to succeed or fail, to survive or fall victim to these technologies, is not yet decided." Indeed. Theologian Reinhold Niebuhr reminds us that we humans tend to overreach, prompted by "the desire to find a way of completing human destiny which would keep man's end under his control and power" (Niebuhr 1996, p. 321). We look to our technologies to give us precisely this control and power. But Niebuhr also noted our capacity for faith that "completes our ignorance without pretending to possess its certainties and knowledge" coupled with our capacity for a humility and contrition that "mitigates our pride without destroying hope" (Niebuhr 1996, p. 321).

Our technologies will keep moving forward. Through them we will inevitably change our world, our selves and our understanding of what we are and what we wish to become. This volume advances an ongoing dialog between religion and technology in the hope that in bringing the wisdom and experience of our forebears together with the aspirations of science and engineering we can find the wisdom to steer those changes well.

Conflicts of Interest: The author declares no conflict of interest.

References

Ellul, Jacques. 1964. *The Technological Society*. New York: Knopf.

Joy, William. 2000. Why the Future Doesn't Need Us. *Wired*. Available online: https://www.wired.com/2000/04/joy-2/ (accessed on 14 July 2017).

Niebuhr, Reinhold. 1996. Human Nature. In *The Nature and Destiny of Man: A Christian Interpretation*. Louisville: Westminster John Knox, vol. 1.

religions

MDPI

Article

Should CRISPR Scientists Play God?

Ted Peters

GTU/CTNS, 2400 Ridge Road, Berkeley, CA 94709, USA; tedfpeters@gmail.com

Academic Editor: Noreen L. Herzfeld

Received: 8 February 2017; Accepted: 5 April 2017; Published: 7 April 2017

Abstract: Will CRISPR usher in a new era of Promethean overreach? CRISPR makes gene editing widely available and cheap. Anti-play-god bioethicists fear that geneticists will play god and precipitate a backlash from nature that could be devastating. In contrast to the anti-play-god bioethicists, this article recommends that laboratory science invoke the Precautionary Principle: pause at the yellow caution light, but then with constant risk-assessment proceed ahead.

Keywords: CRISPR; Cas9; Prometheus; play god; stem cells; bioethics; germline intervention; Precautionary Principle

---

The year 2016 witnessed the World Premier of Liam Scarlett's ballet interpretation of Mary Shelly's *Frankenstein: Or, The Modern Prometheus*. The San Francisco Ballet's *Encore* says, "both book and ballet tell a disturbing, tragic tale about the consequences of abandonment, the risks of tampering with the creation of human life, and, most of all, the power of love, both given and withheld" (San Francisco Ballet 2017, p. 31). Will CRISPR gene editing lead our next generation into a Promethean if not Frankensteinian tragedy?

Sun Microscystems Bill Joy feared such a tragedy in the year 2000 when he wrote, "Our most powerful 21st-century technologies—robotics, genetic engineering, and nanotech—are threatening to make humans an endangered species" (Joy 2000). Joy warned that bio-machines smarter than we *Homo sapiens* would supersede us and then eliminate us. Where Joy was negative, today's transhumanists are positive. Super-biology will lead us to super-intelligence, and super-intelligence to a new post-human species. "Let us cast aside cowardice and seize the torch of Prometheus with both hands," says Transhumanist Manifesto author Simon Young (Young 2006, p. 40). Some fear Prometheus, while others greet the Greek Titan with open arms.

The Promethean hubris of the present generation to create super-intelligence is destined to overreach, to put in place the very mechanisms for our own demise. When we humans play god, nature will retaliate and make us suffer for it. So goes the Promethean myth. So goes the argument of anti-play-god bioethicists. This is not my position. Yet, it is a position repeatedly voiced when the subjects of genomics and genetic engineering are brought up.

Does the Promethean myth apply to gene editing with CRISPR technology? The alarm is already sounding. *Modern Prometheus* is the book title for a light treatment of otherwise heavy science. Science writer Jim Kozubek prophesies that "we will rewrite our own genetic code" (Kozubek 2016, p. 63). Although to date theologians have been *oh hum* about CRISPR, at least one religious spokesperson, Jim Eckman, worries that genetic manipulation might violate the divine image in the human species. This means, ethically, that we should abandon the semi-mythical technological imperative due to fear of another myth, the Promethean myth.

> Human civilization must critically examine the scientific (technological) imperative. Simply because society can pursue a particular medical, reproductive or genetic procedure does not mandate that it must! Especially in the area of genetics, "can" does not mandate "ought." The potential for power and control and its obvious abuse mandates an examination of this

imperative. Perhaps with some of these procedures, such as gene editing, it would be wise to not do them at all. (Eckman 2015)

According to such anti-play-god bioethicists, the yellow caution light means stop, do not race ahead.

We bioethicists find ourselves at a cross roads. What color is the traffic light? The technological imperativists or positive Private-Prometheans want to see a green light, to proceed with speed. The anti-play-god Private-Prometheans want to see a red light, to keep all traffic stopped. The proceed-with-caution bioethicist looks both ways on yellow, but drives forward. I recommend the third.

In what follows I argue for the following: *proceed with caution.* Don't stop. Keep driving ahead while perpetually assessing the risk; watch out for pot holes and avoid swerving into a ditch. This applies to germline intervention as well as somatic genome editing therapy.

Methodologically, I recommend that we proceed with developing and applying CRISPR/Cas9 while invoking the Precautionary Principle (PP). There is no warrant either theologically or ethically for putting up a red stop light to halt this particular technology. Theologically, I observe this: human creativity belongs inherently to the *imago Dei*, because we are created by the God who does new things (Isaiah 65:17). Philip Hefner rightly describes the human being as God's "created co-creator" (Hefner 1993, pp. 35–42). Ethically, I observe this: human relationship to God and to one another belongs inherently to the *imago Dei* (Herzfeld 2002, p. 87), so human creativity must always be thought of in terms of our relationship to self, God, and the world. The implication is this: if gene editing has the potential for improving human health and if gene drive has the potential for restoring the health-giving fertility of our natural environment, then the divine image of God at work in us will lead us to toward embracing CRISPR's benefits. If we think of human society as the divine image on Earth, then our creative advance in human health and ecological health through advancing medical technology would be a morally fitting expression of that divine image.

1. A Conflict of Myths in the Heart of Science

Two myths are competing with one another to grab the attention of the bioethicist, the green light myth of the technological imperative—that is, Prometheus positively interpreted—and the red light myth of anti-play-godism—that is, Prometheus negatively interpreted. The technological imperative is known commonly by its moral command, "if we can do it, then we should do it." The Promethan myth with its heir, Victor Frankenstein, frequently leads to a counter proscription, "thou shalt not play god."

The term *myth* here refers specifically to a conceptual set of presuppositions which frames a domain of discourse; a myth provides a screen or strainer through which information is filtered before it gets formulated. This definition of myth differs from other definitions such as (1) myth is a false story or (2) myth is an account of creation. At the intersection of science and culture, (3) a myth is a conceptual set, a worldview, a persistent framework for interpreting new experience (Peters 2017, pp. 96–97). Regarding CRISPR, the technological imperative partners with the positive interpretation of Prometheus whose hubris or pride led him to steal fire from the gods, while the anti-play-god lesson to be learned from the Promethean myth stands counter.

What is the technological imperative? Ask the super geeks. "The concept that new technologies are inevitable and essential and that they must be developed and accepted for the good of society. This philosophy is naturally promoted by super geeks in high-tech companies" (PC Magazine 2017). The technological imperative and the positive embracing of Prometheus lead to the same moral conclusion: if we can do it, let's do it. The light is green. Proceed with haste. This technological imperative is a myth, an ethical framework which keeps society on an accelerating treadmill toward ever advancing progress for the very sake of progress itself.

The counter to the technological imperative is the Promethean myth with its negative commandment: thou shalt not play god. The light is red. When applied to genetic engineering, the admonition against playing god means, "stop!" Leon Kass, former chair of the U.S. President's Council of Bioethics, puts up such a red stop light. "Not everyone cheers a summons to a post-human future. Not everyone likes the idea of remaking Eden or of man playing God" (The President's Council on Bioethics 2003)

This phrase, "play god," sports at least three meanings. First, to play god means that scientific researchers investigate the inner sanctum of nature, revealing its previously hidden secrets. Second, to play god in the field of medicine is to wield the power of life and death; doctors become godlike to those on whom their very life depends. The third use of this term applies directly to genetic engineering: laboratory scientists play god when they alter life and influence the future evolution of the human species (Peters 2003, pp. 9–15; Peters 2005, pp. 124–25). From within the framework of the Promethean myth, bioethicists put up red lights by commanding: thou shalt not play god! This is not a theological commandment. Rather, it is derived from pagan mythology and applied to secular ethics. Because Zeus put a stop to Prometheus after the Titan had stolen fire from the gods, some of today's ethicists want to put a stop to the unbridled technologization of human life as we have inherited it from our evolutionary past.

Nearly a half century ago pioneer bioethicist Paul Ramsey warned us, "Men ought not to play God before they learn to be men, and after they have learned to be men they will not play God" (Ramsey 1970, p. 138).

More recently theologian Cynthia Crysdale has observed that the moral import of Prometheus' myth is to let nature take its course without technological intervention. "Most people who invoke this language envision a world of nature created by God, with its own distinctive sets of laws. Creation, according to this view, has a certain order instilled in it by God. The counterpart of the admonition that we ought not to play God is the positive injunction to 'let nature take its course'" (Crysdale 2003, p. 245). On the one hand, Crysdale shows respect for this anti-play-god red light. "The valid religious insight here lies in the recognition of the human tendency to overreach ourselves. The caution is against the hubris of the human spirit which assumes no limits." On the other hand, she argues that nature itself is not static but rather is changing and evolving with new things emerging. This means morally that we should take risks to advance the welfare and flowering of our species and our ecosphere. "In a world that is subject to emergent probability, the moral question becomes not whether to 'play God', whether to intervene in nature or not, but which kinds of interventions are legitimate and which kinds are not" (Crysdale 2003, p. 251). In short, take the risk and proceed with caution. "The best we can hope for is to set up new conditions of possibility for what might emerge, with due humility and caution" (Crysdale 2003, p. 256). Crysdale's traffic light is yellow, it appears to me.

Neither the technological imperative nor the Promethean myth are major scriptural themes. In its wisdom literature, the Bible comes close to warning us against Promethean hubris: (Proverbs 16:18) "Pride goes before destruction, and a haughty spirit before a fall." If Allen Verhey is correct in defining distinctively *Christian* bioethics—"Scripture is the measure, the *canon*, for any bioethics that would be Christian. Attention to scripture as somehow normative for bioethics is what makes Christian bioethics Christian" (Verhey 2005, p. 297)—then the Christian bioethicist is not mandated biblically either to adherence or repudiation of one or both myths. Discernment and sound judgment, however, demonstrate the wisdom of precaution.

With regard to CRISPR/Cas9, I would like to avoid such myths and proffer the following mandate: *proceed with caution*. Don't stop. Keep driving ahead, constantly assessing the harm-benefit risk. Watch out for pot holes and avoid swerving into a ditch.

2. Remind Me: What Is CRISPR/Cas9 Again?

Here is what you don't need to know. CRISPR stands for Clustered Regularly Interspaced Short Palindromic Repeats. What does this mean? In the past, our human genomes incorporated palindromic DNA repeats from bacteria and archaea which became an adaptive method for strengthening immune systems. The summary point to get is this: palindromic repeats of DNA base pairs provide targets for the geneticist to shoot at.

The CRISPR archer shoots at these targets with Cas9 arrows. What's Cas9? It's an endonuclease capable of cleaving DNA. When combined with specific RNA in a system it can either insert or delete specific genetic sequences. If Cas9 is the arrow, the CRISPR archer can fire it to a specific target on a DNA strand, cut it, insert a prescribed sequence of nucleotides, and then re-connect the DNA strand. We call this "gene editing" for short.

Here is the upshot. CRISPR/Cas9 technology can be used for highly specific and convenient gene editing, either inserting sequences in target genes, deleting genes, or turning genes off. The overwhelming scientific consensus is that this technology will usher in an age of cheap and easy genetic manipulation. If we don't like the DNA nature has bequeathed us, we can employ CRISPR/Cas9 to edit it to our standards.

There is good reason for our scientists to applaud with vigor. According to Jennifer Doudna, one of the CRISPR pioneers, "The simplicity of CRISPR-Cas9 programming, together with a unique DNA cleaving mechanism, the capacity for multiplexed target recognition, and the existence of many natural type II CRISPR-Cas system variants, has enabled remarkable developments using this cost-effective and easy-to-use technology to precisely and efficiently target, edit, modify, regulate, and mark genomic loci of a wide array of cells and organisms" (Doudna and Carpentier 2014).

Some bioethicists, in contrast to the scientists, are not applauding. Arthur Caplan flashes the yellow caution light. "In addition to the discussion about human germline editing, CRISPR raises or revives many other ethical issues, not all of which concern only humans, but also other species and the environment" (Caplan et al. 2015). George Annas flashes the red light. "The core challenge is what the new technology means to the human species. Is it a technology that affects our understanding of humanity and opens the door to a neo-eugenics agenda that could threaten the survival of the species?" (Annas 2016). If CRISPR/Cas9 threatens species survival, then this warrants a red stop light.

A Promethean transhumanist will grin with glee at this. CRISPR/Cas9 could provide a tool in the tool box the transhumanist needs to build a more intelligent species, a post-human species which will leave today's *Homo sapiens* in the archives of evolutionary history. A bioethicist, on the other hand, trembles with fear that such playing god will lead to a recklessness that might put an end to our species before a superior one can emerge. How should we parse the issues?

3. Therapeutic Editing of Somatic Cells

Rather than threaten the existence of the human species, CRISPR/Cas9 shows promise for cancer researchers to improve human health and wellbeing. Everyday our immune system engages cancer threats with a defense. When the defense is compromised, cancer wins. On the front line is the T cell which, like Achilles, leads the immune system into the battle against cancer. In persons with metastatic non-small lung cancer for whom chemotherapy and radiation have failed, scientists have observed that T cells are sabotaged from within by a Quisling enzyme, PD-1. By sending CRISPR/Cas9 into these T cells, clinicians are hoping to snip out the PD-1 gene and liberate the T cell. The T cell should then triumph once again in the cancer siege (Cyranoski 2016; Kozubek 2016, p. 265; Couzin-Frankel 2016).

What we are talking about here is *somatic genome editing therapy*. As scientists move from theory to clinical application, we can foresee some applications to remove cells—such as blood or bone marrow cells—from a person's body, alter the genomes in these removed cells, and then return them to same individual. Because the edited cells would be outside the body (ex vivo), the success of the editing could be verified before the cells were replaced in the patient. Such ex vivo application of CRISPR/Cas9 technology reduces drastically any risk to the patient's safety.

That's ex vivo editing in the Petri dish outside the body. Such genome editing could also be performed directly in the body (in vivo) by injecting a genome-editing tool into the bloodstream or target organ. There is a risk: gene-editing tools introduced into the body might not find their target gene within the intended cell type efficiently (NASEM 2017, pp. 72–78). The result could be little or no health benefit to the patient, or perhaps even unintended harm. The risk of unintended consequence of in vivo editing is higher than that of ex vivo, prompting increased concern for the patient's safety.

"Despite these challenges, however," say the ethicists studying CRISPR on behalf of the National Academy of Sciences, Engineering, and Medicine (NASEM), "clinical trials of in vivo editing strategies are already under way for hemophilia B and mucopolysaccharidosis I" (NASEM 2017, p. 4).

Safety and efficacy are routine bioethical concerns, and they apply here. Taking safety and efficacy into account, we note that no serious ethical argument is being made to proscribe somatic genome editing therapy (NASEM 2017, pp. 82, 105, 112). NASEM advocates proceeding with caution with somatic genome editing therapy.

4. The Special Case of Germline Intervention

Other prospects give bioethicists nightmares, however. Caplan (above) reminds us of previous bioethical debates over germline intervention (Peters 2003, pp. 145–58). With CRISPR/Cas 9, that debate is back.

The terms used during the era of the Human Genome Project in the 1990s were "germline modification" and "human inheritable genetic modification." Today, "gene editing" could be applied to animal germlines and human germlines, so once again the question arises: is this ethical? "Where ethicists become most concerned is when germ cells are the target of CRISPR. Any changes in the germ cells can be potentially passed down to future generations, essentially introducing those changes into the human population" (Novella 2015).

Here is the way NASEM formulates the issue.

> The technology [of germline modification] is of interest because thousands of inherited diseases are caused by mutations in single genes. Thus, editing the germline cells of individuals who carry these mutations could allow them to have genetically related children without the risk of passing on these conditions...Germline editing is highly contentious precisely because the resulting genetic changes would be inherited by the next generation, and the technology therefore would cross a line many have viewed as ethically inviolable....Policy in this area will require a careful balancing of cultural norms, the physical and emotional well-being of children, parental autonomy, and the ability of regulatory systems to prevent inappropriate or abusive applications.... It would be essential for this research to be approached with caution, and for it to proceed with broad public input. (NASEM 2017, pp. 5, 93–99).

Let me parse the issue. What we are talking about is altering the genetic code in germ cells—in eggs or sperm—that will influence future generations of a given species. Scientifically and ethically, this sounds like a great idea. Suppose we would snip out of the germline the gene for Huntington's disease located on the short arm of chromosome 4. Huntington's is a neurodegenerative disorder leading to mental decline, dementia, uncontrollable body movements, anxiety, depression, and aggression. In 1993, Huntington's was traced to a mutation leading to a trinucleotide repeat—that is, three DNA bases (cytosine-adenine-guanine, or CAG) get repeated multiple times (... CAGCAGCAG ...). So, looking at this, it is reasonable to ask: Should we snip out this allele from the germ cells, so that all children born later will be free of the Huntington's gene? In fact, if scientists do this systematically, we might eliminate Huntington's disease from the human gene pool. And, further, if scientists should perform this task for, say, another 2000 genetically based diseases, then ... what?

Two decades ago, the bioethicists said, "Whoah!" Why? Are the bioethicists heartless? Do bioethicists want to see Huntington's patients suffer? No, that is not the reason. Their judgment was based on what we don't know. What we don't know is the long-term effect of such large-scale changes in the genome. Genes work with other genes and other DNA in delicate systems like Swiss watches, mutually influencing one another. To eliminate one set of gears in an old fashioned Swiss watch would cause it to self-destruct. Might this analogy apply to the human genome? We don't know yet. Without this knowledge, clinical geneticists cannot measure the risk.

Without knowing the level of harm-benefit risk, the question arising among bioethicists is this: should we proceed to modify the germline in human beings (and plants or animals too)? On most days when such questions arise, the average bioethicist can get by with a single-word vocabulary. All he or she needs to do is pronounce the word "No," with emphasis, and the job is done. If a bioethicist were to say, "Yes" too often, he or she would be shunned by colleagues as having sold out to the industry.

I recommend we try this on for size: "Yes, but not yet." That's a longer sentence than merely the word, "No". "Yes, but not yet" might be the most appropriate ethical counsel we could offer to those geneticists attempting to ascertain the risk level of CRISPR editing.

5. Applying the Precautionary Principle to Gene Editing

I recommend that we pause when the yellow light is flashing, but we proceed with our own gene driving. The yellow light should remind us of the PP, originally formulated for ecological ethics but equally applicable to genetics. Here is a UN working definition of the Precautionary Principle.

> When human activities may lead to morally unacceptable harm that is scientifically plausible but uncertain, actions shall be taken to avoid or diminish that harm. Morally unacceptable harm refers to harm to humans or the environment that is threatening to human life or health, or serious and effectively irreversible, or inequitable to present or future generations, or imposed without adequate consideration of the human rights of those affected. The judgment of plausibility should be grounded in scientific analysis. Analysis should be ongoing so that chosen actions are subject to review. (UNESCO 2005, p. 14)

I prefer the so-called Wingspread version of the Precautionary Principle as it was formulated at the 1992 United Nations Conference on Environment and Development: "When an activity raises threats of harm to human health or the environment, precautionary measures should be taken even if some cause and effect relationships are not fully established scientifically. In this context the proponent of the process or product, rather than the public, should bear the burden of proof" (Urban Governance 1998). Although the PP applied originally to ecological ethics, I think it might apply equally well to gene editing.

The PP is a variation on the non-maleficence principle, because it opens a temporal space to explore the possibilities that harm might be done. But, exploring possibilities cannot go on indefinitely. At some point, researchers need to leap forward. The PP should be a temporary principle, whereas the Beneficence Principle—heal whenever the opportunity presents itself—should be permanent. Hence, "Yes, but not yet."

NASEM pauses at the yellow light, but then drives through. "Heritable germline genome editing trials must be approached with caution, but caution does not mean they must be prohibited (NASEM 2017, p. 102).

In short, when today's scientists engage in therapies that might yield consequences for generations to come, the burden of proof regarding safety must be borne now. Rather than march forward and risk falling off a cliff, the burden of proof requires that we locate as many of the cliffs as possible before marching. Invoking the PP is like looking both ways before proceeding through the yellow light.

6. Public Contributions to Ethics

Some concerned scientists, led by Edward Lanphier, president of Sangamo and chairman of the Alliance for Regenerative Medicine in Washington DC, speak out on both safety and the public's contribution. "In our view, genome editing in human embryos using current technologies could have unpredictable effects on future generations. This makes it dangerous and ethically unacceptable. Such research could be exploited for non-therapeutic modifications. We are concerned that a public outcry about such an ethical breach could hinder a promising area of therapeutic development, namely making genetic changes that cannot be inherited" (Lamphier et al. 2015). Note that such scientists provide two reasons for precaution. First, unpredictable consequences risk negative impact. This in itself warrants appeal to the PP. Second, scientists want to avoid offending the public who might shut off the supply of their research money for non-germline research. That is, "I'll be moral if you pay me to be." An appeal to gain public funding supplements the inherently ethical warrant, apparently.

Here is the hinge on which both the ethical and public image arguments swing: the distinction between genome editing in somatic cells and in germ cells. Virtually everyone would approve morally of therapeutic gene editing in somatic cells such as the cancer research mentioned above. But, germline cells should be treated as if they have laboratory leprosy. A voluntary moratorium in the scientific community could be an effective way to discourage human germline modification and raise public awareness of the difference between these two techniques. Such a moratorium would obey the PP while giving the public time to join the applause for our laboratory geneticists. But, if we are to declare a moratorium on germline gene editing, what will be our ethical argument?

Let me distinguish between the safety ethic and the ethical appeal to the Promethean anti-play-god position. They are not the same. Here is the safety argument: because of a foundational commitment to non-maleficence—do no harm!—medical researchers should pursue risk assessment to maximize protection of patient safety. If safety is put at too high a risk, then CRISPR editing should be postponed until that risk can be reduced. The mandate to protect safety through risk-assessment goes virtually unquestioned.

Nevertheless, this safety argument differs significantly from the Promethean argument against gene editing. The anti-play-god position puts a red stop light in front of Prometheus as well as Frankenstein in order to protect our inherited nature. If we violate nature, then nature will unleash punishment in the form of increased suffering. According to the anti-play-god argument, no amount of risk assessment can protect us from the self-destruction heaped upon us due to our hubris, our overreach into the sacred depths of nature. Let's examine the decisive assumption of this anti-play-god position, namely, nature as we have inherited it is sacred and should not be violated with technological alteration.

7. Is the Human Genome Metaphysically Off-Limits to Gene Editing?

Should we think of the human genome as sacred and unchangeable? "Is the human genome sacred? Does editing it violate the idea that we're made in God's image or, perhaps worse, allow us to 'play God'?" (Joseph 2016)

No. The human genome is not sacred, nor is it immoral to edit it (Peters 2003; Peters et al. 2008). Neither Prometheus nor Frankenstein should dictate our ethics. In the myth of Prometheus it is Zeus who punishes the Titan for stealing what belongs to the Olympian gods, whereas in the Frankenstein sequel nature replaces Zeus and exacts punishment against human hubris or pride. Should we today fear nature as the ancient Greeks feared Zeus?

No, because nature is not sacred, at least for biblical believers. "Creation is the work by which God establishes and sustains the existence of beings that are other than God," writes biblical scholar Ian McFarland (McFarland 2014, p. 107). Neither we human beings nor our genomes are divine, sacred, untransformable. In addition, as theologian Cynthia Crysdale (above) notes, God's creation is already changing and evolving with new things emerging. Nature is already on the move, so to speak. Therefore, no one violates the being of God let alone the created order through technological innovation. Moral values are formulated by ethicists in light of their vision of a future that is good for humanity and good for the encompassing creation. Neither Zeus nor nature should paralyze us with trepidation.

In short, there is no theological or metaphysical reason to presume that the genome we have inherited either individually or as a species is so sacred that we should put up a stop light saying, "Don't Change the Genome." DNA is not the essence of the human being, either individually or collectively. Altering the genome in our somatic cells for therapeutic reasons is akin to surgical removal of an infected appendix or implantation of a stent in the heart. If genome alteration improves health and wellbeing, then we should thank God for giving us the medical scientists who can provide this healing.

The bioethical issues raised by CRISPR/Cas9 are more practical than metaphysical or anthropological. Again, what is at stake is caution accompanied by scientific and technological advance.

8. Gene Drive: A Yellow or Red Light?

One prospect exciting futurists is the application of CRISPR/Cas9 technology to *gene drive*. Gene drive—promoting genetic changes to spread in a population in the absence of selective advantage—could become beneficial when controlling vector-borne disease such as malaria and for restoring an environment already threatened by a nonindigenous organism.

The CRISPR controversy reminds us that the other creatures with whom we humans share our planet have also become an ethical concern. We might consider invoking precaution regarding the possible environmental impact of removing from mosquitoes the capacity to spread malaria. On the one hand, we can anticipate future applause for eliminating the malaria, yellow fever, and Zika viruses. On the other hand, unless properly regulated and contained, this research has risk; it has the potential to rapidly alter our ecosystems in irreversible and damaging ways.

> Proof-of-concept in a few laboratory studies to date is not sufficient to support a decision to release gene-drive modified organisms into the environment. The potential for gene drives to cause irreversible effects on organisms and ecosystems calls for a robust method to assess risks. A phased approach to testing, engagement of stakeholders and publics, and clarified regulatory oversight can facilitate a precautionary, step-by-step approach to research on gene drives without hindering the development of new knowledge. (NASEM 2016)

Proceed with constant risk-assessment. This is what the Precautionary Principle exacts on us, I believe.

9. Objecting to the Precautionary Principle

Some scientific researchers object to invoking PP because it appears to tie their hands. "Precautionary approaches to governance of emerging technology call for constraints on the use of technology whose outcomes are characterized by high levels of complexity and uncertainty" (Kaebnick et al. 2016, p. 710). Scientists and technology innovators are impatient with the PP because it threatens to paralyze development and use of even beneficial new technologies such as CRISPR. Invoking the PP too often takes the form of scaremongering. Can reasonable caution be made compatible with support for science? Why not?

A corollary objection is that PP is too vague (NASEM 2016; UNESCO 2005, p. 51). It's ambiguous. Defenders of PP counter by declaring that critics may be demanding more than PP can deliver. PP was never meant to provide an algorithm for decision-making. Rather, PP's value is better understood as fostering an attitude, disposition, or cautious approach that includes sharpening or broadening the scrutiny of any proposed project.

In light of these objections and responses, I recommend we press for increased clarity regarding what PP intends. Distinguishing reasonable caution to avoid Promethean recklessness should not be all that difficult.

Bioethicists who invoke PP recognize that scientific progress does not advance in a vacuum. It functions within society, within the ecosphere. When it comes specifically to gene drive, PP advocates ask that authorities engage relevant publics and foster attention to values, questions, priorities, and safety concerns. In a democratic society, stakeholders require consultation. Further, ecological risk assessment regarding long term impact should precede the initial proposal for a technology such as gene drive (NASEM 2016).

Some PP bioethicists want to slow the pace of technological development. Researchers should follow phased testing that monitors step-by-step progress. Researchers should advance to future phases only after gaining evidence regarding potential outcomes. It appears to me that invoking the PP at this stage of technological development should be evaluated on a case by case basis and not be thought of as a rule or policy.

10. Conclusions

Harvard entomologist E. O. Wilson gives the Promethean war cry—waving the technological imperative flag while trumpeting the positive Promethean war hoop—that causes bioethicists to shudder and cower in abject fear: "We are about to abandon natural selection, the process that created us, in order to direct our own evolution by volitional selection—the process of redesigning our biology and human nature as we wish them to be" (Wilson 2014, p. 14). Should this green light position prevail, one might expect the elimination of governmental regulations, IRBs, and bioethics committees. Such unbridled Promethean recklessness would lead only to reactive punishment, exacted not by Zeus but by nature, at least according to the prevailing myth.

How can today's bioethicist earn an honest living by protecting us from both the green light of the technological imperative and the anti-play-god red light while still fostering progress in human health and wellbeing? I offer four recommendations for both scientists and their ethicist friends.

First, encourage the scientific community to remain in the conversation regarding bioethics. Don't separate the professions. Ethicists must welcome those scientists—especially the NASEM scientists—who have already foreseen many of the ethical issues and are motivated to proceed with caution. The Promethean version of the technological imperative has not as of this writing overly contaminated CRISPR/Cas9 research, even though it is an ever present threat.

Second, bioethical research projects should be funded to examine long range impact of germline modification via CRISPR or other genome modification methods. Such specifically ethical research should incorporate up-to-date scientific findings along with the applicability of the Precautionary Principle, harm-benefit analysis, cost-benefit analysis, and such. Classical bioethical principles—non-maleficence, beneficence, autonomy, and justice—should provide the categories within which research results are reported.

Third, bioethicists should encourage the existing willingness within the scientific community to give serious consideration to the Precautionary Principle. Prudence—not the technological imperative—should be our watchword here. Prudence with a yellow light should inform public policy and bioethics consultants. If the public is willing to withhold research money for genetic therapies, then researchers might become even more precautious regarding germline editing. Such a funding threat would have no impact on private business selling CRISPR-based services, however.

Fourth, ethicists and the supporting public should promote increased research into prognosticating the future impact on the environment and the wider ecosphere, i.e., continue research on risk assessment. Looking ahead is indispensable. We should look ahead before driving through the flashing yellow light.

In short, CRISPR/Cas9 puts us momentarily at a traffic stoplight. We have three options. The positive Promethean or transhumanist option is to race through a green light toward our post-human destination. The anti-play-god Promethean option is to hope that the light will remain red so all traffic remains stopped. The proceed-with-caution bioethicist looks both ways on yellow, but drives forward. I recommend the third.

Conflicts of Interest: The authors declare no conflict of interest.

References

Annas, George J. 2016. The mythology of CRISPR. *Science* 354: 189. [CrossRef]

Caplan, Arthur L., Brendan Parent, Michael Shen, and Carolyn Plunkett. 2015. No time to waste—the ethical challenges created by CRISPR. *Science and Society* 16: 1421–26. [CrossRef]

Couzin-Frankel, Jennifer. 2016. Worries, confusion after cancer trial deaths. *Science* 354: 1211. [CrossRef] [PubMed]

Crysdale, Cnythia W. 2003. Playing God? Moral Agency in an Emergent World. *Journal of the Society of Christian Ethics* 23: 243–59. [PubMed]

Cyranoski, David. 2016. First trial of CRISPR in people. *Nature* 535: 476–77. [CrossRef] [PubMed]

Doudna, Jennifer A., and Emmanuelle Carpentier. 2014. Genome Editing: The new frontier of genome editing with CRISPR-Cas9. *Science* 346: 1258096. [CrossRef] [PubMed]

Eckman, Jim. 2015. The Ethics of Gene Editing. *Issues in Perspective*, May 16. Available online: https://graceuniversity.edu/iip/2015/05/the-ethics-of-gene-editing/ (accessed on 28 November 2016).

Hefner, Philip. 1993. *The Human Factor: Evolution, Culture, and Religion*. Minneapolis: Fortress Press.

Herzfeld, Noreen L. 2002. *In Our Image: Artificial Intelligence and the Human Spirit*. Minneapolis: Fortress Press.

Joseph, Andrew. 2016. God and the genome: A geneticist seeks allies among the faithful. *STAT*, October 13. Available online: https://www.statnews.com/2016/10/13/genome-religion-ethics-ting-wu/ (accessed on 28 November 2016).

Joy, Bill. 2000. Why the Future Doesn't Need Us. Wired, April. Available online: https://www.wired.com/2000/04/joy-2/ (accessed on 28 November 2016).

Kaebnick, Gregory E., Elizabeth Heltman, James P. Collins, Jason A. Delborne, Wayne G. Landis, Keegan Sawyer, Lisa A. Taneyhill, and David E. Winickoff. 2016. Precaution and governance of emerging technologies. *Science* 354: 710–11. [CrossRef] [PubMed]

Kozubek, Jim. 2016. *Modern Prometheus: Editing the Human Genome with CRISPR-Cas9*. Cambridge: Cambridge University Press.

Lamphier, Edward, Fyodor Urnov, Sarah Ehlen Haecker, Michael Werner, and Joanna Smolenski. 2015. Don't Edit the Human Germline. *Nature* 521: 117. Available online: http://www.nature.com/news/don-t-edit-the-human-germline-1.17111 (accessed on 6 April 2017).

McFarland, Ian A. 2014. *From Nothing: A Theology of Creation*. Louisville: Westminster John Knox.

NASEM (National Academy of Science, Engineering, and Medicine). 2016. Gene Drives on the Horizon: Report in Brief. Available online: http://nas-sites.org/gene-drives/files/2015/08/Gene-Drives-Brief06.pdf (accessed on 28 November 2016).

NASEM (National Academy of Science, Engineering, and Medicine). 2017. *Human Genome Editing: Science, Ethics, Governance*. Washington: The National Academic Press (pre-publication).

Novella, Steven. 2015. CRISPR and the Ethics of Gene Editing. Science Based Medicine, December 2. Available online: https://www.sciencebasedmedicine.org/crispr-and-the-ethics-of-gene-editing/ (accessed on 28 November 2016).

PC Magazine. Encyclopedia: Technology imperative. Available online: www.pcmag.com/encyclopedia/term/64252/technology-imperative (accessed on 6 April 2017).

Peters, Ted. 2003. *Playing God? Genetic Determinism and Human Freedom*, 2nd ed. London and New York: Routledge.

Peters, Ted. 2005. Playing God. In *Encyclopedia of Science, Technology, and Ethics*, 4 vols; Edited by Carl Mitcham. New York: Thomson Gale, vol. 3, pp. 1424–27.

Peters, Ted, Karen Lebacqz, and Gaymon Bennett. 2008. *Sacred Cells? Why Christians Should Support Stem Cell Research*. New York: Roman and Littlefield.

Peters, Ted. 2017. *God in Cosmic History: Where Science and History Meet Religion*. Winona: Anselm.

Ramsey, Paul. 1970. *Fabricated Man: The Ethics of Genetic Control*. New Haven: Yale.

San Francisco Ballet. 2017. *Encore*. San Francisco: Encore Media Group, Program 3.

The President's Council on Bioethics. 2003. Beyond Therapy: Biotechnology and the Pursuit of Happiness. Available online: https://bioethicsarchive.georgetown.edu/pcbe/reports/beyondtherapy/fulldoc.html (accessed on 31 October 2016).

UNESCO (United Nations Educational, Scientific, and Cultural Organization). 2005. The Precautionary Principle. Available online: http://unesdoc.unesco.org/images/0013/001395/139578e.pdf (accessed on 15 December 2016).

Urban Governance. 1998. Wingspread Statement on the Precautionary Principle. Available online: http://www.gdrc.org/u-gov/precaution-3.html (accessed on 15 December 2016).

Verhey, Allen. 2005. What Makes Christian Bioethics Christian? Bible, Story and Communal Discernment. *Christian Bioethics* 11: 297–315. [CrossRef] [PubMed]

Wilson, Edward O. 2014. *The Meaning of Human Existence*. London: W.W. Norton.

Young, Simon. 2006. *Designer Evolution: A Transhumanist Manifesto*. Amherst: Prometheus Books.

religions   MDPI

Article

The Catholic Church and Technological Progress: Past, Present, and Future

Brian Patrick Green

School of Engineering and Markkula Center for Applied Ethics, Santa Clara University, 500 El Camino Real, Santa Clara, CA 95053, USA; bpgreen@scu.edu

Academic Editor: Noreen Herzfeld
Received: 18 February 2017; Accepted: 17 May 2017; Published: 1 June 2017

Abstract: Over 2000 years the Catholic Church has slowly developed a posture towards technology which is predominantly techno-optimist and techno-progressive, and yet the Church does not have this reputation today. Concomitantly, Church institutions and individuals have made crucial contributions to the advance of science and technology, yet despite this practical effort to better human development, Christian theology has been remarkably uninterested in the subject of technology. This lack of interest is no longer tenable; scholars of religion and theologians should seriously engage technology because it is empowering humanity in ways that were previously reserved only for gods. This blind spot has not only hampered the Church's ability to understand itself and our world, but also impeded the ability of the Church to fulfill its mission. Pope Francis's 2015 encyclical *Laudato Si* has begun to address this neglect, but is best understood in the context of Christian history, not only as written, but more so as practiced.

Keywords: Catholic; Christian; history; technology; theology; ethics; *Laudato Si*; Pope Francis

1. Introduction

Tertullian, criticizing the role of philosophy in religion, famously asked "What has Athens to do with Jerusalem (Tertullian 1914, chp. 7)?" While his attitude might find sympathy amongst some religious fundamentalists, for most of history it has been anathema to the majority Christian scholars and theologians. And yet, I assert, even among those scholars and theologians unsympathetic to Tertullian's saying, his sentiment remains in force in theology with respect to one field of human rationality even today.

Harking back to Aristotle's tripartite division of reason into theory, practice, and production; while many Christians have come to accept theoretical reasoning (philosophy, theology, and science) and practical reasoning (ethics) as deeply intertwined with their faith, in matters of *techne*—rational production, engineering, technology—sentiments ranging from uncertainty to ignorance to disdain are still widespread. Building upon Aristotle's notion of *techne*, I define technology as a means to an end, which consists of both applied conceptual techniques (e.g., mathematics, the scientific method, the concepts of engineering) and the purpose-laden material products (e.g., tools, artifacts, structures) of human reason and labor, including the skills, practices, and knowledge necessary to create and utilize those rational products.

To paraphrase Tertullian we might yet ask "What has technology to do with theology?" or, more anachronistically, "What has Silicon Valley to do with Jerusalem (or Rome)?" The standard, accepted, answer throughout most of Judeo-Christian history would have been "not very much." But contemporary advances in technology are demonstrating that this response is inadequate (Green 2014b, 2016b). As we create technologies capable of destroying the world and remaking ourselves, we tread into what was formerly the exclusive realm of God. Surely this *novum* is worthy of consideration (Jonas 1984, p. 1).

In ancient Greece and Rome, artisans and workers were looked down upon for their bondage to tools and manual labor (Plutarch 1932; Xenophon 1971, vol. 1, chp. IV.2, pp. 22–23; Aristotle 1984). But Western Christian theology evolved away from this ancient overt disdain for the manual arts and developed into a spectrum of perspectives on labor and technology. On one hand, labor and technology existed because of original sin, and therefore working was living a punishment, continuing the imperfection of this world (Boas 1948, p. 24; Ambrose 1961, chp. 10; Ovitt 1986, p. 488). On the other hand, through work we could improve this world, and while not achieving perfection, we could come closer to it, as St. Augustine argues: material progress shows God's beneficence and providence (Ovitt 1986, p. 492; Augustine 2009, chp. 24). Of note is that the first end of the spectrum was a theoretical tradition, which while disparaging work, or neglecting it, did not reject it. The second is a practical tradition, one of deep love and respect for manual labor, and even a love for innovation and technological progress. It is quietly embedded in the Bible, present in the religious tradition, and dramatically apparent in the history of technology in Western Europe. The first tradition has faded with time, yet the second has not come to clearly replace it, leaving something of a vacuum, which I hope to help fill; therefore the second tradition is the one which I will examine here.

In our contemporary world, one may legitimately wonder "What is the Catholic Church's stance towards technology?" It seems, for example, that in its resistance to reproductive technology and control the Church must be retrograde and wish to return to the technological past. And when combined with its continual critique of the modern world, whether in the *Syllabus of Errors*, *Rerum Novarum*, *Humanae Vitae*, *Dignitas Personae*, or *Laudato Si*, little defense is obvious against this assertion. The Church just plain seems to be opposed to modernity, especially technological modernity.

However, this is a much too simplistic evaluation of the Church's long history with technological advance. The question of the Church's stance on technology must first be disaggregated, because technology is not one thing, and the Catholic Church evaluates different technologies in different ways.

The connections between Christian theology and technology have not yet been thoroughly explored; indeed, in the last few decades there are just the beginnings of what could be called a *theology of technology*. Some older examples would include works by Nicholas Berdyaev (Berdyaev 1932), Jacques Ellul (Ellul 1964), Lynn White (White 1978), Paul Tillich (Tillich 1988), and Carl Mitcham and Jim Grotes (Mitcham and Grotes 1984). This field, however, in response to a clear need in society, has recently begun to grow at a rapid pace. More recent works include those of Albert Borgmann (Borgmann 2003), Noreen Herzfeld (Herzfeld 2009), Brad Kallenberg (Kallenberg 2011, 2012), David F. Noble (Noble 1998), and Brent Waters (Waters 2016). There remains, however, immense work to be done.

In this paper I will take a predominantly "high-altitude" perspective, occasionally dipping into the weeds, looking at the past, present, and future of the relationship of Christianity and technology. I will argue that technological development (and the science which underlies it) is integral to the successful fulfillment of the Christian vocation in the world. I will look particularly at Catholic Christianity, but I believe that the findings are broadly applicable to Christianity as a whole, though with some diversity of perspectives.

In response to the question "What is the Catholic Church's stance towards technology?" I will argue that "technology" should be divided into a spectrum ranging from "good" to "neutral" to "bad" technologies, and that (because technology is a means to an end) the hallmark of the morality of a technology relates to whether it facilitates good or bad moral actions. I will argue that the Church is in favor of technologies which facilitate good moral actions, and opposed to those which facilitate bad moral actions, as those actions are understood in its tradition. I will argue that the history of the Catholic tradition as actually practiced is important for interpreting contemporary more theoretical documents regarding technology. And in response to the anachronistic paraphrase of Tertullian, I will argue that Silicon Valley has a lot to do with Jerusalem (and Rome).

2. The Past Relationship of the Catholic Church and Technology

For much of human history, religions in general have been promoters of technology, ranging from megalithic circles to ornate religious structures, the printing press, and the invention of hypertext (involving Roberto Busa, S.J., and Thomas J. Watson of IBM) (America Magazine 2011). Historically, the Catholic Church and its members have done immense work towards advancing science and technology. Indeed, many aspects of the Christian worldview helped form the basis for science, and these presuppositions are likewise crucial for technological progress (Moritz 2009; Artigas 2000; Barbour 1990; Brooke 1991, pp. 18–33; Davis 1999; Hodgsen 2005; Rescher 1987).

The Bible engages with the idea of technological advancement in several places; though at the largest scale some have noted that the Bible begins in the Garden of Eden, and ends in the City of God, thus (since both are holy) apparently blessing, or at least not damning, technological progress (Thiel 2015). We already see the role of technology in the first chapters of Genesis. While the question of the existence of technology in the Garden of Eden has provoked contention in the past, with Jacques Ellul vehemently disagreeing with his contemporaries on the issue (Ellul arguing that there was no technique or work before the Fall) (Ellul 1984, chp. 8, p. 125), there is no question that technology does at least appear after eating from the forbidden tree, with Adam and Eve creating rough garments of leaves (Genesis 3:7). In Genesis 3:21, immediately prior to their expulsion from Eden, God gives Adam and Eve new clothing, gifting higher technology (animal skins) to replace their shabby improvised clothing made of leaves. This gift of animal skin clothing also implies a new technological dependency upon the instrumental exploitation of animals, and by extension all of nature, as a result of—or perhaps as a remediation for—sin. Continuing in Genesis we witness Noah's Ark as an example of a technological artifact saving humanity and animal creation from destruction, thus playing an integral role in God's plan (Gen. 6:14–8:19). Upon leaving the Ark, Noah immediately builds an altar for burnt offerings to God, illustrating the role of technology in divine worship and thanksgiving (Gen. 8:20). In contrast, in the Tower of Babel narrative we see humanity abusing technology for the sake of competing with God, rather than cooperating, and they are duly punished (Gen. 11:1–10). These contrasting stories show the ambivalence of technology and its dual-use capacity: it can be used for good or evil. The Hebrew Scriptures continue to fruitfully engage technological production, for example in the Exodus descriptions of the Ark of the Covenant, and 1 Kings and 1 Chronicles descriptions of Solomon's Temple.

In the New Testament it is worth noting several passages relevant to technology. In Luke 10:37, Jesus calls his disciples to "go and do likewise" and John 14:12 states "Very truly, I tell you, the one who believes in me will also do the works that I do and, in fact, will do greater works than these ... " (all quotations NRSV (NRSV Committee 1989)). This exhortation to imitation and greater works is primarily a moral claim, but in our contemporary world it is also a technical claim because technology empowers us to perform moral works of great magnitude. For example, as a healer, Jesus went about "curing every disease and every sickness" (Matt. 9:35, also 10:1), and "the blind receive their sight, the lame walk, the lepers are cleansed, the deaf hear, the dead are raised" (Matt. 11:5). Indeed, Jesus goes so far as to command his disciples to "cure the sick, raise the dead, cleanse the lepers" (Matt. 10:8). One might think that modern medical technology fulfills some of this commandment, though perhaps not yet all of it. Likewise, the Green Revolution in agriculture, led by Lutheran agronomist Norman Borlaug, vastly multiplied humanity's food supply and might in some way "do likewise" following Jesus's multiplications of the loaves and fishes (Matt 14:13–21 and 15:32–16:10, Mark 6:31–44 and 8:1–9, Luke 9:10–17, and John 6:5–15). In Borlaug's 1970 Nobel Prize lecture he cited the Bible five times, and relied upon several other Biblical allusions and moral principles (Borlaug 1970). While these technological advances might seem far from Jesus's actions, in Matthew 7:16 Jesus says that we can determine true prophets "by their fruits." True prophets will produce good actions in the world; words matter less than results. In the realm of technology we might ask, then, how practically prophetic engineers are who contribute to sanitation, transportation, communication systems, and other vital public goods. While they may not praise God with their lips, they do with their actions, and according to this verse, that is the more important way.

Some of the most clearly pro-technology passages in Scripture are those which call God an artificer (Greek, *technites*, Wis. 7:22, 8:5–6, Heb. 11:10) (Gaine 2016) and which also clearly point out that Jesus was a carpenter (or "builder," Greek *tektonos*, Matt. 13:55, and *tekton* Mark. 6:3). In updated terms, we might say that God is an engineer or a technologist. For Christians of all times and places this serves to bless the manual arts and lift them up, unlike how those professions were considered in ancient Greece and Rome (Kallenberg 2012, pp. 44–45). Simon Francis Gaine, O.P. (Gaine 2016, pp. 497–500), points out that this Biblical description of God as artificer is further expounded in both Augustine (Augustine 1968, vol. 50, p. 241) and particularly Thomas Aquinas, who found it to be a very fruitful analogy (Aquinas 1948, I 14.8, I 27.1 ad. 3, I 39.8, I 44.3, I 45.6, III 3.8; Kovach 1969; Aquinas 1955–1957, IV 13, IV 42).

There are, of course, other verses and interpretations which degrade manual labor as a curse (Gen. 3:17–19), but, interestingly, while these verses could be interpreted in ways which squelch innovation, they typically are not. Indeed, in the context of the expulsion in Genesis 3, God's condemnation of Adam and Eve to hard labor and the concomitant gifting of higher technology seems to point us exactly towards technology as remediation for sin. To seek higher technology would seem to follow God's example. And many Christians, including monks, have taken this example to heart over the last 2000 years.

St. Benedict, one of the patron saints of engineers, founded his monasteries not only on prayer, but also on work, following the guiding principle of "*ora et labora*." And so, following their founder, monks took on such civil and mechanical engineering activities as metalworking, building flood control earthworks, draining swamps, and building reservoirs and mills. Monasteries were responsible for many of Europe's cultural and technological "firsts." Beginning in the 6th century, monastic communities created the first large-scale European system of schools, libraries, scriptoria, and infirmaries; the importance of which cannot be underestimated for the collection, preservation, production, and transmission of technical knowledge. The remains of the first known tidal-powered water wheel have been found in Ireland, at Nendrum Monastery Mill in Strangford Lough, dating to the early 7th to late 8th centuries (Manning et al. 2007). Modern musical notation originated with Guido d'Arezzo, O.S.B., in Italy, c. 992–1033 AD (Encyclopædia Britannica 2017). The first impact-drilled well, and first Artesian well in Europe, was drilled by Carthusian monks in Artois, France, in 1126 (Gies and Gies 1994, p. 112). Monastic beers date into the distant past, the first systematized approach to wine quality control was by Dom Pierre Perignon, O.S.B., in the 17th cent., and the liqueur Chartreuse was invented in 1737. These advances involving alcohol may seem insignificant but they are not, as they had direct connection to the development of food preservation, chemistry, and microbiology.

Contemporarily with the early monasteries, St. Isidore of Seville, a Doctor of the Church, wrote his encyclopedia, the *Etymologies*, in the early 600s which helped preserve crucial ancient knowledge, including many kinds of technology. While St. Isidore made an overtly disparaging connection concerning the origin of the Latin word for "*mechanicus*," drawing its etymology from the Greek word *moichos* for "adulterer" (Kallenberg 2012, pp. 45–46), in his thoroughness and enthusiasm for all knowledge he practically encouraged the preservation of technology after the fall of the Western Roman Empire. This is a prime example of a theologian simultaneously speaking ill of technology, while also cultivating it. For his efforts in systematizing knowledge, in 1997 Pope John Paul II named St. Isidore as the patron saint of the internet and computers (Don Miller 2017; Kelly 2010).

By the early 9th century, holiness and technological progress were becoming overtly connected. For example, the Utrecht Psalter depicts the armies of God using a rotary sharpening wheel, while their enemies using a stationary sharpening stone, thus connecting higher technology to Godliness (White 1978, pp. 185–86). This depiction persists into the Eadwine Psalter in 1100s, thus showing the continuity of the association of holiness and technology.

As the High Middle Ages approached, construction advanced dramatically. Churches are full of technology: stone construction and carving, cement and metal, metallurgy to produce tools, wood carving, ceramics, quarrying and mining of minerals and precious stones, glass chemistry and technology, trade and transportation technology, and so on. As just one example, pipe organs—known in the ancient world, but considered profane outside of Western Europe—became prominent components of Western churches. By 950 AD Winchester Cathedral in England had an organ with 400 pipes the operation of which required 70 men to continuously pump 26 bellows (White 1978, pp. 65, 186–87). Following in the spirit of high-tech construction, in the 12th century a religious order of brothers devoted to engineering grew in France. The *Frères Pontifes*, or Brothers of the Bridge, built such spans as the Pont Saint-Bénézet (Pont d'Avignon) and Pont St. Esprit. These engineering brothers made dramatically innovative use of flattened arches and dual-sided cutwaters to reduce scour, two traits of bridges used even today (Gies and Gies 1994, pp. 150–51).

In the 1120s, Hugh of St. Victor, of the St. Victor Monastery in Paris, wrote his *Didascalicon* in an attempt to rehabilitate the manual arts in the eyes of theology. In it, following Aristotle, Hugh parses the wisdom of philosophy into three kinds: theoretical, ethical, and mechanical. However, far from neglecting or disparaging the mechanical arts, Hugh is so bold as to assert that the mechanical arts have a role in human salvation (Kallenberg 2012, pp. 48–51). This growing overt optimism about technology is noteworthy. While previously, practically speaking, the Church and individual Catholics were quite technologically progressive, theology had mostly ignored the subject. Now, ambivalence was undeniably becoming optimism.

As the Middle Ages progressed, it gradually became apparent that their technology had surpassed the technology of the ancients, and Roger Bacon went so far as to extrapolate yet further advance and thereby predicted a future with "ships, automobiles, airplanes, and submarines" (White 1978, p. 81). The growing medieval universities provided a venue for the further intense progress of science and technology. Prominent natural philosophers and scholars of this period include St. Albert the Great, who reputedly created a talking brass head (Chambers 1728). Brazen (brass or bronze) heads were also attributed to such luminaries as Roger Bacon (Butler 1948) and Bp. Robert Grosseteste (Gower [1390] 2013, vol. 2, ll. 234–43), and St. Thomas Aquinas reputedly once smashed one, fearing it was demonic (Knight and Lacey 1828). These tales are no doubt exaggerated, but they do indicate something of the esteem natural philosophers had at this time. However, ambivalence, ignorance, and uncertainty towards technology and labor remained. For example, in the *Summa Theologiae*, despite being quite forward about analogizing God to an artificer, St. Thomas Aquinas devoted just two articles (out of thousands) to the virtue of "art," exhibiting at best a benign neglect of the issue (Aquinas 1948, I–II 57.3, 4; Durbin 1981).

The development of all-mechanical clocks in Europe in the late 1200s and early 1300s provided a powerful impetus for the continued growth of a technological economy. Before the 13th century, clocks with escapement mechanisms were known in the world (e.g., Su Sung's Kaifeng Clock (Gies and Gies 1994, pp. 89–91)), but were very rare and therefore easily lost to time. When Catholic churches and monasteries across Europe adopted clocks for timekeeping, the clock making and repair industry grew rapidly, thus promoting, replicating, and refining the technology (Gies and Gies 1994, pp. 210–15). While in the Greek East time-keeping was thought to profane the eternity of holy spaces, in the West clocks came to symbolize temperance, orderliness, and virtue (White 1978, pp. 181–204).

The Catholic Church and Catholic scientists and technologists were vital in the development of the scientific method (which is itself a technique for acquiring knowledge), for promoting advances in architecture and structural engineering, for conducting geographic exploration, and many other endeavors. To summarize the period until the 20th century, I will just list a few prominent scholars: Evangelista Torricelli, 1608–1647, inventor of the barometer, Blaise Pascal, 1623–1662, mathematician and developer of the mechanical calculator, etc.; Bl. Bp. Nicolas Steno, 1638–1686, father of stratigraphy; Andre-Marie Ampere, 1775–1836, pioneer of electrodynamics; Ab. Gregor Mendel, 1822–1884, the father of genetics; Louis Pasteur, 1822–1895, the father of microbiology; and Fr. Georges Lemaitre,

1894–1966, father of Big Bang cosmology. So integral is technological practice to the Catholic faith that engineers have four patron saints: St. Benedict of Nursia, St. Ferdinand III of Castille, St. Joseph, and St. Patrick (CatholicSaints.Info 2008). Additionally, several engineers have been declared saints, blessed, or venerable, including: Blessed Alberto Marvelli, Blessed Jan Franciszek Czartoryski, Saint Rocco Gonzalez, and Venerable Jerzy Ciesielski (CatholicSaints.Info 2013). Indeed, the Pope's title as "Pontiff" means "bridge builder."

While the history presented so far lauds the positive relationship of the Catholic Church and technology, it should also be noted that the Church has historically opposed some technologies. In particular, the Church has condemned weapons technologies. The Second Lateran Council of 1139 banned the use of the crossbow against fellow Christians (White 1978, p. 82). The ban was ineffective, however, the idea of weapons which are intrinsically immoral and against the laws of war continues to this day and can be found in many international treaties, such as the 1675 Strasbourg Agreement (banning poison weapons), the 1899 and 1907 Hague Conventions, the 1925 Geneva Protocols (restricting chemical weapons), the 1972 Biological Weapons Convention, the 1983 Convention on Certain Conventional Weapons, and the 1993 Chemical Weapons Convention. Future conventions might attempt to limit or ban cyberwarfare, nuclear weapons, lethal autonomous weapon systems or artificially intelligent weapons systems, nanotechnological weapons, etc.

Nuclear weapons have attracted immediate and repeated denunciations from the Vatican. The day after Hiroshima, the Vatican condemned the existence of the atomic bomb and wished that its makers had followed the wisdom of inventors like Leonardo da Vinci (who reputedly refused to make an especially devilish weapon he had imagined) and destroyed the weapon before it was used (Chicago Tribune 1945). In 2015, "Marking the 70th anniversary of the use of nuclear bombs by the United States . . . Pope Francis reiterated the Vatican's long-standing call for a total ban on nuclear arms and other weapons of mass destruction" (Martín 2015). Weapons technologies facilitate death and destruction, and as such facilitate grave objective evils, even if under certain circumstances war might be justifiable (as in just war theory). In particular, weapons which are indiscriminate or disproportionate are morally unjustifiable.

The Church has not only condemned weapons technologies, however. More controversially, the Church has condemned technologies involving human reproduction, such as condoms, the contraceptive pill, intrauterine devices (IUD), implantable hormonal contraceptives, in vitro fertilization (IVF), pre-implantation genetic diagnosis (PGD), sterilization, abortion, gamete donation, gestational surrogacy, and so on. While some praise these technologies for freeing sexual activity from the burden of procreation, or as refining procreation in the laboratory and assisting those with fertility problems, the Church sees this "liberation" as instead an enslavement to the lower appetites, rejecting the higher good of human life for the lower good of carnal pleasure.

While the condemnations of weapons and technologies of reproductive control stand out to the modern mind, they also stand out in the history of the relationship between the Catholic Church and technology not because they are the rule, but because they are the exception. The overall history of the Church has been one of collecting (both spatially and temporally), preserving, promoting, producing, and consuming technologies. Very few technologies have been singled out for rejection; the vast majority of technologies, those deemed beneficial and life-affirming, have been enthusiastically accepted.

3. Present

In this section I will summarize the Church's present relationship with technologies by taking a deeper look at *Laudato Si*, and some of the traditional influences that operate within that encyclical (Pope Francis 2015). While this section specifically concerns the "present" the past will be crucial for interpreting current Catholic teaching.

As seen in the previous section, the Catholic Church has a *de facto* tradition of encouraging technologies which promote life and discouraging technologies which hinder life. I say *de facto*, because as pointed out before, the Church is traditionally intellectually somewhat ambivalent on technology in theory, while being enthusiastic in practice.

Historically, what Catholic scholarly ethical work has been done on technology has tended to be at the extremely specific level, in the evaluation of particular technologies, such as reproductive technologies. That in itself is significant, though—most new technologies have a presumption of innocence upon them, and therefore only certain classes of technologies are deemed worthy of concern. Large-scale philosophizing and theologizing about technology has not been a major subject because morally bad technologies are the exception, and typically minor ones, to the rule.

At a general level, the Catholic Church's relationship with technology can be summarized as this: some technologies are good, some are neutral, and some are bad. This might seem too simple, but this concept is foundationally related to the first principle of practical reason, often paraphrased as "Good is to be done and pursued, and evil is to be avoided" (Aquinas 1948, I–II 94.2), and acts as a principle to systematize the Church's entire relationship with technology. This moral axiom is deeply embedded into the history of the Church, and parallels can be found both in the Hebrew Scriptures (Deut. 30:19) and in the early Christian *Didache* (1:1), both of which explicitly divide the human path into one of life and one of death. God clearly instructs that humanity should choose life.

At the most basic level, good technologies facilitate good actions and bad technologies facilitate bad actions. If good is to be done and pursued, then good technologies also ought to be pursued. And if evil is to be avoided, then technologies which facilitate evil ought to be avoided too. Dual-use technologies, which can facilitate either good or bad actions, require careful institutional governance.

Examining Pope Francis's recent encyclical *Laudato Si* can help to elucidate the meaning of this otherwise quite abstract principle. *Laudato Si* clearly praises and encourages some technologies:

> We are the beneficiaries of two centuries of enormous waves of change: steam engines, railways, the telegraph, electricity, automobiles, aeroplanes, chemical industries, modern medicine, information technology and, more recently, the digital revolution, robotics, biotechnologies and nanotechnologies...It is right to rejoice in these advances and to be excited by the immense possibilities which they continue to open up before us, for "science and technology are wonderful products of a God-given human creativity (Pope John Paul II 1981)" ... Technology has remedied countless evils which used to harm and limit human beings. How can we not feel gratitude and appreciation for this progress, especially in the fields of medicine, engineering and communications? (Pope Francis 2015, no. 102)

Pope Francis further describes some good technologies:

> Technoscience, when well directed, can produce important means of improving the quality of human life, from useful domestic appliances to great transportation systems, bridges, buildings and public spaces...Who can deny the beauty of an aircraft or a skyscraper? Valuable works of art and music now make use of new technologies (Pope Francis 2015, no. 103).

The Pope includes a very specific request for the development of better energy technologies and encourages technologists to pursue this line of inquiry, saying: "Worldwide there is minimal access to clean and renewable energy. There is still a need to develop adequate storage technologies" (Pope Francis, no. 26). These remarks are fascinating in the context of Christian history. The Pope is aligned with the tradition of such optimistic thinkers and practitioners as the Nendrum monks, Hugh of St. Victor, and the Brothers of the Bridge. In the world, there are problems to solve and technology can solve them. Technology should be put to good use helping people: that is what it is *for*.

However, the Pope does not think of technology as an unconditional blessing. While optimism and belief in progress are warranted, dangers still lurk. While the Pope encourages new technologies, *Laudato Si* also acknowledges that there are moral ambiguities in the potential actions facilitated by technology.

We have the freedom needed to limit and direct technology; we can put it at the service of another type of progress, one which is healthier, more human, more social, more integral. Liberation from the dominant technocratic paradigm does in fact happen sometimes, for example ... when technology is directed primarily to resolving people's concrete problems, truly helping them live with more dignity and less suffering (Pope Francis, no. 112).

Despite the ambiguities of technology we should not resign ourselves to pessimism: "There is also the fact that people no longer seem to believe in a happy future... Let us refuse to resign ourselves to this, and continue to wonder about the purpose and meaning of everything..." (Pope Francis 2015, no. 113). We ought to believe in a happy future *and work* to make it happen. Fascinatingly, this directly parallels technology entrepreneur Peter Thiel's notion of "definite optimism"—optimism in a better future because we will make it that way by our own work (Thiel 2015; Thiel and Masters 2014). The pope agrees, but does not limit optimism to the technological level: our optimism is in the purpose and meaning of it all, not just the technology.

Further, this has significant ethical implications:

All of this shows the urgent need for us to move forward in a bold cultural revolution. Science and technology are not neutral; from the beginning to the end of a process, various intentions and possibilities are in play ... Nobody is suggesting a return to the Stone Age, but we do need ... to appropriate the positive and sustainable progress which has been made, but also to recover the values and the great goals swept away by our unrestrained delusions of grandeur (Pope Francis 2015, no. 114).

There are also technologies which are morally ambiguous, and others which are clearly morally bad because they facilitate evil actions. The Pope says:

Yet it must also be recognized that nuclear energy, biotechnology, information technology, knowledge of our DNA, and many other abilities which we have acquired, have given us tremendous power. More precisely, they have given those with the knowledge, and especially the economic resources to use them, an impressive dominance over the whole of humanity and the entire world. Never has humanity had such power over itself, yet nothing ensures that it will be used wisely, particularly when we consider how it is currently being used. We need but think of the nuclear bombs dropped in the middle of the twentieth century, or the array of technology which Nazism, Communism and other totalitarian regimes have employed to kill millions of people, to say nothing of the increasingly deadly arsenal of weapons available for modern warfare (Pope Francis 2015, no. 104).

Powerful technologies can empower differentially, and in this case a few decision-making humans—whether technologists, business leaders, politicians, or military leaders—become extremely powerful, with the rest of humanity subject to their whim. If we had the ethics and institutional structures to properly control these powers, the differential might be less worrisome, but because we do not, our straits are dire indeed. CS Lewis noted this problem of differential empowerment due to technology in his 1943 book *The Abolition of Man*, where he states "what we call Man's power over Nature turns out to be a power exercised by some men over other men with Nature as its instrument" (Lewis 1944).

Technology—as described by the Pope as a total category of human endeavor—is ultimately morally ambiguous because it contains within itself too many sub-categories. Good and bad technologies must be separated, individually evaluated, and then treated distinctly, depending on their moral salience. And the more powerful that a technology is, the stronger that moral salience will be.

Emerging weapons technologies, then, are of particular concern and here the Pope could easily borrow a phrase from the technologist Bill Joy, who warned of emerging weapons technologies in 2000, calling them weapons of "knowledge-enabled mass destruction" (Joy 2000). Technologically advanced arsenals make war more deadly than ever before and therefore more important to avoid than ever before. Pope Francis states: "War always does grave harm . . . risks which are magnified when one considers nuclear arms and biological weapons . . . Politics must pay greater attention to foreseeing new conflicts and addressing the causes which can lead to them" (Pope Francis 2015, no. 57). The danger of technological war has been a growing concern of the Popes since World War Two. Francis begins *Laudato Si* by recalling Pope John XXIII's 1963 encyclical *Pacem in Terris* which sought multilateral nuclear disarmament, one which would be "thoroughgoing and complete, and reach men's very souls (Pope John XXIII 1963, no. 113)". Pope Francis also cites Pope Paul VI's 1971 *Octogesima Adveniens* on the emerging ecological crisis, calling it a "'a tragic consequence' of unchecked human activity: 'Due to an ill-considered exploitation of nature, humanity runs the risk of destroying it and becoming in turn a victim of this degradation'(Pope Paul VI 1971, no. 4)."

One must also mind the Pope's continual rejection of the "technocratic paradigm" in the encyclical (106–14), but absolutely not confuse the technocratic paradigm with technological progress itself. As is clearly shown above, Pope Francis explicitly desires specific forms of technological progress; however it must be a directed progress, one towards good and away from evil. The technocratic paradigm is too complex to describe fully here (others such as Jacques Ellul, (Ellul 1964), Romano Guardini (Guardini 1998), Neil Postman (Postman 1992), Pope Benedict XVI (Pope Benedict XVI 2009), Michael Hanby (Hanby 2015), etc., have said much already), but in one aspect it can be understood as the belief that every problem is merely one of efficiency, and that therefore technology can solve every problem, without the intervention of ethics. The technocratic paradigm thus explicitly violates the entire Catholic tradition on the interaction of ethics and technology; hence it is not a suitable paradigm for a Catholic approach to technology.

As seen in the previous section, the Catholic Church has done an enormous amount of conceptual and physical work towards the advance of science and technology throughout history. It still does today, most notably through its educational and healthcare systems. For example, Catholic Universities with engineering schools specifically direct technological development in ways that promote human life and health. At just one university, Santa Clara University in California, the Frugal Innovation Hub helps develop technologies for the developing world and the Miller Center for Social Entrepreneurship helps social entrepreneurs in the developing world start and grow their businesses, thus benefitting their communities and nations (Frugal Innovation Hub n.d.; Miller Center for Social Entrepreneurship n.d.).

In conclusion, some might say that the Catholic Church's approach to nuclear weapons, other brutal weapons, environmentally unsustainable technologies, artificial birth control, some reproductive technologies, and embryonic stem cell research is "anti-technology," but these critics would be mistaking the exception for the rule. The Church's response to this criticism would be that it is not "anti-technology" but rather "anti-bad-technology" and that only good technologies ought to progress. Obviously, there is debate possible on what qualifies as "good technology" and "bad technology," but that is a separate debate. In any case, this is a significant point: for nearly its entire history the Church has stood for the preservation and advancement of knowledge and technology, with exceptions only for a few of those technologies which it evaluates as preventing or harming human life. *Laudato Si* is best interpreted in light of this tradition.

4. Future

Quoting Pope Benedict XVI, in *Laudato Si* Pope Francis clearly states that in regard to our precarious future: "The work of the Church seeks not only to remind everyone of the duty to care for nature, but at the same time 'she must above all protect mankind from self-destruction' (Pope Benedict XVI 2009, no. 51, 79)" . This is not an aberrant comment in the encyclical; several times Pope Francis states that "An outsider looking at our world would be amazed at such behaviour, which at times appears self-destructive" (Pope Francis 2015, no. 55), and that we should "escape the spiral of self-destruction which currently engulfs us" (Pope Francis 2015, no. 163).

These statements are powerful: doom is approaching, we are causing it, and we must work to stop it. Thus Pope Francis challenges "all people of good will (Pope Francis 2015, no. 62)" to act to protect humanity from our impending fate. This includes not only technological solutions to the problems created by our technology, but even more so moral solutions, and ultimately, a change of heart. God does not just want our righteous actions; God wants our souls.

This deep internal conversion requires that we—not just a few, but many people—make the necessary ethical decisions and strengthen the necessary institutions to create our better world. Echoing the philosopher Hans Jonas (Jonas 1984, p. 23), Pope Francis says:

> We stand naked and exposed in the face of our ever-increasing power, lacking the wherewithal to control it. We have certain superficial mechanisms, but we cannot claim to have a sound ethics, a culture and spirituality genuinely capable of setting limits and teaching clear-minded self-restraint (Pope Francis 2015, no. 105).

The Pope knows that " ... a technology severed from ethics will not easily be able to limit its own power" (Pope Francis 2015, no. 136) and therefore, in the priorities of current action, ethical development must come first, before all else. We are technically strong, but morally and politically weak. We live in a fragile world that " ... challenges us to devise intelligent ways of directing, developing and limiting our power" (Pope Francis 2015, no. 78). As I tell my students in every course I teach: formerly human action was constrained by our weakness; now we must learn to be constrained by our good judgment, our ethics (Green 2015b). Only when one has immense power must one learn to control it. For humankind, that time has arrived. If we cannot come to control our power we risk extinction.

Ancient philosophers and theologians could disparage or ignore the subject of technology because humans were weak (Green 2015c). Formerly we had to use our own muscles to physically hit people to kill them; now with nuclear weapons, with a phone call we can end civilization in 30 minutes. And while we hypertrophy our destructive capabilities, we still allow untold numbers of children to die every day from easily preventable conditions such as malnutrition and disease. We are strong in our capacity for evil, and weak in our capacity for good. This is precisely the situation that centuries of Catholic moral teaching has sought to avoid.

Pope Francis knows we are morally weak, and we lie to ourselves about our moral weakness:

> As often occurs in periods of deep crisis which require bold decisions, we are tempted to think that what is happening is not entirely clear... Such evasiveness serves as a license to carrying on with our present lifestyles... This is the way human beings contrive to feed their self-destructive vices: trying not to see them, trying not to acknowledge them, delaying the important decisions and pretending that nothing will happen (Pope Francis 2015, no. 59).

What is needed is not so much better technologies, but morally better human beings. In humanity's headlong rush to prioritize technical power, we have concomitantly failed to prioritize goodness and holiness. Morality without power is helpless, it is useless to others—we cannot protect our fellow human beings or aid the fulfillment of their humanity. But power without morality is even worse—in this case we can do much to our fellow human beings, but what we choose to do is evil. It can only lead to death, not only of our fellows, but of ourselves. What we need is a balance of morality and power, where we are powerful enough to help each other and good enough to actually do it.

The Pope knows we need better people, morally speaking, not just better technology. We must "love our neighbors" and help each other as we can. But better technology should be a tool for these "better people," who ought not use outdated technology to inefficiently pursue the noble ends assigned by their religion. A truly prudent "better person" would use the best means available, including the best technology—existing or awaiting invention—to maximize their beneficial impact on the world. And here the dialogue of theologians with scientists, engineers, and technologists becomes not just an interesting endeavor, but a mission. While the world contains much danger, it also contains much hope. Christians should resurrect their own tradition of technological optimism and development for the sake of helping others.

In addition to the constant Christian call to the Corporal and Spiritual Works of Mercy, to help the poor, and everyone, through moral guidance, education, healthcare, and other social welfare programs, there are three areas of technological endeavor which at this point in history might best express the Church's mission to "above all protect mankind from self-destruction."

Mitigating and adapting to global catastrophic and existential risk—As noted by Popes Benedict and Francis, the Church must protect humankind. Climate change, nuclear weapons, synthetic biology, nanotechnology, artificial intelligence, and so on, all threaten the future of humanity with extinction. If the Church wants to promote the continued existence of humanity, then Catholics should engage intensely to protect humankind and alleviate and limit these existential dangers. Many people, both religious and secular are already engaged in this work, but Catholics should be especially zealous in it (Bostrom and Cirkovic 2008; Future of Humanity Institute n.d.; Global Catastrophic Risk Institute n.d.; Green 2014a, 2016a; Long Now Foundation n.d.).

Limiting the negative effects of transhumanism—Humanity could be destroyed by death, or by transformation into something no longer human. Transhumanism seeks to modify human nature into enhanced forms superior to all who now exist. At its core, enhancing humanity to be the best that it can naturally be is good. Health extension is good, growth in knowledge is good, growth in goodness is good—Pope Pius XI noted these good goals in regards to the eugenics movement in *Casti Conubii* in 1930 (Pope Pius XI 1930, pp. 66–71). But in its worst forms it becomes idolatry (replacing God with lower goods) and risks great evil; in particular it risks using evil means to achieve what might be otherwise subjectively good ends, such as instrumentalizing the lives of some humans to serve as ends to others. The movement should be studied, its excesses opposed, and many are already working on this subject (Cole-Turner 2011; Green 2015a; Meilaender 2013; Mercer and Trothen 2015; O'Donovan 1984).

Encouraging space exploration and settlement—The first two threats, extinction and transformation, are dangers which can be dealt with directly, as above, or indirectly, by progress away from them, i.e., escape. It should not be forgotten that in the depths of Christian history, remote settlements such as monasteries preserved civilization during dark times. In our time, for some risks (e.g., runaway greenhouse effect, artificial intelligence, nanotechnology, synthetic biology), nothing on Earth can serve as an adequately remote settlement (though the ocean surface, underwater (Turchin and Green 2017), underground, and Antarctica have all been proposed as refuges (Baum et al. 2015; Turchin 2016); refuges off-planet are the next step. The previous two areas of endeavor are limiting, but this one is freeing. Space exploration might seem far removed from the realities of Earthly life, where the Beatitudes and command to "go and do likewise" might typically predominate, but the Catholic Church has encouraged exploration, both physical and intellectual, from the beginning. Ever since Jesus gave the Great Commission in Matthew 28:18–20, missionaries have explored much of the Earth, and with only a few uncontacted tribes remaining, we might well ask what is next. Among the many options, Brother Sun and Sister Moon, and many sibling orbital objects await. Not only has the Church institutionally already encouraged space exploration with Pope Paul VI's message for the Apollo 11 Moon landing (NASA 1969) and Pope Benedict XVI's prayer for and conversation with the International Space Station (Patterson 2011), but also many individual Christians have been physically engaged with space exploration, the encouragement of it, and in writing articles, books, and novels (Consolmagno 2000; George 2005; Green 2015d; Levinson and Waltemathe 2016; Peters 2013; Russell 1996; Vakoch 2000).

These are just a few of the tasks of the future, as mentioned before, all the traditional tasks of the Beatitudes and Works of Mercy still remain in effect. But as we "grow up" as a species our household chores become harder. The question for future Christians might be thought of as this: who do we want to "grow up" to be? The Bible calls us to become like God, but primarily in what way? Through technology we can become more like God in terms of our power. Through goodness we can become more like God in holiness. But clearly, goodness and holiness must be our first priority. Ethics should judge technology, must judge it, or we will face disaster and even extinction. For God, who is Existence Itself, no amount of power could destroy Him. But for humankind our existence is not guaranteed. We are intrinsically contingent and we are capable of great evil. In our evil we have grown powerful enough to threaten our own existence. Only through goodness can we grow wise enough not only to maintain our lives, but even to flourish.

5. Conclusions

Within contemporary Christianity there is a spectrum of responses towards technology, ranging from the radically optimistic progressivism of the Mormon transhumanists to the technological skepticism of the Amish. Where is the Catholic Church on this spectrum, and furthermore, where *should* it be?

Historically speaking, in practice, the Church has been extremely technologically optimistic and progressive, perhaps more so than any other organization in the history of planet. From installing formerly "profane" pipe-organs and clocks in churches to confidently searching for scientific truth wherever it is to be found (knowing that "truth cannot contradict truth"—that all discoveries will be reconcilable with the Catholic faith), the Church has exuded scientific and technological optimism.

However, this is not the current perception—why? The first problem, the question of this paper, is the lack of an adequate philosophy and theology of technology. In the past we did not need a detailed theology of technology as long as the practices of technology advanced on their own, in ethical ways. However, now that these practices have become questionable we now need to understand the theoretical basis for our actions, to properly guide our new works. Rome and Silicon Valley have not yet figured out just how much they need to talk. Lacking systematic theoretical underpinnings, the Church cannot help but respond in an *ad hoc* and sometimes confused fashion to each new wave of technological development, waves that have become a tsunami. Recent Popes have begun to remedy this lack, but vast work remains.

The second problem, I believe, is that as humanity has grown in power there is more and more to say "no" to. When one is weak, there is little to reject, for little can be done at all, but when one is powerful much must be rejected because there are so many wrong choices that can be made. One does not need to counsel babies against murder and war, precisely because they cannot do such things, but one does need to counsel heads of state against them, precisely because they can.

This growth in power has made the Church come to seem negative about technology, but it is only an apparent negativity. The primary response of the Church to technology has historically been and remains an enthusiastic "yes!" Pope Paul VI's 1967 encyclical *Populorum Progressio* strongly presents this view, its very name in English being *On the Development of Peoples*, and it considers not only the moral and economic development of the world, but also the role of technology in that development (e.g., (Pope Paul VI 1967, no. 25, 65)), while still rejecting technocracy (e.g., (Pope Paul VI 1967, no. 34)

I believe that Christians should be a particular kind of techno-progressive, specifically one which seeks to use technology for the sake of human development. Specifically, as with all issues of moral salience, we need to direct technological developments towards good and away from evil (Green 2016a). In some cases this will mean resisting certain technologies, particularly ones which harm people such as weapons, or technologies with dire side-effects such as ones which contribute to climate change. In other cases this will mean vigorously pursuing technologies that help people, such as technologies that improve health, education, public safety, and which contribute to all aspects of human welfare. This idea of differential technological development has made something of a splash in secular philosophy in the last few years (Bostrom 2014, p. 281), while it has been embedded in Catholic teaching for centuries.

Jesus, as a carpenter, knew a bit about engineering. But he didn't save humanity through his own carpentry, he saved us through his death on and resurrection from on a grisly piece of carpentry that humans made, called the Cross. From this we should be made aware of the ambiguous nature of much technology—many technologies are dual-use. Carpentry can be used to promote life or death, and as we explore emerging technologies we would do well to remember that dual use technologies may require governance, and ultimately it is the human heart that most requires governance. It is we who should be morally good, not just our technology that should be technically good.

As we grow in power it becomes more and more apparent that technology, the rational production of material goods, has a vital role in human action in this world. It also has theological relevance, as we seem to become more godlike in our power, while remaining human in our ethics. When we harken back to Tertullian, who asks the relational question of religion and rationality, I hope that we can now see that rational production—engineering and technology—has been ignored by theology for too long. The archetypes represented by Athens (or Silicon Valley) and Jerusalem (or Rome) are not separate cities now, and they never were. There is only one city, and we are all living in it—everyone, religious or not and technologist or not—together.

Acknowledgments: I would like to thank Dr. Noreen Herzfeld for inviting me to write this manuscript for her special issue on religion and technology, Dr. Barbara Sain for arranging the conference at which a draft of this paper was presented: "A Culture of Ethics: Engineering for Human Dignity and the Common Good," University of St. Thomas, St. Paul, Minnesota, October 6–8, 2016, and the anonymous reviewers and editors for their helpful comments.

Conflicts of Interest: The author declares no conflict of interest.

References

Ambrose. 1961. *Hexaemeron*. Translated by John J. Savage. New York: Fathers of the Church, Inc.

America Magazine. 2011. The Jesuit Who 'Invented' Hypertext. August 15. Available online: http://www.americamagazine.org/issue/784/signs/jesuit-who-invented-hypertext (accessed on 12 February 2017).

Aquinas, Thomas. 1948. *Summa Theologiae*. 3 vols. Translated by the Fathers of the English Dominican Province. New York: Benziger Bros.

Aquinas, Thomas. 1955–1957. *Summa Contra Gentiles*. Edited by O. P. Joseph Kenny. New York: Hanover House, Available online: http://dhspriory.org/thomas/ContraGentiles.htm (accessed on 17 April 2017)

Aristotle. 1984. Politics. In *The Complete Works of Aristotle*. Edited by Jonathan Barnes. Princeton: Princeton University Press, pp. 2121–22.

Artigas, Mariano. 2000. *The Mind of the Universe: Understanding Science and Religion*. Philadelphia: Templeton Foundation Press, p. 22.

Augustine. 1968. De Trinitate 6.10. In *Corpus Christianorum Series Latina*. Edited by W. J. Mountain. Brepols: Turnhout.

Augustine. 2009. Of the Blessings with Which the Creator Has Filled This Life, Obnoxious Though It Be to the Curse. In *De Civitate Dei*. Buffalo: Christian Literature Publishing. Available online: http://www.newadvent.org/fathers/120122.htm (accessed on 23 May 2017).

Barbour, Ian G. 1990. *Religion in an Age of Science*. London: SCM Press.

Baum, Seth D., David C. Denkenberger, and Jacob Haqq-Misra. 2015. Isolated Refuges for Surviving Global Catastrophes. *Futures* 72: 45–56. [CrossRef]

Berdyaev, Nicholas. 1932. The Spiritual Condition of the Contemporary World. Available online: http://www.berdyaev.com/berdiaev/berd_lib/1932_377.html (accessed on 17 April 2017).

Boas, George. 1948. *Essays on Primitivism and Related Ideas in the Middle Ages*. Baltimore: The Johns Hopkins University Press.

Borgmann, Albert. 2003. *Power Failure: Christianity in the Culture of Technology*. Grand Rapids: Brazos Press.

Borlaug, Norman. 1970. The Nobel Peace Prize Lecture: The Green Revolution, Peace, and Humanity. *Nobelprize.org*, December 11. Available online: http://www.nobelprize.org/nobel_prizes/peace/laureates/1970/borlaug-lecture.html (accessed on 13 February 2017).

Bostrom, Nick. 2014. *Superintelligence: Paths, Dangers, Strategies*. Oxford: Oxford University Press.

Bostrom, Nick, and Milan M. Cirkovic. 2008. *Global Catastrophic Risks*. Oxford: Oxford University Press.

Brooke, John Hedley. 1991. *Science and Religion: Some Historical Perspectives*. Cambridge: Cambridge University Press.

Butler, Eliza Marian. 1948. *The Myth of the Magus*. Cambridge: Cambridge University Press, pp. 156–58. Available online: http://bit.ly/2oLjXMS (accessed on 17 April 2017).

CatholicSaints.Info. 2008. Patrons of Civil Engineers. November 2. Available online: http://catholicsaints.info/patrons-of-civil-engineers/ (accessed on 13 February 2017).

CatholicSaints.Info. 2013. Saints Who Were Civil Engineers. September 18. Available online: http://catholicsaints. info/saints-who-were-civil-engineers/ (accessed on 13 February 2017).

Chambers, Ephraim. 1728. Androides. In *Cyclopedia*. Available online: https://archive.org/details/Cyclopediachambers-Volume1 (accessed on 13 February 2017).

Chicago Tribune. 1945. Vatican Views Atomic Bomb 'Unfavorably'. August 8. Available online: http://archives. chicagotribune.com/1945/08/08/page/2/article/vatican-views-atomic-bomb-unfavorably (accessed on 17 February 2017).

Cole-Turner, Ron. 2011. *Transhumanism and Transcendence: Christian Hope in an Age of Technological Enhancement.* Washington: Georgetown University Press.

Consolmagno, Guy, S. J. 2000. *Brother Astronomer: Adventures of a Vatican Scientist.* New York: McGraw Hill.

Davis, Edward B. 1999. Christianity and Early Modern Science: The Foster Thesis Reconsidered. In *Evangelicals and Science in Historical Perspective*. Edited by David N. Livingstone, Darryl G. Hart and Mark A. Noll. Oxford: Oxford University Press, p. 77.

Durbin, Paul T. 1981. Aquinas, Art as an Intellectual Virtue, and Technology. *The New Scholasticism* 55: 265–80. [CrossRef]

Ellul, Jacques. 1964. *The Technological Society.* New York: Vintage Books.

Ellul, Jacques. 1984. Technique and the Opening Chapters of Genesis. In *Theology and Technology: Essays in Christian Analysis and Exegesis*. Edited by Carl Mitcham and Jim Grotes. Lanham: University Press of America, chp. 8; pp. 123–37.

Encyclopædia Britannica. 2017. Encyclopædia Britannica: Guido d'Arezzo, Italian Musician. Available online: https://www.britannica.com/biography/Guido-dArezzo-Italian-musician (accessed on 13 February 2017).

Frugal Innovation Hub. n.d. Available online: https://www.scu.edu/engineering/labs--research/labs/frugal-innovation-hub/ (accessed on 17 February 2017).

Future of Humanity Institute. n.d. Available online: https://www.fhi.ox.ac.uk/ (accessed on 17 February 2017).

Gaine, Simon Francis. 2016. God Is an Artificer: A Response to Edward Feser. *Nova et Vetera* 14: 495–501. [CrossRef]

George, Marie I. 2005. *Christianity and Extraterrestrials? A Catholic Perspective.* New York: iUniverse, Inc.

Gies, Frances, and Joseph Gies. 1994. *Cathedral, Forge, and Waterwheel: Technology and Invention in the Middle Ages.* New York: HarperCollins.

Global Catastrophic Risk Institute. n.d. Available online: http://gcrinstitute.org/ (accessed on 17 February 2017).

Gower, John. [1390] 2013. The grete clerc Grosseteste. In *Confessio Amantis: Book 4*. Edited by Russell A. Peck. Translated by Andrew Galloway. Rochester: River Campus Libaries. First published 1390. Available online: http://d.lib.rochester.edu/teams/text/peck-gower-confessio-amantis-book-4 (accessed on 13 February 2017).

Green, Brian Patrick. 2014a. Are Science, Technology, and Engineering Now the Most Important Subjects for Ethics? Our Need to Respond. Paper presented at 2014 IEEE International Symposium on Ethics in Engineering, Science, and Technology, Chicago, IL, USA, 23–24 May.

Green, Brian Patrick. 2014b. What Has Technology to Do with Theology?: Towards a Theology of Technology. Paper presented at "What Has Athens to Do with Jerusalem?" Dominican Colloquium, Berkeley, CA, USA, 16–20 July.

Green, Brian Patrick. 2015a. Transhumanism and Roman Catholicism: Imagined and Real Tensions. *Theology and Science* 13: 187–201. [CrossRef]

Green, Brian Patrick. 2015b. Pope Francis, the Encyclical Laudato Si, Ethics, and Existential Risk. *Institute for Ethics and Emerging Technologies*, August 16. Available online: http://ieet.org/index.php/IEET/more/green20150816 (accessed on 17 February 2017).

Green, Brian Patrick. 2015c. Transhumanism and Catholic Natural Law: Changing Human Nature and Changing Moral Norms. In *Religion and Transhumanism: The Unknown Future of Human Enhancement*. Edited by Calvin Mercer and Tracy Trothen. Westport: Praeger, pp. 201–15.

Green, Brian Patrick. 2015d. Astrobiology, Theology, and Ethics. In *Anticipating God's New Creation: Essays in Honor of Ted Peters*. Edited by Carol R. Jacobsen and Adam W. Pryor. Minneapolis: Lutheran University Press, pp. 339–50.

Green, Brian Patrick. 2016a. Emerging Technologies, Catastrophic Risk, and Ethics: Three Strategies for Reducing Risk. Paper presented at IEEE International Symposium on Ethics in Engineering, Science, and Technology, Vancouver, BC, Canada, 13–14 May.

Green, Brian Patrick. 2016b. Catholicism and Technological Progress: Past, Present, and Future. Paper presented at the conference of A Culture of Ethics: Engineering for Human Dignity and the Common Good, University of St. Thomas, St. Paul, MN, USA, 6–8 October.

Guardini, Romano. 1998. *The End of the Modern World*. Wilmington: ISI Books.

Hanby, Michael. 2015. The Gospel of Creation and the Technocratic Paradigm: Reflections on a Central Teaching of *Laudato Si*. *Communio* 42: 724–47.

Herzfeld, Noreen. 2009. *Technology and Religion: Remaining Human in a Co-Created World*. West Conshohocken: Templeton Press.

Hodgsen, Peter E. 2005. *Theology and Modern Physics*. Aldershot: Ashgate, p. 16.

Jonas, Hans. 1984. *The Imperative or Responsibility: In Search of an Ethics for the Technological Age*. Chicago: University of Chicago Press.

Joy, Bill. 2000. Why the Future Doesn't Need Us. *WIRED*. Available online: https://www.wired.com/2000/04/joy-2/ (accessed on 17 February 2017).

Kallenberg, Brad J. 2011. *God and Gadgets: Following Jesus in a Technological Age*. Eugene: Cascade Books.

Kallenberg, Brad J. 2012. The Theological Origins of Engineering. In *Engineering Education and Practice: Embracing a Catholic Vision*. Edited by James Heft and Kevin Hallinan. Notre Dame: University of Notre Dame Press, pp. 41–55.

Kelly, Brian. 2010. Patron Saint for the Internet, Isidore of Seville. *Catholicism.org*, January 8. Available online: http://catholicism.org/patron-saint-for-the-internet-isidore-of-seville.html (accessed on 17 April 2017).

Knight, John, and Henry Lacey. 1828. Roger Bacon. In *The Worthies of the United Kingdom; or Biographical Accounts of the Lives of the Most Illustrious Men, in Arts, Arms, Literature, and Science, Connected with Great Britain*. London: D. Sidney for Knight and Lacey, p. 48. Available online: https://books.google.com.hk/books?id=QjhkAAAAcAAJ&pg=PA39#v=onepage&q&f=false (accessed on 13 February 2017).

Kovach, Francis J. 1969. Divine Art in St. Thomas Aquinas. In *Arts liberaux et Philosophie Au Moyen Age*. Montreal: Institut d'etudes medievales, Paris: Vrin, pp. 663–71.

Levinson, Paul, and Michael Waltemathe. 2016. *Touching the Face of the Cosmos: On the Intersection of Space Travel and Religion*. New York: Connected Editions.

Lewis, Clive Staples. 1944. *The Abolition of Man*. New York: Harper Collins, p. 55. Available online: https://archive.org/stream/TheAbolitionOfMan_229/C.s.Lewis-TheAbolitionOfMan_djvu.txt (accessed on 17 February 2017).

Long Now Foundation. n.d. Available online: http://longnow.org/ (accessed on 17 February 2017).

Manning, Conleth, Thomas McErlean, and Norman Crothers. 2007. Crothers. In *Harnessing the Tides: The Early Medieval Tide Mills at Nendrum Monastery, Strangford Lough*. London: The Stationery Office.

Martín, Inés San. 2015. On Hiroshima anniversary, the pope called for a total ban on nuclear arms. *Cruxnow*, August 10. Available online: https://cruxnow.com/church/2015/08/10/on-hiroshima-anniversary-the-pope-called-for-a-total-ban-on-nuclear-arms/ (accessed on 13 February 2017).

Meilaender, Gilbert. 2013. *Should We Live Forever? The Ethical Ambiguities or Aging*. Grand Rapids: Eerdmans.

Mercer, Calvin, and Tracy J. Trothen. 2015. *Religion and Transhumanism: The Unknown Future of Human Enhancement*. Santa Barbara: Praeger.

Don Miller, OFM. 2017. Saint Isidore of Seville. In *Franciscan Media*. Available online: https://www.franciscanmedia.org/saint-isidore-of-seville/ (accessed on 17 April 2017).

Miller Center for Social Entrepreneurship. n.d. Available online: http://www.scu-social-entrepreneurship.org/ (accessed on 17 February 2017).

Mitcham, Carl, and Jim Grotes. 1984. *Theology and Technology: Essays in Christian Analysis and Exegesis*. Lanham: University Press of America.

Moritz, Joshua. 2009. Rendering unto Science and God: Is NOMA Enough? *Theology and Science* 7: 370–71. [CrossRef]

NASA. 1969. Apollo 11 Goodwill Messages. Available online: https://history.nasa.gov/ap11-35ann/goodwill/Apollo_11_material.pdf (accessed on 17 February 2017).

Noble, David F. 1998. *The Religion of Technology: The Divinity of Man and the Spirit of Invention*. New York: Alfred A. Knopf.

NRSV Committee. 1989. *The Holy Bible*. New Revised Standard Version; New York and Oxford: Oxford University Press.

O'Donovan, Oliver. 1984. *Begotten or Made?* Oxford: Oxford University Press.

Ovitt, George, Jr. 1986. The Cultural Context of Western Technology: Early Christian Attitudes towards Manual Labor. *Technology and Culture* 27: 477–500. [CrossRef]

Patterson, Thom. 2011. The surprising history of prayer in space. *CNN Belief Blog*, July 7. Available online: http://religion.blogs.cnn.com/2011/07/07/the-surprising-history-of-prayer-in-space/ (accessed on 17 February 2017).

Peters, Ted. 2013. Astrotheology. In *Routledge Companion to Modern Christian Thought*. Edited by Chad Meister and James Bielby. London: Routledge.

Plutarch. 1932. Marcellus. In *The Lives of the Noble Grecians and Romans*. New York: The Modern Library, p. 376.

Pope Benedict XVI. 2009. *Caritas in Veritate*; Vatican City: Libreria Editrice Vaticana. Available online: http://w2.vatican.va/content/benedict-xvi/en/encyclicals/documents/hf_ben-xvi_enc_20090629_caritas-in-veritate.html (accessed on 17 April 2017).

Pope Francis. 2015. *Laudato Si*. Vatican: Libreria Editrice Vaticana. Available online: http://w2.vatican.va/content/francesco/en/encyclicals/documents/papa-francesco_20150524_enciclica-laudato-si.html (accessed on 17 February 2017).

Pope John Paul II. 1981. Address to Scientists and Representatives of the United Nations University. Paper presented at Apostolic Journey to Pakistan, Philippines I, Guam (United States of America II), Japan, Anchorage (United States Of America II), Hiroshima, Japan, 16–27 February.

Pope John XXIII. 1963. *Pacem in Terris*; Vatican City: Libreria Editrice Vaticana. Available online: http://w2.vatican.va/content/john-xxiii/en/encyclicals/documents/hf_j-xxiii_enc_11041963_pacem.html (accessed on 17 February 2017).

Pope Paul VI. 1967. *Populorum Progressio*; Vatican City: Libreria Editrice Vaticana. Available online: http://w2.vatican.va/content/paul-vi/en/encyclicals/documents/hf_p-vi_enc_26031967_populorum.html (accessed on 17 February 2017).

Pope Paul VI. 1971. *Octogesima Adveniens*. Vatican City: Libreria Editrice Vaticana, Available online: http://w2.vatican.va/content/paul-vi/en/apost_letters/documents/hf_p-vi_apl_19710514_octogesima-adveniens.html (accessed on 13 February 2017).

Pope Pius XI. 1930. *Casti Conubii*; Vatican City: Libreria Editrice Vaticana. Available online: http://w2.vatican.va/content/pius-xi/en/encyclicals/documents/hf_p-xi_enc_19301231_casti-connubii.html (accessed on 17 February 2017).

Postman, Neil. 1992. *Technopoly: The Surrender of Culture to Technology*. New York: Alfred A. Knopf.

Rescher, Nicholas. 1987. *Scientific Realism*. Dordrecht: Reidel, p. 126.

Russell, Mary Doria. 1996. *The Sparrow*. New York: Ballantine.

Tertullian. 1914. *De Praescriptione Haereticorum*. Translated by T. Herbert Bindley. London and Bungay: Richard Clay and Sons.

Thiel, Peter. 2015. Against Edenism. *First Things*, June 11. Available online: https://www.firstthings.com/article/2015/06/against-edenism (accessed on 15 February 2017).

Thiel, Peter, and Blake Masters. 2014. *Zero to One: notes on Startups, or How to Build the Future*. New York: Crown Business, pp. 59–81.

Tillich, Paul. 1988. *The Spiritual Situation in our Technical Society*. Edited by J. Mark Thomas. Macon: Mercer University Press.

Turchin, Alexey. 2016. The Map of Shelters and Refuges from Global Risks (Plan B of X-risks Prevention). Available online: http://immortality-roadmap.com/sheltersmaps2.pdf (accessed on 17 April 2017).

Turchin, Alexey, and Brian Patrick Green. 2017. Aquatic Refuges for Surviving a Global Catastrophe. *Futures* 89: 26–37. [CrossRef]

Vakoch, Douglas A. 2000. Roman Catholic Views of Extraterrestrial Intelligence: Anticipating the Future by Examining the Past. In *When SETI Succeeds: The Impact of High Information Contact*. Edited by Allen Tough. Bellevue: Foundation for the Future, pp. 165–74.

Waters, Brent. 2016. *From Human to Posthuman: Christian Theology and Technology in a Postmodern World*. London: Routledge.

White, Lynn, Jr. 1978. *Medieval Religion and Technology: Collected Essays*. Berkeley: University of California Press.

Xenophon. 1971. *The Economist of Xenophon. Bibliotheca Pastorum*. Translated by Alexander D. O. Wedderburn and W. Gershom Collingwood. New York: Burt Franklin.

religions

MDPI

Article

Incarnating the Unknown: Planetary Technologies for a Planetary Community

Whitney A. Bauman

Department of Religious Studies, Florida International University, 11200 SW 8th Street, DM 301A,
Miami, FL 33199, USA; wbauman@fiu.edu; Tel.:+1-305-348-3348

Academic Editor: Noreen Herzfeld
Received: 1 February 2017; Accepted: 5 April 2017; Published: 12 April 2017

Abstract: This article suggests that current technological development is based upon outdated ways of understanding human beings as "exceptional" to the rest of the natural world. As such, these technologies help serve to reify certain human lives at the expense of others. I argue that such exceptionalism depends upon an understanding of transcendence that is totally other. Using examples such as "Earthrise" and the UN's International Treaty on Outer Space, I argue that an immanent understanding of "the other" renegotiates how we understand our embeddedness within the rest of the evolving planetary community. As part of renegotiating a planetary anthropology, we must also begin rethinking technologies as for the planet (not just for humans).

Keywords: Planetarity; new materialisms; wicked problems; earth ethics

1. Introduction

> The systems involved are complex, involving interaction among and feedback between many parts. Any changes to such a system will cascade in ways that are difficult to predict; this is especially true when human actions are involved [1].

The complexity of "wicked" problems, such as those that Bill Joy alludes to in the epigram of this article, means that we humans have to come to terms with the fact that we don't have all the solutions. Like so many other things within human histories and cultures and within individual lives, salvation often comes from beyond. Not an invisible, supernatural beyond, but from the unknown or what Ernst Bloch called the "not yet" [2]. Moments of creative insight, moments of clarity, moments of innovation and change, moments of great love for another, as well as moments of fear and trepidation, often come from beyond to lure us into new ways of thinking, relating, and becoming. This "delayed messianism" may be at the heart of the meaning of the incarnation of hope in the world: in order to create a different possible planetary community, we need something from beyond to help us shift towards new ways of becoming [3]. We humans seem to be incapable of saving ourselves, so we often look to religion and/or science to save us from ourselves.

Our contemporary contexts were forged through waves of colonization, forced and voluntary migrations, and revolutions in the technologies of communication, production, and transportation. Many contemporary identities were forged through the very threat of global annihilation, at the creation of the atomic bomb and in the fighting of two world wars, but also through the hope that emerged as the Apollo space mission sent back images of our "little blue" planet in the late 1960s. Around the same time as this space mission, one of the first planetary treaties not concerned merely with the peace of nations was forged by the United Nations: the Outer Space Treaty [4].

This article explores how an engagement with images such as "Earthrise" and documents such as the Outer Space Treaty might help to forge planetary technologies for a planetary community, which moves beyond national and religious understandings of identities and boundaries. This shift in our understanding moves us from ideas of transcendence based upon an omni-God in whose image we are created. This type of transcendence projects a space of removal, a disembodied objectivity, from which we humans (or at least some of us) can recreate the world in our own image. It treats the entire planetary community (including many humans) as means toward a colonizing end. Instead, what if we thought of an immanent, embodied form of transcendence: viz., that which is beyond our planet. Forced from a transcendent space of beyond into an immanent understanding of beyond, our interactions with the "other" becomes embodied in outer space. Such an immanent "other" could provide the grounds on which we might begin to think of what a planetary community might mean. Just as the "Earthrise" image has been used to forge a sense of a common planet, so the space treaty identifies outer space as a commons that is "for all." Of course, this "for all" may have meant for all humans, but as our understanding of the planetary community widens to embrace our embeddedness with all other life on this planet, we can begin to see it as a commons for all life on this planet. Furthermore, this new, planetary understanding of the commons means that we can't only think of resources as commons for the planetary community, but that we must begin to think of imagination and technologies for the future, as *for* the entire planetary community.

Might there be planetary technologies that help us understand our own human "animality"? [5] Might technologies help us to understand better our own enmeshment with the plant, animal, and mineral bodies on this 4.5 billion year old planet in ways that the sciences of ecology and evolution have not yet made possible? Might there be planetary technologies for our oceans, lands, atmosphere, and waters? This is precisely the shift that outer space as an unknown "other" might be a catalyst for: a shift away from national, religious, and other types of isolated identities, and towards that of planetary creatures with a common planetary future. As has always been the case in major transitions in recorded human history, these shifts will require new technologies that are not merely extensions of old ways of thinking about humans, but that re-write human relationships (in this case) as creatures co-evolving with multiple planetary others.

2. Immanent Transcendence: The Planetary Outside/Beyond

Many of the problems associated with technology come from the idea of human exceptionalism [6]. This is the idea that, either through being created in the image of God or through the capacity of reason, humans are somehow exceptional to, or transcend in some way, the rest of the natural world. It is this space of removal that then allows humans, so it goes, to manage and enhance the world around us through our technologies. The problem is that we are embedded within the processes of the rest of the natural world and that whatever humans co-create returns to affect the world in various ways. This is precisely one of the things Bill Joy warns against in his article about the unknown effects of Artificial Intelligence [1]. The unknown consequences of our actions, paired with our own embeddedness in the world, means that these technologies change our very humanity as well. In other words, the changes we make, because we are embedded in the process of ongoing evolution, also change us. The assumption of a space of objective removal is a false projection on the part of some human beings, and when this space is projected, it often smuggles in hidden cultural and historical assumptions that then begin to shape the world in the image of those historical and cultural assumptions. Many philosophers and theorists have addressed this problem of perceived transcendence, in particular as it relates to reason, science, and technology.

Martin Heidegger, for instance talks about the problem as one of enframement vs. poeisis [7]. Enframement is a closing off of the becoming world into the confines of human (mostly instrumental) reason. This turns the entire world (and eventually humans therein) into resources and things that become "standing reserve" for the furthering of the project of human reason. Such a cutting off of the world into the confines of human reason ends up destroying (through reification and putrification) the open-ended process of nature naturing. Heidegger suggests, in response, that the appropriate way to look at and understand "nature" is that of poesies: as an open-ended, emergent, self-organizing process.

Horkheimer and Adorno provide a similar analysis in their *Dialectic of Enlightenment* [8]. According to them, the problem of reason and in particular instrumental reason and the assumption of a neutral objective space, is that it essentially is a human solipsism. In other words, the entire world and all therein cannot be confined to human reason and the attempt to confine it to human reason ends up reifying nature, and eventually degrading the entire world. Even more, since humans are part of nature, reason eventually becomes an objectifying ouroboros, eating its own tail and making chaos and death out of all life, including human life. The mechanical model, with its emphasis on efficient causality and instrumental reason, and which is discovered through dispassionate objective reason, ends up killing the world.

Feminist philosophy of science has offered similar critiques that insist that bodies, histories, and cultures all matter. It is not just that transcendent objective ideals, forms, or reason are a human problem, but more specifically they are a male problem. Even more to the point, they are a Euro-Western, elite male problem. The idea of transcendence mimics the dispassionate male God who creates through no labor but with word alone *ex nihilo* [9]. This type of theology is the projection writ large of the ideal (male ruling class) human onto the cosmos. Thinkers such as Sandra Harding have thus argued that what we really need is a "strong objectivity" that takes into account the scientists' embodied subjective realities and histories [10]. If all knowledge is located, then we must know something about the gender, sex, sexuality, race, history and culture of the one producing knowledge in order to be objective in this strong sense. Critical race, post-colonial, queer, affect, and other theorists have added to the unraveling of the transcendent ideal of objective reason. Part of the impetus for doing so comes from the continuation of scientific exploration itself.

In many ways, the narrative of "the death of nature" in terms of how nature becomes merely dead matter moved by external forces still has explanatory power [11]. The shifts in cosmology that began with Copernicus and were confirmed by Galileo began to fracture the idea of the "heavens" as a place where some divine power might reside. This "dis-enchantment" was even further realized in the material world around us through Newton's mechanical understanding of physics. In many ways, the Industrial Revolution was the outcome of these more mechanical materialistic understandings of the natural world. However, there were always conflicting voices and the "death" was never quite realized. Bruno, Copernicus, and Galileo were all, in the end, religious peoples and their scientific endeavors did not, for them, negate the mystery inherent in the natural world, but rather in many ways their findings made the world more mysterious. The shifts made possible by the telescope made the universe a much larger place of which we are but a small part, which now includes a 13.8 billion-year-old universe with millions of galaxies spinning through space, not to mention the fact that we know very little about the dark matter and energy that make up the majority of our cosmos, nor do we know whether we are merely one of many universes in existence. Evolution, though used early on to combat theological dogmas, especially by the likes of Thomas Henry Huxley and Ernst Haeckel, suddenly place humans within a 4.5 billion-year process of planetary evolution, which includes religious ideas, thoughts, songs, and language just as much as it includes quantum realities, chemicals, living cells, bacteria, and everything else that we know as "nature" made up by the elements of the periodic table.

Even further, neuroscientists are beginning to understand just how relational we are in that every interaction we have changes our neuronal structures: our inside is deeply intertwined with what is outside our bodies. The Human Microbiome Project now understands the human body not as isolated individuals, but as ecosystems made up mostly of non-human cells. We are more consciously aware of our embeddedness in a planetary community and in a vast cosmos than at any other point in the history of humanity that we know of. Furthermore, the boundaries between energy/matter, human/animal, male/female, living/dead are now more challenged and made mysterious by the very sciences that at times purport to demystify the world they study. Science itself, then, challenges the narrative that nature is dead. Indeed all the way up to the early 20th century, scientists such as Wilhelm Bölsche, Gustav Fechner, and Ernst Haeckel (among others) were arguing about whether or not the methodological and epistemological foundations of the natural sciences ought to be reductive materialism, idealism, dualism, or some form of non-reductive materialism that included both energy/matter, mind/brain, body/soul [12–14]. Right up to the time of the second world war of the 20th century, scientists had not yet agreed that nature was "dead stuff." This was all to change with the war efforts that conscripted nearly all chemists and physicists into a technology transfer model of science which produced things: first for the war machine, then for industrial agriculture, then for advances in communication, transportation, and production technologies. It was really the world wars, then, that cemented the reductive, instrumental model of the natural sciences that was assumed nearly universally by scientists until Rachel Carson published *Silent Spring* in the 1960s and the modern environmental movement began [15].

What I am arguing here is that the model of reductive materialism and the "industrial" type of technology that comes out of such a model is more of a historical blip on the radar than the norm for the natural sciences. It lasted, largely unchallenged, from around WWII until the early 1960s. This was a mere 20 years. Emergent theorists, feminist philosophers, critical theories, new materialisms, and many voices from within the area of "religion and ecology" and "religion and nature" have been lifting up the problems of reductive materialism and the need for a new understanding of the natural world that includes humans, cultures, thoughts, and histories, just as much as it includes atoms, chemicals, quarks, rivers, and forests. However, the methods of reductive and productionist science that opt for the economic benefits of technology transfer have not really shifted to match our current understanding. We are still, largely, producing technologies for human advances alone and based upon the assumptions of instrumental reason, efficient causality, and human mastery. In other words, we are still acting as if there are transcendent places of objective removal, from which we (like an omni-God in whose image we are made) can (re)create the world *ex nihilo*. The end result of imagining humans as a transcendent from or exceptional to the rest of the natural world is that we recreate the world, through our technologies, in our own image. Instead, what we need is an understanding of transcendence (something beyond us) that doesn't negate our embeddedness and immanence.

Perhaps one type of immanent transcendence can be gleaned from the first images of our planet from outer space in 1968, taken by Apollo 8. This "Earthrise" image was the first time we had really seen our earth as a unified planet from the outside. All histories, all cultures, all wars, all art, all animals, plants, minerals that ever existed all of the sudden seemed radically connected in a way that had never before been pictured. Yet, this was an immanent, embodied transcendence: the astronauts taking the picture were no more objective than the billions of people on the earth that they could not see or detect from the outside. The astronauts were outside the planet, yes, but still embodied and no more omniscient than anyone on the planet. Their own cultures and histories still shaped the ways in which they interpreted the images they were seeing, just as everyone else interprets it from their own socio-historical and biological locations. There are at least three lessons to be learned about immanent-transcendence from this image.

The first I have already mentioned: whatever objectivity might mean, it does not mean seeing all life on the planet at once as if from a god's eye view. There is no way to see all the differences and perspectives when one gets too far away: and this suggests something important about the way human knowledge works. It is always perspectival, partial, and depends upon the ability to relate to other people, places, animals, plants, minerals, and things. No relation, no knowledge.

The second is that objective spaces that assume removal gloss over difference and diversity. In other words, we may know something by going to other cultures and going to places outside of the planet, but it always needs to be understood from within our own historical-social context, and within the context of the larger planetary community. Otherwise instead of understanding ourselves as learning from the other, we act as if we can speak fully for the other.

Third, and related to the first two points, the Earthrise image challenges all narratives that lay claim to universal knowledge. All of the earthly narratives, whether religious, philosophical, or scientific are now shown to be but many different understandings of a world we hold in common. Any claim to universality needs to explain how intimate knowledge of the farthest reaches of the universe might be possible for a species that exists and persists primarily in one planet, in one solar system, and in one galaxy.

We are all beneficiaries of a cosmos and planet of which we are but a part: the human ideal of objectivity that seeks to see it all as a monotheistic god might, eventually leads to an attempt to create the world in its own image. This, as we have seen, creates a lot of planetary problems (e.g., global climate change). This may seem like an odd argument, seeing as how many sciences, including the ones that tell us we are part of a 13.8 billion-year expanding universe, lay claim to objectivity. However, I would also argue (along with Bruno Latour, for example) that in actuality sciences are giving voice to many more perspectives other than the human, and serving as spokespersons for those (chemical, atomic, ecosystemic, cosmic, etc.) voices [16]. It is part of the process of allowing multiple perspectives to come together in creation of a common world, not a dictating how and for whom that world ought to become. Rather than seeking to colonize from an outside space, the stories of the sciences are those of immanent, embedded "others" constructing a commons that together transcend all located perspectives, and thus cannot be reduced to one perspective. The "Earthrise" image helps us to imagine such a commons, while the International Space Treaty sought to articulate that commons. Together, they provide us with a good source for imagining what a planetary, immanent transcendence might mean.

The bulkily named "Treaty on Principles Governing the Activities of States in the Exploration and Use of Outer Space, including the Moon and Other Celestial Bodies" was a United Nations document that came into effect in 1967 [4]. During the Cold War era, it boldly claimed that, "the exploration and use of outer space shall be carried out for the benefit and interests of all countries and shall be the province of all mankind." Further, it claimed that "outer space is not subject to national appropriation by claim of sovereignty, by means of use or occupation, or by any other means," and that "states shall not place nuclear weapons or other weapons of mass destruction in orbit or on celestial bodies or station them in outer space in any other manner" [4]. There were several other clauses and statements in the treaty, but these are the general ones setting up outer space as a commons.

In 1967 so much was unknown about space and what our possibilities might be in terms of space travel. Even though today so much is still unknown, we have an international space station, many countries have sent people to space, we have sent powerful telescopes further and further out in to space, rovers have landed on Mars, and the first "commercial" space vehicle is under construction. It remains to be seen how far into the future our immediate solar system will serve as a commons "for all" (humankind and earthkind), but for the foreseeable future, it does. The outside of our frame of planetary reference is a commons, a place for peaceful exploration rather than industry and personal gain. The outside of our embodied frame of reference (the planet) is not some blank "space" onto which we can project whatever we want: it too exists in a context of 13.8 billion years of cosmic expansion, yet it transcends us in that it is the outside of our earthly, historical, social, and daily lives. This is the type of immanent transcendence that might be a good starting point for understanding ourselves as first and foremost "planetary citizens" among other humans and the more than human world, rather than first and foremost as a member of one or another religion, nation, or other type of tribe [17]. This is the type of immanent transcendence that, as a "commons" does not allow individuals (or a people) to use it as an Archimedean point from which to recapitulate and reform (indeed terraform) the whole planet; rather it must be inclusive of the multiple perspectives and embodiments that make up our planet (as it is a commons and not the property of any one). In other words this is a commons, which pre-existed human beings and even the planet earth, and of which we are but a part. It is ultimately a reference point that we can use not to recreate the world as if "*ex nihilo,*" but rather from which we can understand ourselves as radically immanent, radically interrelated, and radically multiple. Indeed, as Randolph and McKay argue, developing an ethics for astrobiology might help us to "protect and expand the richness and diversity of life" here on planet Earth as well ([18], p. 33). Just as new types of "religious" and "ethical" understanding of ourselves ought to be derived out of an awareness of our planetary identity, so too new "scientific" and "technological" understandings ought to follow from this.

3. The Flattening of Life without Homogenization

Some have argued that the loss of transcendence and so-called "collapse into immanence" has led to a rise in reductive materialism and mechanical models of nature, and a collapse into individualism ([19], pp. 539–93). However, I would argue that the type of transcendence that takes us away from embodiment and contextuality, and the type of objectivity that relies on such transcendence is actually a collapse into certainty, materialism, and individualism. Let me explain a bit further. As Bruno Latour has pointed out the problem with objectivity which is the "outside" of subjectivity, or the problem of "transcendence" which is the outside of "immanence" is that the whole is then fully defined: all that exists can be understood as existing between these two poles [16]. A monotheistic God which transcends the earth is the container of possibilities for what that earth might become; a universal Reason with universal laws is the container for what nature can possibly become.

If, instead, we move to a model of immanent transcendence, it implies an emergent ontology in which the possibilities of the future of life are radically open to multiple different directions [20]. This may be understood as the "poesies" Heidegger argued for, or it may be understood as the rhyzomatic ontology that Deleuze and Guattari argued for [21]. Such immanence is not a prison, rather it opens us up to multiple possibilities for future becoming. As Latour notes, "Deprived of the help of transcendence, we at first believe we are going to suffocate for want of oxygen; then we notice that we are breathing more freely than before: transcendences abound" ([16], p. 187). Furthermore, such collapse into immanence re-places us into a world of evolving relations, as assemblages within the planetary community.

Whether we use the metaphor and models of "assemblages," of "New Materialisms" or of "object oriented ontologies," the point of such rethinking of identity, things, and relationships is to make events and processes primary and to challenge any type of essentialism that would cut us off from the rest of the planet (and thus suggest some type of transcendence of self vs. other) [21–23]. In other words, we are assemblages of the evolution of multiple histories, ecologies, biologies, chemicals, minerals, plants, and animals. According to the Human Microbiome Project, our bodies are better thought of as ecosystems rather than individual organisms [24]. Neurologically, our inside is connected with our outside in that our neural structures change with every interaction we make. The boundaries between biotic and abiotic, plant and animal, human and other animals are constantly challenged. All of this we know, yet we still have a model for understanding technologies as instruments used toward specific goals (mostly for the benefit of human beings). Our scientific, religious, philosophical, and cultural traditions in general, all condition us to live as if: humans are above the rest of nature, there are clear boundaries between self and other, there are distinct species boundaries, things can be known discretely, and actions can be isolated to individual causes. What we need, rather, is a shift in our perspective toward understanding ourselves as embedded and evolving with, rather than as exceptions to, the rest of the planetary community.

So much of our lives is determined by the biological, historical, and cultural processes that build up over time, long before our own existences. We are simply thrown into these processes at birth. What is meant by male or female, race, or personal "success," what it means to be a person, ideas of family, ideas of the "good life," all of these ideas and/or roles pull and tug our bodies, luring them toward certain ways of becoming rather than others [25]. These ideas, norms and habits can also be labeled technologies that shape and form the embodied world in which we live. We would not ever say that we rationally choose to adopt these technologies as we were thrown into a life that was already marked by them. What makes us so sure that we can rationally adopt any technology? It turns out, we may not be the rational selves we think we are. Technologies design our lives toward certain ways of becoming rather than others and we likely can no more "rationally adopt" or reject them than we can rationally choose when and where we are born.

Deep-seated emotions, feelings, and affectations are shaping us on a daily basis. This is, at least, the idea of "affect theory" [26]. In short, we have for too long in the modern and postmodern world assumed a rationalized version of the body: if the problem is bad information, let us just input new information and changes will follow. This is an old assumption based upon an Enlightenment understanding that proper education and rationality will lead to "correct" decision-making. Al Gore is a recent, perfect example of the failure of this way of thinking. In his documentary, "An Inconvenient Truth," the assumption is that we just need to understand better the evidence and the information on climate change, and we will begin to behave differently and demand different politics around energy consumption. But, the truth is, we have never really been rational just as we have never really been modern (and by extension postmodern) [27]. We are more like assemblages of processes that pre-date us, feeling our way through moments based upon what lures us and what repels us. Affects are not just emotions, but deep-seated tendencies that shape and form how we are able even to express our emotions and vitality.

One of the promises of affect theory, is that we can begin to acknowledge how little we do is based upon rational choice. Accordingly, we might begin to address the underlying structures that push and pull us toward some ways of becoming more than others. Furthermore, dismantling the ideal of the "rational individual," which relies upon that transcendent objective space that enables us to negate our historical and biological embodiment, helps open us on to the planetary community in which we are embedded. In other words, human exceptionalism is based upon one form of objective removal or another: *imago Dei*, Language, Reason [6]. In its challenge to all of these "technologies," affect theory encourages us to pay more attention to the ways in which our living, breathing, eating, defecating, copulating, dying, evolving bodies are connected with the rest of the natural world in ways that shape us well beyond what we might rationally examine. We are "in the midst" and not above the fray of the bubbling process of nature naturing. How might we then begin to create technologies that affirm and reinforce our evolving interconnectedness with the planetary community, rather than developing technologies based upon the idea that reason allows us to distance ourselves from this process of nature naturing? We need to start thinking about planetary technologies.

4. Planetary Technologies, Delayed Justifications

If the outside or the beyond of the planet is understood as a planetary commons, then it seems that our ability to think about our planet should result from collective imagining. How might our collective imaginings incarnate in the world around us? How do our visions translate to technological and scientific advances that promote the entire planetary community rather than just human beings (or some human beings)? How do these collective imaginings shape and change our embodiments and our relations? These are some of the questions we might begin to ask ourselves from a position of located, immanent transcendence. Indeed, ever since the "Earthrise" image, we have had the capacity to be imaginatively on the "outside looking in." With the exception of the handful of astronauts who actually get to experience this with the naked eye, most of us will only experience this as mediated through technologies. But it is a powerful experience nonetheless. Rather than imagining that we are "without" location when we examine images of the earth from outer space, it is rather helpful always to remember that we are exactly looking at it from an embodied perspective, and without that body there would be no imagining. Just as one might have some type of out-of-body experience, there is no way to speak of it unless he/she returns to the body that experiences this, so too with this experience of looking at the world "from the outside."

We need this embodied space of "outside" so that we can begin to imagine ourselves as planetary creatures or citizens among many other creaturely, planetary citizens (both human and non). Such images, when they are always coupled with the embodied realities of the planet and the different ways different bodies experience the world based upon geographical location, race, class, gender, sex, sexuality, ability, history, and culture, can be a powerful tool for imagining ourselves beyond parochial, nationalistic, or other exceptional identities of imagined superiority.

Revelation, in its monotheistic forms, works by a breaking in from beyond to uncover a new possible reality. Deconstruction, in the western philosophical forms and in Vedic forms of breaking through illusion, allows us to see other possibilities for how we might interpret the world around us and our places therein. Tricksters and iconoclasts help us to uncover possibilities that are there for realizing, if we only break open the stale ways in which we have come to understand the world around us. These methods for understanding reality anew in ways that we might begin to live differently all depend upon some sort of beyond: but not on a beyond that is unrelated to the here and now. It is rather, like the possibilities of multiverses, which exist right on top of us; it is an immanent and intertwined form of transcendence [28].

How might our technologies, rather than recapitulating the human worlds that we know and understand, begin to foster us to live in other ways? What would technologies that help us to deconstruct business as usual and reconstruct ourselves as planetary citizens look like? Perhaps we need technologies for healthy forests, technologies for integral oceans, and technologies that promote the thriving of the human microbiome rather than mere instrumental technologies that help humans transform the world into "things" that are useful and instrumental for us. To be certain, we will also need to question what a successful technology is: it cannot just be measured on the instrumental value for human life, and the amount of money it may potentially generate. We also need to rethink, in other words, where justification comes from.

Currently technologies, built upon efficient causality and designed with instrumental reason, are based upon justifications that come from the present or immediate future. Instant gratification comes to mind: there is an isolated problem, concern, desire, or need, and this or that technology steps in to answer or fulfill. Success in this model is based on how well it addresses the issue in isolation, often without much understanding of the ways in which its effects ripple out to affect multiple earth bodies in different ways and throughout time. The so-called "green revolution" is a great example. The problem: not enough food to feed a growing human population. The solution: industrialize agriculture the world over in order to increase crop yields in so-called "developing" countries. The unintended outcome: a lot of people made a lot of money, and even in developing countries the larger farmers who could afford the new technologies made out well; however, with the increase in commodity crop production the price of said commodities fell, forcing smaller farmers out of business and thereby leading to the consolidation of land into fewer and fewer hands, and an increase in poverty for some [29]. Furthermore, industrial agriculture has led to severe water, air, and land pollution, and also has increased the CO_2 and other greenhouse gas levels contributing to climate change. Yet, the technologies as they were developed—to increase crop yields—justified their purpose. The meta-analysis of how those technologies have changed the face of the planet and daily life are still being measured. Similarly, Bill Joy is arguing for us to pay close attention to the unintended consequences of Artificial Intelligence (AI) in his article outlining what he perceives to be future dangers [1].

What we need, then, is technological development that understands that our interactions in the world lead to so-called "wicked" problems that do not have clear-cut solutions and that lead to unintended consequences [30]. The justification and cost-benefit analysis of a given technology's "goodness" can only come from the future, from outside of the present looking back. The Iroquois' "seventh generation principle" gets at this type of analysis: that we should only do something when we have thought about its effects for the next seven generations. Rob Nixon's *Slow Violence* also draws attention to the ways in which technologies fan out in the ecosystem over generations, affecting especially the poorest of bodies around the world [31]. We need to map these geographies of violence over generations to reveal the ways in which technologies might be judged "better" or "worse." More importantly, we should start thinking more about how to build in critical adaptation into technology transfer. As we become aware of problems that arise, companies that have perpetuated the unintended problem(s) should be largely responsible for monetarily spearheading the solutions to said problem(s). Technologies need to become as organic, varied and adaptable as the rest of life on the planet, rather than used merely to secure a certain way of being in the world for certain peoples. The idea of "cradle to cradle" technologies, in which the waste of one technology becomes the material for yet another, come to mind here [32]. Biomimicry, in which we look to how things are "done" in nature to make more sustainable technologies, also comes to mind [33]. Technologies should be about creating new possibilities for a thriving planetary community, rather than securing a particular way of being in the world.

The possibilities of creating alternative worlds is nothing new to the world of fiction, and particularly science fiction. It is also important for almost every religious tradition: something is not right with the world we inhabit, and we can come up with a radically different way of living together on this planet. J. Cameron Carter speaks of the imaginative work that needs to be done in terms of developing "parallel visions" for planetary becoming [34]. *Para*, in the Greek, as Carter notes, is "next to." It is precisely not an anti-vision of the world, as anti-visions often mirror the structures they develop against. This is something Catherine Keller also argues: instead of an anti-apocalypse, we need a counter-apocalypse [35]. It is also not a "post" vision, as "post" whatever is merely a line of continuation from what comes before. Rather, it is an acknowledgement of many different realities existing side by side, simultaneously. It is opening us up to the reality of and the possibilities of a multiverse [28].

The problem with most technologies as they exist and persist, is that they are largely geared toward recreating the world in which we live: perhaps in a "better" way than before, but they are often not critical of the dominant structures in societies. What might an egalitarian, earth-friendly, technology that helped us to create different spaces for planetary becoming look like? Some visionaries have attempted this type of thinking toward a radically different future: Buckminster Fuller and Paolo Soleri come to mind. These technologies create a world in which way more life than merely some human life matters and is taken into consideration. The extending of our circle of moral concern past the human and to the rest of the natural world, ought also to be an extension of our technological concern beyond merely the human. Still, for the most part, technologies are developed to make some human lives easier or last longer; in this way, these technologies continue to reify the human as exceptional to the rest of the natural world, and thus all life as fodder toward human ends. Developing a planetary technology would begin to understand that every technology has the power to open up new ways of being in the world; every technology has the potential to create new relations among humans and between humans and the rest of the natural world. In a sense, every technology has the ability to co-construct new meaning-making practices and ways of living within the planetary community. It is this call toward alternative ways of becoming that technological creation must heed if we don't want to continue the reification of all life on the planet for the betterment of a few human beings.

Conflicts of Interest: The author declares no conflict of interest.

References

1. Bill Joy. "Why the Future Doesn't Need Us." *WiRED*, 1 April 2000. Available online: https://www.wired.com/2000/04/joy-2/ (accessed on 11 April 2017).
2. Ernst Bloch. *The Principle of Hope.* Cambridge: MIT Press, 1986, vol. 3.
3. Jacque Derrida. *Specters of Marx.* New York: Routledge, 1994.
4. United Nations, Office for Outer Space Affairs. "Treaty on Principles Governing the Activities of States in the Exploration and Use of Outer Space, including the Moon and Other Celestial Bodies." 1966. Available online: http://www.unoosa.org/oosa/en/ourwork/spacelaw/treaties/introouterspacetreaty.html (accessed on 11 April 2017).
5. Mel Chen. *Animacies: Biopolitics, Racial Mattering and Queer Affect.* Durham: Duke University Press, 2012.
6. Anna Peterson. *Being Human: Ethics, Environment and Our Place in the World.* Berkeley: University of California Press, 2001.
7. Martin Heidegger. *Question Concerning Technology and Other Essays.* New York: Harper and Row, 1977.
8. Max Horkheimer, and Theodor Adorno. *Dialectic of Enlightenment.* Stanford: Stanford University Press, 2002.

9. Whitney Bauman. *Theology, Creation and Environmental Ethics*. New York: Routledge, 2009.
10. Sandra Harding. "Rethinking Standpoint Epistemology: What is 'Strong Objectivity'?" In *Feminist Epistemologies*. Edited by Linda Alcoff and Elizabeth Potters. New York: Routledge, 1993, pp. 49–82.
11. Carolyn Merchant. *The Death of Nature: Women, Ecology and the Scientific Revolution*. New York: HarperCollins, 1980.
12. Gustav Fechner. *Nanna Oder Über das Seelenleben Der Pflanzen*. Leipzig: Leopold Voss, 1848.
13. Wilhelm Bölsche. *Love Life in Nature: The Tory of the Evolution of Love*. New York: Albert & Charles Boni, 1926, vol. 2.
14. Ernst Haeckel. *Monism as Connecting Religion and Science: The Confession of Faith of a Man of Science*. London: Adam & Charles Black, 1895.
15. Rachel Carson. *Silent Spring*. New York: Houghton Mifflin, 1962.
16. Bruno Latour. *Politics of Nature: How to Bring the Sciences into Democracy*. Cambridge: Harvard University Press, 2004.
17. Whitney Bauman. *Religion and Ecology: Developing a Planetary Ethic*. New York: Columbia University Press, 2014.
18. Richard Randolph, and Christopher McKay. "Protecting and Expanding the Richness and Diversity of Life: An Ethic for Astrobiology Research and Space Exploration." *International Journal of Astrobiology* 13 (2014): 28–34. [CrossRef]
19. Charles Taylor. *A Secular Age*. Cambridge: Harvard University Press, 2007.
20. Terrence Deacon. *Incomplete Nature: How Mind Emerged from Matter*. New York: WW Norton, 2012.
21. Gilles Deleuze, and Felix Guattari. *A Thousand Plateaus: Capitalism and Schizophrenia*. Minneapolis: University of Minnesota Press, 1987.
22. Jane Bennett. *Vibrant Matter: A Political Ecology of Things*. Durham: Duke University Press, 2010.
23. Timothy Morton. *Realistic Magic: Objects, Ontology, Causality*. Ann Arbor: University of Michigan, 2013.
24. National Institute of Health. "Human Microbiome Project. " Available online: http://hmpdacc.org/ (accessed on 11 April 2017).
25. Pierre Bourdieu. *The Field of Cultural Production*. New York: Columbia University Press, 1993.
26. Donovan Schaefer. *Religious Affects: Animality, Evolution and Power*. Durham: Duke University Press, 2015.
27. Bruno Latour. *We Have Never Been Modern*. Cambridge: Harvard University Press, 1993.
28. Mary-Jane Rubenstein. *Worlds without End: The Many Lives of the Multiverse*. New York: Columbia University Press, 2014.
29. Vandana Shiva. *Staying Alive: Women, Ecology and Development*. London: Zed Books, 1989.
30. Horst W. J. Rittel, and Melvin Webber. "Dilemmas in a General Theory of Planning." *Policy Sciences* 4 (1973): 155–69. [CrossRef]
31. Rob Nixon. *Slow Violence and the Environmentalism of the Poor*. Cambridge: Harvard University Press, 2013.
32. William McDonough, and Michael Braungart. *Cradle to Cradle: Remaking the Way We Make Things*. New York: North Point Press, 2002.
33. Janine M. Benyus. *Biomimicry: Innovation Inspired by Nature*. New York: HarperCollins, 1997.
34. J. Cameron Carter, and Keri Day. "Conversation on the Flesh, Spirit, and the Black Sacred." Paper presented at the Lecture at the American Academy of Religion Meeting, San Antonio, TX, USA, 19 November 2016.
35. Catherine Keller. *Apocalypse Now and Then: A Feminist Guide to the End of the World*. Minneapolis: Fortress, 1996.

religions |MDPI|

Article

The Glorified Body: Corporealities in the Catholic Tradition

Cory Andrew Labrecque

Faculty of Theology and Religious Studies, Université Laval, Pavillon Félix-Antoine-Savard, (bureau 714), 2325, rue des Bibliothèques, Québec, QC G1V 0A6, Canada; cory-andrew.labrecque@ftsr.ulaval.ca

Received: 5 August 2017; Accepted: 25 August 2017; Published: 28 August 2017

Abstract: The rise of new technologies—robotics, artificial intelligence, and nanotechnology among them—gave the American computer scientist Bill Joy certain pause for deep concern; these, he cautioned, carry the very real potential to push humankind toward extinction. In this essay, I explore an often understated reference in conversations on the promises and shortcomings of said technologies: the disposability of the human body. The Catholic tradition, in particular, boasts a rich and extensive collection of teachings on the theology of the body, which addresses, among other things, the significance of the body for human identity, its relationship to the soul, our (restrained) rights and mastery over it, its (proper) uses over the course of life, its relationship with other bodies, the value of its limitations, and its postmortem fate. Here, I engage the Church's understanding of the centrality of the body alongside currents in transhumanist philosophy which champion technologies that neglect, or intentionally seek to discard, the body in the name of progress.

Keywords: theology of the body; resurrection; throwaway culture; glorified body; transhumanism

In his *Phenomenology of Perception*, the philosopher Maurice Merleau-Ponty affirms that "the body is our anchorage in a world" (Merleau-Ponty 1990, p. 128). In other words, we gain access to the world because of—and through—the body. Importantly, he refuses to reduce the body to something that we simply *have*, declaring that "I am not in front of my body, I am in it, or rather I *am it*" (Merleau-Ponty 1990, p. 133). The idea that we *are* our bodies, which Merleau-Ponty contends has been vastly undervalued in philosophy, is echoed over and again in John Paul II's seminal contribution to the Catholic Church's teaching on corporeality. In accord with Merleau-Ponty, the pope made plain that since the human person expresses him or herself by means of the body, he or she *is*, in this sense, the body (Paul 2006, n. 55:2). "Together with the spirit," John Paul II wrote in stark opposition to dualistic renderings, "the body determines man's ontological subjectivity and participates in his dignity as a person" (Paul 2006, n. 45:1).

In contrast, proponents of transhumanism (such as Nick Bostrom, James Hughes, and Max More)—a vision and movement that is of increasing interest to academics across the disciplines—persistently bemoan the deficiencies of our material existence, urging that we must ultimately liberate ourselves from our confining, mortal bodies. "We will ignore the biological fundamentalists," More asserts, "who will invoke 'God's plan,' or 'the natural order of things,' in an effort to imprison us at the human level. We will move through the transhuman stage into posthumanity, where our physical and intellectual capacities will exceed a human's as a human's capacities exceed an ape's. To fully flower, self-transformation requires a rebellion against humanity" (More 1993).

In order to assure some degree of continuity from one stage to another (and it is *cognitive* rather than *bodily* continuity that matters to transhumanists), More is convinced that self-directed change is "more likely to result in continuous development rather than disruption of self since the outcome will better reflect our values and goals" (More 1993). By a process that he calls "transbiomorphosis," the human body is expected to be gradually replaced with a magnificently engineered synthetic life-sustaining vessel that is far more "worthy of our evolving intelligence" (More 1993). This portrayal of the human body as irrelevant or encumbering, and its diminution to a mere "container for the mind, the true locus of personal value" (Campbell 2009, p. 2) reflect a functionalist approach to personhood that prizes cognitive capacity over and above all else.

In this paper, I compare and contrast transhumanist and Roman Catholic conceptions of the human body, paying attention to how these two worldviews evaluate the relevance of the human body for individual identity and for the way we connect to the material world writ large. This comparative study sheds light on how indifference toward, or disregard for, the corporeal—articulated by transhumanist philosophers in light of biotechnological advancement—risks atomizing, mechanizing, or disposing bodies, especially marginalized and non-conforming bodies that fall short of the posthuman ideal. I hope that the content herein prompts a broader, yet ever more urgent, conversation among scholars of religion, theologians, ethicists, and transhumanist philosophers on the necessity of the human body and the parameters (if any) of its mutability as strides are made in fields such as biomedical engineering and regenerative medicine. Evidently, our understanding of the body as disposable or indispensable has important implications for the way we think about human–human, human–nonhuman, and human–environment relationships.

1. Technological Soteriology and Morphological Freedom

It is one thing to speak about biotechnological interventions to aid or even enhance the human body, but it is quite another to propose that these interventions should aim at moving beyond the body altogether. The want to transcend or, better, the want to be delivered from the limitations of humanhood, a fundamental tenet of transhumanist philosophy, sometimes amounts to just this. There is no real need for the human body, many transhumanists argue; in fact, the vulnerabilities wrought upon us by the human body are obstacles to our proper flourishing and they are surmountable. "Your body is a deathtrap," Bostrom writes in his *Letter from Utopia*, "this vital machine and mortal vehicle, unless it jams first or crashes, is sure to rust anon . . . oh, it is not well to live in a self-combusting paper hut!" (Bostrom 2008, pp. 3–4).

Ironically, when it comes to the quest for immortality, a number of transhumanists—including Bostrom (Leonard 2013)—have signed up for cryonics, which offers a person the option of vitrifying the body (or just the head) until the day when we have the biotechnological means to revive, restore, and improve it (Alcor Life Extension Foundation 2017). However scornful one might be toward the human body and its lamentable imperfections, if one wishes to maintain some continuity in identity then to dispose of the body, at least at this time, risks oblivion unless there is some other way to assure that the person before and after technological self-transformation is still one persisting entity, albeit qualitatively different (More 1993). More seems to suggest that the real pressing concern is in making sure that said transformation is always *self-directed*. This morphological freedom—that is, one's right to maintain or modify the self as he or she desires (Sandberg 2001)—flows out of the transhumanist proclivity for the autonomy of persons over their own bodies. As an aside, it is interesting to note that some transhumanists make a point to restrain this right by considering the harms that self-modification might cause to others. It is this self-direction, More says, that sustains continuity because "continuity requires that later stages of an individual *develop* out of earlier stages, rather than simply usurping their place" (More 1993). It is not always clear in the transhumanist literature whether an eventual rift in (psychological) continuity as the posthuman emerges is something that can or should be avoided altogether.

Some proponents of mind uploading—that is, "transferring an intellect from a biological brain to a computer" (Humanity+ 2016)—suggest that while embodiment might matter, having a specifically *human* body does not. "For the continuation of personhood," Bostrom writes, "it matters little whether you are implemented on a silicon chip inside a computer or in that gray, cheesy lump inside your skull, assuming both implementations are conscious" (Humanity+ 2016). Therefore, "an upload could have a virtual (simulated) body giving the same sensations and the same possibilities for interaction as a non-simulated body. With advanced virtual reality, uploads could enjoy food and drink, and upload sex could be as gloriously messy as one could wish. And uploads wouldn't have to be confined to virtual reality: they could interact with people on the outside and even rent robot bodies in order to work in or explore physical reality" (Humanity+ 2016).

Among the many advantages envisaged for an upload, some transhumanists include that it "would not be subject to biological senescence; back-up copies of uploads could be created regularly so that you could be re-booted if something bad happened (thus your lifespan would potentially be as long as the universe's); you could potentially live much more economically as an upload since you wouldn't need physical food, housing, transportation, etc., [...]; you would think faster than in a biological implementation [. . .]; you would thus get to experience more subjective time, and live more, during any given day; you could travel at the speed of light as an information pattern, which could be convenient in a future age of large-scale space settlements; [and] radical cognitive enhancements would likely be easier to implement in an upload than in an organic brain" (Humanity+ 2016). Similarly, the development of intelligent machines and the want to create human–robot fusions, a phenomenon that Bill Joy comments on in his article, *Why the Future Doesn't Need Us*, brings to the fore a comparable indifference or outright aversion to the *human* body (Joy 2000).

Herein lies an important debate in transhumanism regarding the necessity of the body for posthumanhood. There is something incongruous about needing the body to build on and enhance it, and the desire to replace the body in its totality in order to combat the tragic forces of ageing and mortality attached to our current material existence. The transhumanist vision, of course, is that enhancement may very well lead to replacement, if the person so chooses to move in that direction. This, though, becomes a delicate matter. John Harris, in his *Enhancing Evolution: The Ethical Case for Making Better People*, is convinced that the future of humankind depends on framing enhancement as a moral duty (Harris 2007, pp. 19–35), but whether replacing the body altogether ought to be a moral duty as well (once the proper technology becomes available) is left up in the air. Whatever the case, both of these propositions seem to impose on individual autonomy and this would not be consistent with transhumanist ethics. Although the enthusiasm, in transhumanist circles, around the biotechnological promise to evolve from human to posthuman is high, it is often tempered—intentionally or not—by this emphasis on autonomy. Most of the transhumanist philosophers I have included here prefer the language of "*self*-directed transformation" and "morphological *freedom*" to an endorsement of enhancing or replacing the body as an ethical *imperative* for the future of (post)humanhood despite the fact that the latter underlies the transhumanist mission.

For Bostrom, at least, there is a certain sense of moral urgency in transcending human nature, which he describes as "a work-in-progress, a half-baked beginning that we can learn to remold in desirable ways" (Bostrom 2005, p. 4; Humanity+ 2016). This does not, and must not, amount to the perception and treatment of *people* as disposable and substitutable (say, by some mass of superhuman beings) (Humanity+ 2016), but hinges on making available to all the option to move beyond the body and its limitations.

2. The Human Body in the Catholic Tradition

Although transhumanism espouses a certain soteriological vision that has seriously engaged scholars of religion and theology (some have contended that transhumanism looks very much like a secular religion), the human body is arguably the site of greatest contention between this worldview and the Roman Catholic tradition.

Centuries of Christian discourse on the relationship between the body and the soul reflect a general discomfort with the body that was certainly prevalent in the early Church (Ramsey 1985, p. 59), but that was ultimately assuaged by an affirmation of the body as part of the created order that God deemed to be "very good" in its entirety (Gen. 1.31). Lamentations about the miseries of our mortal existence (including the loss of human control over the body)—introduced to humanhood after the Fall—abounded in the writings of the Church Fathers; many have correlations with the overall malaise regarding the human condition that characterizes the transhumanist movement. It was Augustine, for instance, who melancholically claimed that "a hard condition is the life of man. What else is it to be born, but to enter on a life of toil? Of our toil that is to be, the infant's very cry is witness. From this cup of sorrow no one may be excused" (Augustine of Hippo 1844, sermon X.2). Subsequently, in *The tCity of God*, he listed a host of "cruel ills" that the whole of the human race is condemned to know (Augustine 1999, XXII.22).

Augustine also echoed, in some sense, the dreadful impotence of mortals in the face of death (what transhumanism refers to as "deathism" (Humanity+ 2016)): "for no sooner do we begin to live in this dying body, than we begin to move ceaselessly towards death. For in the whole course of this life (if life we must call it) its mutability tends toward death [...] so that our whole life is nothing but a race towards death, in which no one is allowed to stand still for a little space, or to go somewhat more slowly, but all are driven forwards with an impartial movement, and with equal rapidity" (Augustine 1999, XIII.10).

Still, Augustine also recognized and celebrated the "countless blessings with which the goodness of God, who cares for all He has created, has filled this very misery of the human race;" among them, he names: human fecundity, the mind (with its gifts of reason and understanding), our ability to love what is good and virtuous, and, of primary importance here, the extraordinariness of the body (although weak and mortal, its function and beauty bear witness to God's providence) (Augustine 1999, XXII.24).

When it came to the principal tenet of theological anthropology that describes all human beings as created in the image and likeness of God, many—though not all—of the Church Fathers believed that it was not in the body, but only in the soul—the seat of reason, free will, and dominion—that one resembled God (Ramsey 1985, pp. 68–69). Irenaeus, however, disagreed. "For by the hands of the Father, that is, by the Son and the Holy Spirit," he proclaimed, "man, and not merely a part of man, was made in the likeness of God. Now the soul and the spirit are certainly a *part* of the man, but certainly not *the* man; for the perfect man consists in the commingling and the union of the soul receiving the spirit of the Father, and the admixture of that fleshly nature which was moulded after the image of God" (Irenaeus n.d., V.VI.1).

The Catholic tradition echoes this teaching on the composite existence of humanhood. In his "Letter to Families," called *Gratissimam Sane*, John Paul II made a point to underline that "it is typical of rationalism to make a radical contrast in man between spirit and body, between body and spirit. But man is a person in the unity of his body and his spirit. The body can never be reduced to mere matter: it is a *spiritualized body*, just as man's spirit is so closely united to the body that he can be described as *an embodied spirit*" (Paul 1994, n. 19). In the text, the pope goes on to warn the reader about the challenges of a new Manichaeism in the world that is putting body and spirit in opposition, resulting in the objectification of human persons (Paul 1994, n. 19).

The understanding of the human person as a *unity* (*corpore et anima unus*) that forms a single nature (Catholic Church 1997, n. 365) is grounded in the Incarnation, which affirms the place and significance of the flesh in salvation history, and is a pillar of the Church's theology of the body. In the Catholic tradition, the body can never be reduced to mere matter nor can it be done away with (not even in the afterlife). It is in the body that one discovers, John Paul II says, "the anticipatory signs, the expression and the promise of the gift of self" (Paul 1993, n. 48). The body, Paul makes plain in his first letter to the Corinthians, is "a temple of the Holy Spirit" and it, ultimately, belongs to God (1 Cor. 6.19–20). The *Catechism of the Catholic Church* affirms that the "human body shares in the dignity of 'the image of God' and "through his very bodily condition he sums up in himself the elements of the material world. Through him they are thus brought to their highest perfection and can raise their voice in praise freely given to the Creator" (Catholic Church 1997, n. 362). Thus, the Church teaches that a person can neither despise nor dispose of his or her bodily life, but must "regard [the] body as good and to hold it in honor since God has created it and will raise it up on the last day" (Catholic Church 1997, n. 364).

One's identity as a person, therefore, is rooted in the composite reality of body and soul. The continuity of personhood even into the afterlife requires, as we shall see, that both body (that is, the "same" body that one knew in his or her mortal life) and soul re-unite after death. The value of the body—which is what the human person *is* rather than what the human person *has* (Paul 2006, p. 681, n. 2:4, n. 5:5–6, n. 55:2)—is unambiguous in the Catholic tradition; the human body is indispensable. Accordingly, "body language" permeates Church teaching: the physicality of the sacraments and the healing narratives are unmistakeable, the Church itself is called the "Body of Christ," and the mystery of the Incarnation—which the Church underscores as "the distinctive sign of Christian faith" (Catholic Church 1997, n. 463)—tells of a God who chooses to dwell among us in the flesh in order to redeem the flesh (Labrecque 2015, p. 309; Catholic Church 1997, n. 1015). Indeed, Tertullian referred to the flesh as "the hinge of salvation" (Catholic Church 1997, n. 1015).

At the same time, the Church is cautious: "if morality requires respect for the life of the body, it does not make it an absolute value. It rejects a neo-pagan notion that tends to promote the *cult of the body*, to sacrifice everything for its sake, to idolize physical perfection [...] by its selective preference of the strong over the weak, such a conception can lead to the perversion of human relationships" (Catholic Church 1997, n. 2289). This is particularly revealing in light of transhumanist approaches to the human body, which at once seem to promote such a cult (in the want to enhance and perfect the body) and then disdain it altogether once, or perhaps *if*, the transhumanist model of enhancement and perfectability outgrows what the human body can bear. Indeed, this is exactly how transhumanists describe *posthumans*: "possible future beings whose basic capacities so radically exceed those of present humans as to be no longer unambiguously human by our current standards [...]. Posthumans could be completely synthetic artificial intelligences, or they could be enhanced uploads, or they could be the result of making many smaller but cumulatively profound augmentations to a biological human" (Humanity+ 2016). Therefore, for transhumanism, the future of humanhood does not need the body; for the Church, humanhood—in the here-and-now, in the future, and in the hereafter—very much depends on it.

3. What If the Mortal Coil Is Shuffled Off in Death? Postmortem Corporeality in the Catholic Tradition

The centrality of the human body is further accentuated in the Church's eschatology. This is especially apparent in its doctrine on the resurrection.

The Church defines death, theologically, as the separation of the body and the soul (Catholic Church 1997, n. 1005). That is, the human person cannot exist outside of his or her composite-ness. The resurrection, then, is understood as a reintegration (Paul 2006, n. 72:3); the soul is returned to the body, which is "recovered and also renewed" (Paul 2006, n. 66:4), but not replaced (Labrecque 2015, pp. 309–10). The Church's teaching on the glorified body, a body that is granted incorruptible life in this reunion (Catholic Church 1997, n. 997), makes plain that, for this faith tradition, matter can indeed be perfected (Ratzinger 1988, p. 192).

The resurrection accounts in the Gospels highlight this recovery-of-the-body motif. The Risen Christ returns with the body that others knew him as, but in a way that is somehow different. Even those closest to Jesus fail to recognize him in this new manifestation regardless of the fact that his mortal body—though transfigured—has come to life again. Interestingly, what the evangelists make painstakingly clear here is that the body of the Risen Christ is truly physical and that it bears the marks of his crucifixion. "Look at my hands and my feet," Jesus says to his disciples upon appearing to them after his death, "see that it is I myself. Touch me and see; for a ghost does not have flesh and bones as you see that I have" (Lk 24.39). The glorified body of Jesus, then, is also a *wounded* body; the wounds are not considered to be mere vestiges of his former vulnerability, but are *identifying* attributes of sacrifice imprinted, as it were, on this newly imperishable body.

This does not seem to be in accord with the idea of enhancement or perfectability espoused by transhumanism; this embodiment of humility—the physical manifestation of humbling in a transfigured body—is in stark contrast with the images of power, hyperfunctionality, and greatness that often characterize the posthuman archetype. Following this, the Church's International Theological

Commission—whose task is to examine pressing doctrinal questions of the day—claims that the aim to use genetic enhancement to create a superhuman being is deeply problematic given that "the spiritual life principle of man—forming the matter into the body of the human person—is not a product of human hands and is not subject to genetic engineering" (International Theological Commission 2004, n. 91). True improvement, the Church teaches, comes with a person's fuller realization of the image of God (International Theological Commission 2004, n. 91). Note the Church's criticism here of proponents of enhancement who single out and instrumentalize the body, completely disregarding other dimensions (such as the spiritual in this case) that constitute human personhood, and whose Manichaean approach inevitably leads to objectification.

At the same time, one cannot deny that descriptions of the glorified body in Catholic literature also point to some ideal of what constitutes the best of bodiliness, whatever the measure of "best" might be. For instance, in *The City of God*, Augustine talks about how all the blemishes and deformities of the body—"whether common ones or rare and monstrous"—will be done away with in the resurrection while "the natural substance shall suffer no diminution" (Augustine 1999, XXII.19). The quality and the quantity of the natural substance of the body is altered so as to produce beauty;" incidentally, bodily beauty, according to Augustine, is found in the proportionality of the parts (Augustine 1999, XXII.19). Similarly, Thomas Aquinas describes the glorified body, in his *Summa Contra Gentiles*, as that which is "raised up to the characteristics of heavenly bodies: it will be lightsome, incapable of suffering, without difficulty and labor in movement, and most perfectly perfected by its form" (Aquinas 1955–1957, IV.86.6). An exception to the rule, as we have seen above, are the wounds of the martyrs, which are not to be seen as blemishes or deformities, but marks of honour and virtue that "add lustre to their appearance" (Augustine 1999, XXII.19). The implications of this particular rendering of the human body in its glorified state are extensive and I would be especially interested in learning how disability studies scholars might approach this kind of construction.

In the end, the Church teaches that one cannot possibly imagine what the relationship between the human person and matter in the world to come might be or what the risen body might look like (Ratzinger 1988, p. 194) although some have speculated, concerning the latter, something rather grand. The hope is not for the superhuman functionality of transhumanist longing, but for "the fullness of the perfection proper to the image and likeness of God" (Paul 2006, n. 66:1). The Church speaks of a new state of being that does not connote, as we have seen, the disincarnation of human persons, but "the spiritualization of their somatic nature" (Paul 2006, n. 66.3, n. 66:5). Here, perfection is best understood as the height of *communion*; that is, the perfect communion of body and soul, and the eschatological communion of God, the person, and the world (Paul 2006, n. 67:2, n. 68:1).

4. The Disposability of the Body in a Culture of Excess

In his encyclical on care for our common home, called *Laudato Si'*, Pope Francis criticizes our "throwaway culture" that delights in excess and is quick to discard and replace (Francis 2015, n. 20–22). Perhaps it is only in such a culture that we might find serious discussions about the disposability of the human body. In a general audience address on this subject, the pontiff proclaimed that "this 'culture of waste' tends to become a common mentality that infects everyone. Human life, the person, are no longer seen as a primary value to be respected and safeguarded, especially if they are poor or disabled, if they are not yet useful—like the unborn child—or are no longer of any use—like the elderly person [. . .]" (Francis 2013). Pope Francis refers to the abandonment of these as "hidden euthanasia" (Francis 2014).

Defining personhood and estimating one's value based on utility and function disqualify those who do not, cannot, will not, or are no longer able to operate at a level that is considered contributive (by whom and to what end are not always clear). The transhumanist ideal of the hyperfunctional posthuman leaves behind the "unenhanced" as a class that will inevitably slip into oblivion if it chooses (which it is very well free to) not to keep up. The body is an impediment to posthuman flourishing, as some transhumanist proponents make plain, and progress will require new and improved "vessels" that are better suited for the development of capacities that radically exceed what we now know. One could very well argue that this recurrent reference to the need for such new and improved vessels clearly implies that, in the end, one can never be rid of a body of some kind.

Transhumanist attitudes regarding the human body seem to be symptomatic of the "throwaway culture" of which Pope Francis speaks. Interestingly, a number of scholars have drawn attention to how this kind of thinking can also be characteristic of modern scientific medicine, which extricates the body from the self, mechanizes it, and renders it manipulable while neglecting a lived experience of illness that involves the whole person (Keenan 1996; Toombs 1988; Zaner 1981). The body-as-machine motif that is prominent in transhumanist discourse can also be detected in the clinical encounter in which the body "can be divided into organ systems and parts which can be repaired, removed or technologically supplemented; it can be tested experimentally, and so forth [...] it omits the person to whom the body belongs, the person whose body it is" (Toombs 1988, p. 201). In this vein, the philosopher S. Kay Toombs describes illness as an experience of bodily alienation (Toombs 1988, p. 202). If "a threat to the body necessarily incorporates a threat to [the] self" (Toombs 1988, p. 207), as she suggests, then it is fathomable to conclude that a complete disposal of the body can only mean an extinction of the self.

The objectification of the body in the clinical encounter, Toombs warns, isolates the body from the self, threatening the patient's autonomy and sense of control (Toombs 1988, pp. 221–22). It is ironic, for our discussion here that, according to Toombs, the body itself is the locus of freedom of choice and self-dominion. The question for transhumanists is whether shedding the human body for a "new and improved vessel" will automatically result in the eradication of at least two of the values that matter most to transhumanism: autonomy and mastery over the self.

In his appeal to a deeper appreciation for an authentic human ecology (emphasized by Pope John Paul II and Pope Benedict XVI before him) that recognizes the irrefutable connection between humankind, the environment, and God, Francis says that "the life of the spirit is not dissociated from the body or from nature or from worldly realities, but lived in and with them, in communion with all that surrounds us" (Francis 2015, n. 216). The material world—the human body and the environment from which it is drawn—is not expendable; to judge it and treat it as such will eventually assure nothing less than annihilation. Christ himself, the pontiff reminds, was "far removed from philosophies which despised the body, matter and the things of the world" (Francis 2015, n. 98). This pressing appeal for a recognition of an "integral ecology" underlines the fundamental importance of the body as that which directly relates us to the environment and to the other human, nonhuman, and inanimate beings that constitute it. This crucial detail is often overlooked in transhumanist literature.

"The acceptance of our bodies as God's gift," Pope Francis writes, "is vital for welcoming and accepting the entire world as a gift from the Father and our common home, whereas thinking that we enjoy absolute power over our own bodies turns, often subtly, into thinking that we enjoy absolute power over creation" (Francis 2015, n. 155). That is, there is a striking parallel between the way we value or undervalue the human body and the way we value or undervalue the material world of which it is part. Perceiving the body as extrinsic to the self to the point of rendering it expendable or perpetually malleable matches, in many ways, the human tendency to disengage from the natural world and to view it primarily as a resource to use or discard as we see fit.

It is on this point that transhumanist philosophy and the Catholic tradition find little accord. For the former, the human body and, ultimately, all things material are manipulable, disposable, and replaceable. For the latter, the human body is essential for an identity rooted in communion that survives even the sting of death. These conceptions of the human body and, by extension, of the material world evidently have much to say about how we ought to relate to and respect bodies—individual bodies and bodies in community—as well as how we ought to relate to and respect the created order.

Conflicts of Interest: The author declares no conflict of interest.

References

Alcor Life Extension Foundation. 2017. What Is Cryonics? *Alcor Life Extension Foundation.* Available online: http://www.alcor.org/AboutCryonics/index.html (accessed on 30 January 2017).

Aquinas, Thomas. 1955–1957. *Summa Contra Gentiles.* Translated by Charles J. O'Neil. New York: Hanover House. Available online: http://dhspriory.org/thomas/ContraGentiles4.htm#86 (accessed on 30 January 2017).

Augustine. 1999. *The City of God.* Translated by Marcus Dods. New York: Modern Library.

Augustine of Hippo. 1844. *Sermons on Selected Lessons of the New Testament.* Translated by Richard Gell MacMullen. Oxford: John Henry Parker.

Bostrom, Nick. 2005. Transhumanist Values. *Journal of Philosophical Research* 30: 3–15. [CrossRef]

Bostrom, Nick. 2008. Letter from Utopia. *Studies in Ethics, Law, and Technology* 2: 1–7. [CrossRef]

Campbell, Alasdair V. 2009. *The Body in Bioethics.* London: Routledge.

Catholic Church. 1997. Catechism of the Catholic Church. *Vatican Website*, August 15. Available online: http://www.vatican.va/archive/ccc_css/archive/catechism/ccc_toc.htm (accessed on 15 June 2017).

Francis. 2013. General Audience. *Vatican Website*, June 5. Available online: http://w2.vatican.va/content/francesco/en/audiences/2013/documents/papa-francesco_20130605_udienza-generale.html (accessed on 15 June 2017).

Francis. 2014. Meeting of the Pope with the Elderly. *Vatican Website*, September 28. Available online: http://w2.vatican.va/content/francesco/en/speeches/2014/september/documents/papa-francesco_20140928_incontro-anziani.html (accessed on 15 June 2017).

Francis. 2015. *Laudato Si'.* Encyclical Letter. *Vatican Website*, May 24. Available online: http://w2.vatican.va/content/francesco/en/encyclicals/documents/papa-francesco_20150524_enciclica-laudato-si.html (accessed on 15 June 2017).

Harris, John. 2007. *Enhancing Evolution: The Ethical Case for Making Better People.* Princeton: Princeton University Press.

Humanity+. 2016. The Transhumanist FAQ 3.0. *Humanity+.* Available online: http://humanityplus.org/philosophy/transhumanist-faq/ (accessed on 25 January 2017).

International Theological Commission. 2004. Communion and Stewardship: Human Persons Created in the Image of God. *Vatican Website*, July 23. Available online: http://www.vatican.va/roman_curia/congregations/cfaith/cti_documents/rc_con_cfaith_doc_20040723_communion-stewardship_en.html (accessed on 15 June 2017).

Irenaeus. n.d. *Against the Heresies.* Grand Rapids: Christian Classics Ethereal Library. Available online: http://www.ccel.org/ccel/schaff/anf01.ix.vii.vii.html (accessed on 15 June 2017).

John Paul II. 1993. *Veritatis Splendor.* Encyclical Letter. *Vatican Website*, August 6. Available online: http://w2.vatican.va/content/john-paul-ii/en/encyclicals/documents/hf_jp-ii_enc_06081993_veritatis-splendor.html (accessed on 15 June 2017).

John Paul II. 1994. *Gratissimam Sane.* Letter to Families. *Vatican Website*, February 2. Available online: http://w2.vatican.va/content/john-paul-ii/en/letters/1994/documents/hf_jp-ii_let_02021994_families.html (accessed on 15 June 2017).

John Paul II. 2006. *Man and Woman He Created Them: A Theology of the Body.* Translated by Michael Waldstein. Boston: Pauline Books.

Joy, Bill. 2000. Why the Future Doesn't Need Us. *Wired*, April 1. Available online: https://www.wired.com/2000/04/joy-2/ (accessed on 30 January 2017).

Keenan, James F. 1996. Dualism in Medicine, Christian Theology, and the Aging. *Journal of Religion and Health* 35: 33–45. [CrossRef] [PubMed]

Labrecque, Cory Andrew. 2015. Morphological Freedom and the Rebellion against Human Bodiliness: Notes from the Roman Catholic Tradition. In *Religion and Transhumanism: The Unknown Future of Human Enhancement.* Edited by Calvin Mercer and Tracy J. Trothen. Santa Barbara: Praeger.

Leonard, Tom. 2013. Three Senior Oxford University Academics Will Pay to Be Deep Frozen When They Die So They Could One Day Be 'Brought Back to Life'. *Mail Online*, June 9. Available online: http://www.dailymail.co.uk/news/article-2338434/Three-senior-Oxford-University-academics-pay-deep-frozen-die-day-brought-life.html (accessed on 3 February 2017).

Merleau-Ponty, Maurice. 1990. *Phenomenology of Perception*. Translated by Colin Smith. Unknown place: Taylor & Francis. Available online: http://www.myilibrary.com.acces.bibl.ulaval.ca?ID=15777 (accessed on 14 June 2017).

More, Max. 1993. Technological Self-Transformation: Expanding Personal Extropy. Available online: http://www.maxmore.com/selftrns.htm (accessed on 14 June 2017).

Ramsey, Boniface. 1985. *Beginning to Read the Fathers*. New York: Paulist Press.

Ratzinger, Joseph. 1988. *Eschatology: Death and Eternal Life*, 2nd ed. Translated by Michael Waldstein. Washington: Catholic University of America Press.

Sandberg, Anders. 2001. Morphological Freedom: Why We Note Just Want It, But Need It. *Anders Sandberg's Pages*. Available online: http://www.aleph.se/Nada/Texts/MorphologicalFreedom.htm (accessed on 14 June 2017).

Toombs, S. Kay. 1988. Illness and the Paradigm of Lived Body. *Theoretical Medicine* 9: 201–26. [CrossRef] [PubMed]

Zaner, Richard. 1981. *The Context of Self: A Phenomenological Inquiry Using Medicine as a Clue*. Athens: Ohio University Press.

![religions logo] *religions*

MDPI

Article

The Disappearing Human: Gnostic Dreams in a Transhumanist World

Jeffrey C. Pugh

Department of Religious Studies, Elon University, Elon, NC 27244-2020, USA; pughjeff@elon.edu

Academic Editor: Noreen Herzfeld
Received: 25 January 2017; Accepted: 18 April 2017; Published: 3 May 2017

Abstract: Transhumanism is dedicated to freeing humankind from the limitations of biological life, creating new bodies that will carry us into the future. In seeking freedom from the constraints of nature, it resembles ancient Gnosticism, but complicates the question of what the human being is. In contrast to the perspective that we are our brains, I argue that human consciousness and subjectivity originate from complex interactions between the body and the surrounding environment. These qualities emerge from a distinct set of structural couplings embodied within multiple organ systems and the multiplicity of connections within the brain. These connections take on different forms, including structural, chemical, and electrical manifestations within the totality of the human body. This embodiment suggests that human consciousness, and the intricate levels of experience that accompany it, cannot be replicated in non-organic forms such as computers or synaptic implants without a significant loss to human identity. The Gnostic desire to escape our embodiment found in transhumanism carries the danger of dissolving the human being.

Keywords: Singularity; transhumanism; Merleau-Ponty; Kurzweil; Gnosticism; AI; emergence; technology

---

1. Introduction

In 1993, the mathematician and science fiction writer Vernor Vinge gave a talk at the Vision 21 symposium sponsored by NASA introducing the idea of the Singularity, an evolutionary moment when we would create the capacity for superhuman intelligence that would transcend the human and take us into the posthuman world (Vinge 1993). His opening statement presciently revealed what was to become our future: "The acceleration of technological progress has been the central feature of this century. We are on the edge of change comparable to the rise of human life on Earth. The precise cause of this change is the imminent creation by technology of entities with greater-than-human intelligence" (Vinge 1993). Vinge's predictions, now finding fulfillment in research programs of machine superintelligence or hybrid forms of human intelligence enhancement, made him a technoprophet.

The discourse around Vinge's vision, and Ray Kurzweil's popularization of ideas like the Singularity, has influenced contemporary technology, helping to create a new category of philosophical and political thinking about what humans are and will be in the future—transhumanism (Kurzweil 2005).[1] Though it shares diverse perspectives, this ideology is dedicated to everything from human enhancement to escaping the biological confines of the body altogether. Transhumanist ideas have become a passion for a growing group of thinkers and scientists working in the areas of genetics, nanotechnology, artificial intelligence, and robotics. Enormous resources are being poured into programs and labs that are working for a future where we can at last free ourselves of bodily limitation, thus ensuring immortality and transcendence

---

[1] The Time magazine cover that took up Kurzweil's ideas was the February 21, 2011 issue, vol. 177.

from the fragility of perishable human bodies (Geraci 2010). This desire to escape the body exhibits a structural and shared concern with ancient forms of Gnosticism, but comes at the cost of dissolving the richly textured experiences that constitute the human being.

2. Technognosticism?

The entire program of scientific and technological practices that shape transhumanism can be understood in religious terms, since transcendence of the mundane—a core animating concern of religion—drives much of the transhumanist agenda. It is not just the escape from the ordinary world, but the human struggle with death and finitude that permeates the work of transhumanists. This is not unique to transhumanism, however; the desire to deny our mortality and survive death has motivated human endeavors from antiquity to the present (Becker 1987).

While transhumanism does not replicate ancient Gnosticism, it does represent the reappearance of a perennial ideology that recurs through history and continues to shape and inform human culture. The Gnostic vision was rooted in the idea that the divine was held captive within the cell of the human body, which existed within the larger prison of Earth. The only way to achieve true freedom was to escape from this captivity and reunite with our true source and being in the realm of light. While not Gnostic in seeing the divine spirit within as the essence of human identity, transhumanism shares this eschatological vision—the end of all things leads to escaping the body.[2]

In the very hope of cybernetic immortality, we are hard at work on technologies of extending ourselves beyond our current bodies. This envisioned future shows up in numerous cultural expressions like the HBO series *Westworld*, or movies like *Transcendence* and *Selfless*, shaping society to accept and embrace the worlds being prepared for us. Sometimes these expressions of material culture take on more dystopian themes, as in the *Matrix* trilogy, or *Blade Runner*, but in the labs and research programs working in AI, nanotechnology, and superintelligence, most conversation around transhumanism focuses on the promise more than the peril. One example of this type of optimism was offered by William Sims Bainbridge when he speculated that "[i]n the distant future, we may learn to conceptualize our biological lives on Earth as extended childhoods preparing us for the real life that follows in cyberspace" (Bainbridge 2014, p. 119). In Bainbridge's imagination, we would transmute from flesh into data, and as information we would travel throughout the universe taking on new bodies. Free from the constraints of our biology, the anticipated world of transhumanists offers us a type of resurrection and immortality (if you die in cyberspace, you can choose a new avatar). This type of vision represents the more extreme end of the transhumanist continuum; nonetheless, it inspires many who are working to create that future.

In his book, *Apocalyptic AI: Visions of Heaven in Robotics, Artificial Intelligence, and Virtual Reality*, Robert Geraci shows how intertwined our technology is with other themes, narratives, and imaginative tropes found in religion such as apocalypticism, dualism, the restoration of perfection from a "fallen" state, and even eternal life. Science and technology is creating virtual worlds in cyberspace where millions prefer to spend their time instead of engaging fully in this one (Geraci 2010, pp. 8–10). We will experience technosalvation through virtual bodies in the worlds we create (Geraci 2010, pp. 78–79). The masters of technology will even use hybridity to create new life forms: "Cyberspace allowed the technocracy to rethink salvation and what it means to be human; properly envisioned, cyberspace created a powerful new human–machine hybrid" (Geraci 2010, p. 12).

---

2   The connection between Gnosticism and current expressions of transhumanism is being noticed with increasing frequency. See, for example, Mark Shiffman's review of Steven Fuller's work in "Humanity 4.5." (Shiffman 2015, pp. 23–30), or Lee A. Johnson. "Return of the Corporeal Battle: How Second Century Christology Struggles Inform the Transhumanism Debate." (Johnson 2015). For a more extended debate about Gnosticism and nature, see Benjamin Lazier. "Overcoming Gnosticism: Hans Jonas, and Hans Blumenberg. The Legitimacy of the Natural World." (Lazier 2003, pp. 619–37).

Technology, then, is not just an escape from a primal and superstitious human past; it is the latest iteration of what humans conceive of when they build cultures. The same themes of finitude, loss, and meaning are as present in our technologies as they were in ancient systems of religion and philosophies like Gnosticism (Geraci 2010, pp. 9–14, 31–38).

3. Are Our Present Bodies Crucial for Human Identity?

Though transhumanist programs range from the therapeutic (genetics, implants) to the full downloading of consciousness, the one constant is transcending the bodily limits of *homo sapiens*. Bodies are central to the transhumanist agenda. If the goal of transhumanists is to enhance the mind and preserve it in a more durable body, we should be thinking deeply about bodies. How our bodies mediate experience, and whether different bodies based in silicon or other materials might alter human experience, such that the distinctly human creature is erased, are crucial issues. Are there sacrosanct boundaries that should be respected as technology increasingly enters and affects our bodies? Is there a line that, once crossed, leads to the death of the human? For many, this may not be a loss because replacing the human body with something better is a step forward in the evolutionary process. No one romanticizes or mourns the loss of creatures before we evolved into *homo sapiens*. If *techno-sapiens* replaces us, it is doubtful anyone will grieve us either.

These are concerns that go to the core of what the human being is and is meant to be in the future. Presuming that some type of reverse engineering of the human brain could be done that would allow for human intelligence to exist in a non-biological platform, running algorithms that are of central importance to the existence of minds, would such a thing really be desirable? There may be a few sticky problems to solve, but achieving hardware parity with the brain at some point in the future is not outside the realm of possibility. Should we be skeptical of migration technologies that would allow consciousness and presumably identity to gradually shift from wetware systems (body–brain) to hardware systems (quantum computers)?

The incorporation of the trope, metaphor, or analogy of the brain as equivalent to a computer is a central article of faith for many who are working to create the posthuman future. It is a given that if we can engineer faster cognition or machine superintelligence in some form that can survive the death of human bodies, this will result in a better world. The pragmatism of efficient causality—the ability to effectively achieve a task—seems to propel our movement into the future.

The type of technological determinism inherent in Moore's Law (i.e., exponential growth in computer processing capacity) will no doubt result in more integrated networks, facilitating communication among billions of people and agents. When we improve on DNA or optical or quantum computing, we will discover capacities that we are not yet aware of (Ceruzzi 2005). Are we, though, trying to replicate something that is of a whole other order than intelligence alone? Our bodies developed through processes of chemical and biological interaction, beginning with the minutest level of things in the universe and scaling up from there in evolutionary time. This process produced a complex and complicated creature with distinct properties. Can these organic processes be replicated in such a way that does justice to where evolution has brought us? Put another way—are we capable of engineering artifacts that can create not just the type of intelligence we find in AI programs, but also the depth of knowing that comes from an embodied consciousness?

4. The Infinite Complexity of Embodiment

Human knowing of the world is a distinctly embodied phenomenon. Human language relies on images and meanings derived from our spatial orientation, movement, perceptions, and bodily feeling. The semantics of all human language relies inescapably upon the images and meanings of the movement of our bodies. Language has the sinews of our bodies behind it in some sense. Such things as gestures and expressions transfigure our bodies into information systems that create worlds and layers of meaning. Through our bodies, we create spaces of signification and symbol that mold and shape cultures. Our entrance into a speaking world is made possible by the body.

We inhabit a world of meaning inherited from the past, a web of experience that was set up at our birth (Merleau-Ponty 2012).

In his account of how human evolution has moved from mimetic through mythic culture to the theoretic understanding of the world, Robert Bellah shows how the very building blocks of those experiences we deem "religious" have their origins in bodily movement and vocal noise (Bellah 2011). Even in our abstract thinking with terms like transcendence/immanence, we experience the realities of in/out or near/far in bodily perceptions as we interact with the environment around us: "Viewed developmentally, experience is better understood as embodied behavior, where embodiment is understood at multiple levels from the neural to the phenomenological and behavior is broadly construed to include linguistic and mental events as well as overt actions. Conceived in this way, there is no way (*pace* the perennialists) to *unequivocally* establish the meaning of experience apart from its expression in embodied behaviors, linguistic or otherwise." (Taves 2009, p. 64). Emotions also factor into this. The joy, pleasure, fear, anger, and anxiety located in the body lead us to create through such things as play and ritual the foundations of religion (Bellah 2011, pp. xiv–3).

Self-organizing and emergent capabilities of biological networks specified and evolved within our particular and distinct world. We cannot escape this without a significant change in how the world itself would be perceived. Our very way of interpreting the environment, of changing that environment, occurs because we are embodied within it. We take our cognitive clues and structure and interpret the world from within the space of our body. We are incarnate knowers. Religion itself, instead of being a *sui generis* phenomenon, is the result of our deeming some human experiences—all of which are embodied—as being of special, even spiritual, significance (Taves 2009, pp. 61–66). For example, we move our bodies from one place to another and "journey" or "path" becomes a part of our religious language. Religion itself emerges from our being embedded within the world.

This is not to say that AI programs are not embodied, because they are to the extent that they are located in silicon or other materials, but they remain disincarnate in the sense that they are nowhere close to human bodies with their distinct biological/organic emergent systems. The question of reducing human experience to minds and information processing is important. Models of artificial intelligence that use pattern and symbol recognition can replicate and will surpass some of what human intelligence accomplishes, but can this capture the complexity of such experiences as empathy, compassion, or love?

Human consciousness operates in a way that goes beyond computational processing alone. Computer scientist and theologian Noreen Herzfeld points to the fact that embodied experience means that it is not just functional concerns of information processing that distinguish us; we are beings continually in a relationship of reciprocity with the world and others. AI researchers going back to Turing—who bases his famous test on relational interaction—understand that "the center of our being is dynamic and cannot be isolated from the bodies, societies, and natural world in which they are embedded" (Herzfeld 2002, pp. 310ff). Relationships are what truly define us.

This is one reason why relationships are of increasing importance to AI programs. The creation of machines that interact with humans has come a long way since COG and Kismet, but the authentic response to another human being involves more than recognition and response. To express an appropriate emotion means drawing on multitudes of human experience where memory creates a continually changing narrative of what gets learned (or not) about suffering, compassion, and empathy (Herzfeld 2015). Memories are not retrieved as intact wholes based on the pattern of one's neural connections, but by assembling the bits of them located throughout the body and then constructing them into the story that one believes to be true. Static memories, unaltered by human experiences, offer us a truncated existence. In this way, memory constitutes more than information to be retrieved; it is the story of persons constructed over time and circumstance in relationship to other bodies (Herzfeld 2013). The body allows for the appearance of novelty.

In organic self-organizing systems, new phenomena emerge not necessarily predicated on constituent parts. Mental properties like memory and empathy, and even consciousness itself, are emergent phenomena of these biological systems, dependent upon, but not predicated on the physical substrates that form them. Human subjectivity itself constitutes a novel property not reducible to its constituent parts (Clayton 2004, pp. 107–39).[3] A crucial aspect of our embodied consciousness is found in our subjective apprehension of the world, aspects of which are our emotions, intuition, and feelings. Can discarnate models emphasizing the brain/mind equals the computer capture what something like an aesthetic experience feels like, or the depths of feelings that are mediated by an experience like forgiveness? We could program something like an aesthetic or moral response, but could we replicate the exact thing that human beings *feel* when they have an aesthetic moment or experience forgiveness? ((Nagel 1974), See also (Chalmers 1997) for a fuller examination of the problem of subjectivity.) The sublime experience of beholding the Sistine Chapel's ceiling when the brilliance of Michelangelo pops out, or the feeling of grief at losing a loved one, are not moments that we can shave off and label religious or even epiphenomenal; they constitute dimensions of the entirety of human experience. What gets left behind if the potential for these types of experiences disappears through the technological manipulation of the human being?

Transhumanism envisions our transcending biology or manipulating matter as a necessary part of the evolutionary process. We should not fear the progress this represents, nor feel anxiety that so much power is in our hands; the ability to enhance our lives only makes them better. For those who believe this usurps the divine power of creation, theologians like Philip Hefner challenge us to consider our role as created co-creators when thinking about science and technology. By emphasizing the *created* aspect of this term, Hefner calls upon theologians to realize their own contingency and reliance on God as they engage in the creative process of evolution. Thinking of ourselves as co-creators of the world allows for our powers to be used in ways that honor our moral and ethical responsibility for the planet (Hefner 1988).

Theologians who have welcomed this opening to partner with transhumanism are exploring how theology can inform and support emerging technologies. Thinking about the role of bodies in Christianity, Calvin Mercer explores how biblical writers understood the body, specifically the resurrected body. Using the resurrected or transformed body as a model of what a posthuman future might look like, Mercer is able to situate the Christian belief of a resurrected body (a very different body) with the ability of personhood existing in a cyborg or hybrid body (Mercer 2015, pp. 29–31). The transformed body does not have to constitute a diminished existence; it can open new doors to the future. The possibilities involved in this type of move give us the opportunity to reframe religion itself: "Perhaps the rise of transhumanism is another occasion to take a step back from anthropocentric religion and theology and reflect on how the religion and theological principles might apply to persons in a posthuman world. More specifically, is Christian theological anthropology flexible enough to view posthuman persons, or for that matter posthumans who do not meet the full criteria for personhood, as in the image of God?" (Mercer 2015, p. 30).

Mercer expresses caution about blanket acceptance of agendas like superintelligence, but he does think that "value loading" of AI programs might allow for more positive outcomes around our new creations. In his call for theological openness to the transhumanist project he embraces a fluidity of what sort of bodies persons will be able to exist in: "And if this creature is a product of the co-creative work of God and humans why would we not embrace it, as long as getting to that future is done in a way that satisfies ethical precepts" (Mercer 2015, p. 30). Given what our bodies have mediated

---

[3] Emergence in the sense that I am using it is the idea that systems of life develop in such a way that the whole cannot be predicted on the parts that constitute it, and that true novel properties emerge in evolution. It is a non-reductive argument in that the parts of the system cannot properly explain properties that are emergent features of a system. One of the most controversial aspects of this process comes when the issue is the relationship of the brain to the mind, especially when the idea of mental properties influencing material properties by a top down causality is invoked (think the Placebo effect). There is no consensus on this idea, some philosophers arguing that the mental states are nothing more than epiphenomenon, but evolution itself shows that we have now arrived at the place where mental properties will control the future of evolution and top down causalities will have much to say about what the future looks like.

to us over time, the interpretations of the world, the emergence of subjectivity, the constellation of experiences that have constructed human identity, is Mercer's optimism that we can replicate the complexity of this in other bodies warranted?

5. Our Bodies Contains Multitudes

Another dimension of human being complicates this optimism for some elements of transhumanism—we are shaped through informational processes taking place within the entire body, not just the brain. Candace Pert points to how the body and mind are connected and how emotions and the knowing associated with them are manifested throughout the body, not just in neuronal connections located within the brain (Pert 1986). Pert's work comes about through her investigation of neuropeptides—peptide structures produced by nerve cells in the brain (though not only there)—and receptor sites in the body that accept neuropeptides. Peptides are strings of amino acids that code for certain chemical interactions within the body. Produced by DNA, peptides move to the axon ball of neurons waiting for the right electrophysical event to release them. Once released, these peptides seek receptors in the body that serve as mechanisms to sort out the information exchanges carried by the electrochemical interactions (Pert 1986, p. 10).

Neuroscience agrees that emotions are mediated by the limbic system of the brain and these are areas that are rich with neuropeptides and their receptors, but they are not the only place where the chemical interactions that affect our consciousness are located. Neuropeptides and their receptors are found everywhere through the body, not just the brain. Research has shown that human monocytes—cells that move through the body—contain these receptor sites as well. These are the chemicals that impact our moods, feelings, and certainly color our perceptions of the world as experienced within our bodies (Pert 1986, p. 13). Cells of the immune system not only have receptors for neuropeptides, but manufacture them as well. There are subsets of immune cells that make beta-endorphins and there is ongoing study showing receptor cells within other organs and the circulation system. Evidence is plentiful that when someone says they have a "gut feeling" about something, they are responding to the interaction of neuropeptides and their receptors that line the human intestine (Pert 1986, pp. 13–14). Experimental work suggests that glial cells may have been monocytes that rose in the bone marrow and circulated around the body until they enter the brain and transform into glial cells (Pert 1986, p. 16).

We may need to think of the mind itself differently—as the information flowing not just through the brain, but through the whole body. The physical substrate of mental properties is the brain *and* the body, as well as an immaterial energy that has to do with information flowing within the entire body. Pert's work suggests that instead of the dualism we seek to escape of mind *and* body, we should perhaps think of ourselves in terms of bodymind.

If Pert and others who are investigating the chemical processes of our bodies are right, then the whole metaphor of the brain as computer needs to be reconsidered. A more nuanced understanding of our consciousness, the impact of immaterial energies on physical substrates, and the informational processing that takes place in the entirety of the human body, would show us that while artificial intelligence may be transferable, human consciousness and personhood is another thing altogether.

Given the complexity of biological systems, this puts the issue of a virtualized consciousness into sharp relief. I can readily envision a virtualized intelligence through some form of information download from our brains, but given that it is the subjective qualia of our experiences that define a significant piece of our personal identity, I find it difficult to see a road to the human/machine cyborg that incorporates the wisdom of the neuropeptides. The qualities of our experiences that lead us to conceive such things as compassion, love, art, relationships, and religion—which itself is descriptive of a world that in some very real sense is "in" us—leads me to think that the nuanced biological complexity of humankind cannot be technologically replicated.

Even in the pursuit of something as worthy as human enhancement, either genetically or through implant technologies, is there a boundary crossed into an essentially different creature than *homo sapiens*? Keeping the intricacy of the human body, we can work on technologies that will reverse aging and other cellular deterioration. Even skeptical theologians see this as a proper use of our creative powers (See, for example, (Cole-Turner 2011)). This does not have to have a deleterious impact on persons, but is there a point in this process where something distinctly human gets lost? If some enhancements deal with intelligence amplification through implants, is there the danger that our brains would rewire to run only on the basis of the implanted programs? We could end up replicating and extending the initial inputs *ad infinitum*, creating a recursive knowing that never changes in interaction with others or the environment. The irony of this would be that in our desire to escape the body we become irretrievably imprisoned by our own technologies, unable to experience any of the novelty of life that has given us our very subjectivity. Without our particular bodies, we disappear.

6. Everything Old is New Again

While transhumanism does not replicate ancient Gnosticism exactly, it is the reappearance of a recurring philosophy that permeates history and continues to shape human cultures. Transhumanism shares the Gnostic notion of bodies and the world being prisons, but it differs from Gnosticism in that our emancipation will come from our commitment to pragmatic and technological solutions (Coenen 2014, p. 767). The ideology reappears, though in different form: "The transhumanist visions are seen as having some plausibility precisely because the views on science, technology, human corporeality, and nature expressed by them are radicalised versions of ideas and beliefs which have strongly shaped Western intellectual history" (Coenen 2014, pp. 766–67).

Even with the goods of enhancement, transhumanism, like Gnosticism, reflects an alienation from the *eros* of the sensuous world. Once life enters artificiality, it risks coming loose from the world itself. The counterfeit of reality is a negation of being. This sounds, perhaps, too much like nostalgia for the time when we knew our place in the universe and the hidden God, *deus absconditus*, resided in heaven, working all things out according to divine providence. The idea of final causes used to comfort us in the darkness, but most do not mourn the disappearance of divine purpose within the processes of nature given our successful scientific and technological abilities. In our hands nature itself becomes a malleable thing, without its own integrity, save as material for us to control and master. Whether the technology is artificial chromosomes, implantable computer chips, or artificial intelligence, the assumed goal is the necessity to escape the confines that nature and time have placed on us.

The assumed deficiency of nature is an ontological claim, but we cannot say with certitude that nature, for all its challenges, does not contain its own purposes. We have developed subjective capacities within our bodies through vast amounts of time that have enhanced our lives. Hope, forgiveness, awe, or wonder are only some of the foundations upon which the sublimity of our lives rests. Human biology has not impeded our growth into this world; it has given us the language and ability to contemplate aspects of it we would not experience without the way our bodies have evolved. Our bodies have been the means to create the rich textures of our lives. Because we no longer have adequate accounts of natural phenomena, rejecting the notion that nature had its own trajectories in the universe's process of becoming, we denigrate what nature has given.

Of course, the response to this is that we will still have bodies, and we will lose none of those capacities, but our new bodies will be better equipped to deal with the challenges of the future. Imagine not having to strip resources from the planet in order to eat, feel warm, or survive; not just humanity, but nature itself will be enhanced in the new world. No one decries the medical advancements that have been able to extend our lives; why should we stand in the way of progress? Yet, nested within the transhumanist vision is the recognition that we will have to become less human to survive: "Emphatically humanist at its core, transhumanism has always, almost religiously, aspired to dissolve the humanist individual, even long before the latter's theoretical decentering became widespread in academia" (Coenen 2014, p. 764).

Wariness concerning where our technology is taking us does not just come from fearful Luddites huddling in the corner. Bill Joy, Nick Bostrom, and Jaron Lanier are scientists and innovators who warn that the unforeseen consequences of our technological explorations may have an existentially detrimental impact on nature and humankind. Every door we open with our technical abilities reveals massive complexities that we should consider more deeply before plunging onward. One only need look at the net of fear we spread over the world by splitting the atom. The concerns about creating superintelligence come from those who are most knowledgeable about the risks (Joy 2000; Lanier 2010; Bostrom 2016). This does not mean that we reject all our science and technology, but we do need to more carefully consider the consequences of our technologies. Yet, despite this caution, in the face of unknown consequences, speed seems to have become an objective necessity for us as we plunge into the future.

In the face of this technological inevitability, those voices expressing concern are not given sufficient attention. Our technology constrains our decision making into avenues that have most to do with mastery and control. However, technical mastery is not the only ideology that shapes the future. Those who control the money enjoy the mastery. Theologian Ted Peters worries that laissez-faire capitalism is so baked into the value systems of the technological ethos that all technological advancement will be directed to the interests of investors, leaving those without power at the mercy of those who possess the ability to control society (Peters 2011, pp. 70–71). This raises the issue of how the reality of transhumanism will look as opposed to the hopeful visions of it. Social Darwinism lurks in the shadows, claiming it can pick the winners and losers. In this case, it is those with the most resources who are able to control the contours of the new human being in the posthuman world. If history is any indication, the dystopian works of science fiction may be more prescient about what the future looks like than we want to think.

That future will be shaped by how we think about the world and our place in it. Certainly, a type of nihilism about a universe devoid of meaning can push us forward; or, we may recover a sense of teleology about the world we are embedded within.[4] Contemplation on nature might give us the picture of something that we need not be alienated from. The universe is not so much things or particles as much as it is a process made up of events, relationships, and experiences that we access in our biological bodies, which, for all their limitations, have brought us to the present. The richness of our interior worlds, our journey to the creation of the aesthetic, occurred because of—not in spite of—our embodiment within the world (Clayton 2004, pp. 163 ff.).

Many transhumanists counter that maximizing our potential is also a response to the universe's lure.[5] It is nature that has brought us to this point, and we should use our powers to improve upon it. However, our track record at improving our environment is consistently at odds with our use of technology. We are more likely to use technology to increase our powers, like intelligence, than the moral and ethical qualities of empathy or care for the natural world. This raises a larger question about whether we have developed sufficient habits, ethics, or wisdom to acquire and use such powers in ways that would not constitute the paths to our disappearance. Is the economic capital presently driving our technologies and science more of an existential threat than we realize? Is it wealth that gets to decide what bodies look like in the future, or which bodies are worth valuing and saving? We risk doing great harm in our desire to do great good.

Though it is inevitable that we will create some type of superintelligence, we will not likely create enhanced compassion to accompany it. Certainly, the ported brain does not seem a likely candidate

---

[4] The philosopher Hans Jonas was deeply concerned about the ways in which modern technology was pushing aside assumptions about ethics and natural purpose. See, for example, "Technology and Responsibility: Reflections on the New Tasks of Ethics." (Jonas 1973, pp. 31–54). See also his treatment of the ways in which Gnosticism still shapes our thinking about the world in "Gnosticism and Modern Nihilism." (Jonas 1952, pp. 435–52).

[5] Kurzweil actually does have this type of teleology in mind when he ascribes a certain type of purpose to the universe. The goal of the universe is increased intelligence. "The purpose of the universe reflects the same purpose as our lives: to move toward greater intelligence and knowledge" (Kurzweil 2005, p. 372; Herzfeld 2013, p. 69). At this point, however, Kurzweil enters into metaphysical speculation that borders on the religious. Such claims as purpose and meaning can be made, of course, but at that point we've left the world of science, and Whitehead's understanding might hold far more wisdom than Kurzweil's.

for capturing this dimension of human experience. Until qualities such as compassion, forgiveness, or empathy become our priority, I suspect that no matter how far we are able to move toward the eschatology of batteries and silicon, our Gnostic dreams of immortality constitute an existential threat to the fragile wonder that is humankind.

Conflicts of Interest: The author declares no conflict of interest.

References

Bainbridge, William Sims. 2014. Progress toward Cyberimmortality. In *The Scientific Conquest of Death*. Buenos Aires: Libros en Red, pp. 107–22.

Becker, Ernest. 1987. *The Denial of Death*. New York: Free Press.

Bellah, Robert N. 2011. *Religion in Human Evolution: From the Paleolithic to the Axial Age*. Cambridge: Belknap Press.

Bostrom, Nick. 2016. *Superintelligence: Paths, Dangers, Strategies*, Reprint ed. Oxford: Oxford University Press.

Ceruzzi, Paul E. 2005. Moore's Law and Technological Determinism: Reflections on the History of Technology. *Technology and Culture* 46: 584–93. [CrossRef]

Chalmers, David. 1997. Facing up to the problem of Consciousness. In *Explaining Consciousness: The 'Hard Problem'*. Edited by Jonathan Shear. Cambridge: MIT Press.

Clayton, Philip. 2004. *Mind and Emergence: From Quantum to Consciousness*. New York: Oxford University Press.

Coenen, Christopher. 2014. Transhumanism in Emerging Technoscience as a Challenge for the Humanities and Technology Assessment. *Teorija in Praska* 51: 754–71.

Ronald Cole-Turner, ed. 2011. *Transhumanism and Transcendence: Christian Hope in an Age of Technological Enhancement*. Washington: Georgetown Press.

Geraci, Robert. 2010. *Apocalyptic AI: Visions of Heaven in Robotics, Artificial Intelligence, and Virtual Reality*. New York: Oxford University Press.

Hefner, Philip. 1988. The Evolution of the Created Co-Creator. *Currents in Theology and Mission* 15: 512–25.

Herzfeld, Noreen. 2002. Creating in Our Own Image: Artificial Intelligence and the Image of God. *Zygon* 37: 303–16. [CrossRef]

Herzfeld, Noreen. 2013. Outsourced Memory: Computers and Conversation. *Perspectives on Science and Christian Faith* 65: 176–86.

Herzfeld, Noreen. 2015. Empathetic Computers: The Problem of Confusing Persons and Things. *Dialog* 54: 34–39. [CrossRef]

Johnson, Lee A. 2015. Return of the Corporeal Battle: How Second Century Christology Struggles Inform the Transhumanism Debate. In *Religion and Transhumanism: The Unknown Future of Human Enhancement*. Edited by Calvin Mercer and Tracy J. Trothen. Westport: Praeger.

Jonas, Hans. 1952. Gnosticism and Modern Nihilism. *Social Research* 1: 435–52.

Jonas, Hans. 1973. Technology and Responsibility: Reflections on the new tasks of ethics. *Social Research* 1: 31–54.

Joy, Bill. 2000. Why the Future Doesn't Need Us. *Wired Magazine*. April. Available online: https://www.wired.com/2000/04/joy-2/ (accessed on 28 December 2016).

Kurzweil, Ray. 2005. The Singularity is Near: When Humans Transcend Biology. New York: Penguin Books.

Lanier, Jaron. 2010. You Are Not a Gadget: A Manifesto. New York: Vintage Press.

Lazier, Benjamin. 2003. Overcoming Gnosticism: Hans Jonas, and Hans Blumenberg. The Legitimacy of the Natural World. *Journal of the History of Ideas* 64: 619–37. [CrossRef]

Mercer, Calvin. 2015. Bodies and Persons: Theological Reflections on Transhumanism. *Dialog* 54: 27–33. [CrossRef]

Merleau-Ponty, Jean. 2012. *Phenomenology of Perception*. Translated by Donald A. Landes. New York: Routledge, pp. 80–81.

Nagel, Thomas. 1974. What is it like to be a bat? *The Philosophical Review* 83: 435–50. Nagel uses the bat to ask the same question. We can understand all the factors that bats use to experience the world, but we no ability to really know that experience.

Pert, Candace. 1986. The Wisdom of the Receptors: Neuropeptides, the Emotions, and Bodymind. *Advances* 3: 8–16.

Peters, Ted. 2011. Progress and Provolution: Will Transhumanism Leave Sin Behind? In *Transhumanism and Transcendence: Christian Hope in an Age of Technological Enhancement*. Edited by Ronald Cole-Turner. Washington: Georgetown University Press.

Shiffman, Mark. 2015. Humanity 4.5. *First Things* 257: 23–30.

Taves, Ann. 2009. *Religious Experience Reconsidered*. Princeton: Princeton University Press, pp. 61–66.

Vinge, Vernor. 1993. Technological Singularity. Available online: http://www.frc.ri.cmu.edu/~hpm/book98/com.ch1/vinge.singularity.html (accessed on 26 December 2016).

religions

MDPI

Article

New Technologies—Old Anthropologies?

Levi Checketts

Graduate Theological Union, 2918 Regent St #D, Berkeley, CA 94705, USA; lchecketts@ses.gtu.edu

Academic Editor: Noreen Herzfeld
Received: 1 March 2017; Accepted: 29 March 2017; Published: 31 March 2017

Abstract: Eighty years ago, Nicholas Berdyaev cautioned that new technological problems needed to be addressed with a new philosophical anthropology. Today, the transhumanist goal of mind uploading is perceived by many theologians and philosophers to be dangerous due to its violation of the human person. I contrast transhumanist "patternist" views of the person with Brent Waters's Augustinian view of the technological pilgrim, Celia Deane-Drummond's evolutionary Thomistic view of humanity, and Francis Fukuyama's insistence on the inviolability of "Factor X". These latter three thinkers all disagree with the patternist position, but their views are also discordant with each other. This disagreement constitutes a challenge for people of faith confronting transhumanism—which view is to be taken right? I contend that Science, Technology and Society (STS) studies can enrich our understanding of the debates by highlighting the transmutation of philosophical view into scientific theory and the intermingled nature of our forms of knowledge. Furthermore, I contend that STS helps Christians understand the evolution of their own anthropologies and suggests some prospects for future theological anthropology.

Keywords: consciousness uploading; Science, Technology and Society studies (STS); theological anthropology; philosophical anthropology; transhumanism

The debate between transhumanists and their opponents, argues Gregory Stock, is "about philosophy and religion. It is about what it means to be human, about our vision of the human future" ([1], p. 303). A brief survey of a few of the articles and books written on the topic suggests he is right. Transhumanists contend that human beings should use the tools of science and technology to enhance themselves beyond what is biologically natural [2]. Their intellectual opponents, sometimes called "bioconservatives", argue that doing so violates human dignity [3], endangers human rights [4], or elevates humanity above their rightful station [5]. Transhumanists in turn retort that the principle of dignity need not exclude the posthuman (i.e. what "humans" are once they are no longer biologically *Homo sapiens*) [6], that rights can be better ensured by enhanced persons [7] and that humanity has no reason to be bounded [2]. As one surveys the literature, it is clear that these agonists are trying to engage with each other, but one gets the feeling they are still speaking past each other. Surely whatever Leon Kass meant by human dignity in relation to finitude excludes Nick Bostrom's more "expanded" concept. C. A. J. Coady's concern about hubris imposes limits unacceptable to Max More's unbounded vision of humanity. The question of enhancement, one must conclude, reduces to simple understandings of what it means to be a person.

I take up but one example of the highly-contested transhumanist goals in this paper, namely the proposal of mind uploading. This is a technological project favored by such technological luminaries as Ray Kurzweil, Hans Moravec, the late Marvin Minsky and Peter Thiel. Currently, Dmitri Itskov is one of a few persons actively pursuing this goal with his 2045 Initiative, a movement to bring together various scientific and technological achievements, including robotics, neuroscience and artificial intelligence, into the singular task of removing persons' consciousnesses from their biological bodies and transferring them to superior computer substrates [8]. Literature supporting this project is diverse, including Moravec's *Mind Children*, Kurzweil's, *The Age of Spiritual Machines*, Steve Fuller's *Humanity 2.0*, and essays by computer programmers, AI researchers and entrepreneurs. The aim of such a project is to liberate humanity from its biological limitations, especially mental and physical weaknesses and the inevitability of death. The uploaded mind would be free from the slowness of neurons, boundaries of memory capacity and biological vulnerabilities to the passage of time.

Accomplishing this task, according to pro-uploaders, requires progress in three technological and scientific areas. First, computer hardware must be up to the task. Running a computer mind requires huge amounts of data storage and powerful and fast processors. However, we are already approaching the low-end estimates of some of the older predictions for uploading in our standards for home computing technology ([9], p. 60). This means the necessary hardware for the task will be available soon and will be inexpensive. Second, computer software must be sophisticated enough to do all that the brain does reliably. According to some software experts, we are far from reaching this goal because software programming suffers from an "inverse Moore's Law" whereby progress slows over time rather than accelerates [10]. However, the intricacies and complexity of the necessary programming seems just to be a matter of time, not of ability. Finally, we must have an improved understanding of the brain and how it functions. "What" the mind is and "how" it works is important information for moving it successfully into a new home. Neuroscience and "brain mapping" is being pursued to this end, but understanding the brain remains the most elusive project so far. To get around this last obstacle, some have proposed "whole brain emulating" whereby a sufficient "map" of the brain created by deep tissue scanning is simply recreated within a computer environment and allowed to function as it would in a physical medium [11]. Although several real obstacles remain, many proponents of this project expect to accomplish all of these ends, and thus feasibly uploading itself, as early as 2045 (hence the 2045 Initiative).

Aside from very real concerns about environmental impact, distribution of technology and existential threats, most opponents of uploading are concerned that doing so crosses important moral boundaries regarding the status of the human person. Some, like Nicholas Agar, believe it to be ontologically impossible and thus "a novel way to commit suicide" ([12], p. 27). Others fear it is possible but will result in a disembodied monstrosity [13]. Others still worry about the harm that can be done from being removed from one's material origins [14]. Nonetheless, those in favor of uploading hold a "patternist" theory of mind, which holds that human identity is reducible to a brain pattern ([9], pp. 116–22). The successful copy of this brain pattern into another "substrate" constitutes having one's identity transferred to another substrate. A mind is therefore analogous to a poem; written on bark, vellum, stone or paper, the text contains the same meaning and (theoretically) significance.

I contend that in these discussions, we see the need for careful anthropological consideration. This is not a novel thought for technological ethics; eighty years ago, Nicholas Berdyaev began considering the challenges we face in our "technological" world and the threat they pose to humanity. His conclusion was that the answer to the technological challenge lies "in the Christian view of [humanity] as such, for we can no longer be satisfied by the patristic, scholastic, or humanistic anthropologies ... Philosophical anthropology becomes a central problem: [human] and machine, [human] and organism, [human] and cosmos, are what is has to deal with" ([15], p. 213).

In this essay, I examine briefly three anthropological views contending against transhumanism that are reminiscent of Berdyaev's concern (NB: not all of these authors write specifically against patternism, but their anthropological views clearly allow no room for mind uploading as a morally worthwhile technological pursuit). I take up the writings of Brent Waters, who holds an Augustinian view of humanity, Celia Deane-Drummond, who adopts a Thomistic anthropology, and Francis Fukuyama, who uses a mostly humanist perspective. I show that within the context of the transhumanist debate, the discordance of these views leaves the reader with no clear answers. Thus, I advocate for outside perspectives informed by work done in Science, Technology and Society (STS) studies. Too many of our backwards-looking anthropological frameworks lead only to struggle and contention about the moral challenge of transhumanism. The work done in STS however, reframes the anthropological debate by contextualizing its evolution, thereby providing a new solution to intractable disputes.

1. A Sampling of Anthropologies

I contend that Berdyaev's call has not truly been answered today. This is not to say that nobody has taken up the anthropological question, but rather that many views are beholden to older anthropological traditions. For example, Jacques Ellul wrote a great deal about humanity's relationship to technology, but his thought remains fairly Augustinian. He suggests, for instance, that Adam did not have to work in the perfect Garden of Eden, so work and technology arise only as a result of sin [16]. W. Norris Clarke, SJ, on the other hand, writes about technology from a Thomistic perspective and suggests it is a genuinely human expression of God's gifts of rationality to human beings [17]. Finally, one must note that the transhumanists themselves consider their own intellectual heritage to be the early humanist movement [2]. One notes, for example, that patternism is a somewhat Cartesian substance dualist view of the human person, who should be free from the suffering and pain attendant to biological bodies. For the rest of this section, I examine three major figure's anthropological views relating specifically to the question of transhumanism and why it is dangerous. Each author corresponds loosely to one of Berdyaev's anthropological models, and each critiques transhumanism from this perspective.

Brent Waters has written extensively on new technologies, and especially the implications of transhumanism and its misplaced conceptions. Waters writes more in line with the philosophy of Hannah Arendt, but as a Protestant theologian, his writing is unmistakably (and undeniably) Augustinian in tone. Waters begins by arguing that the "technoculture" we live in leaves us homeless and estranged ([18], p. 122). This homelessness affects everyone, but Waters argues that we Christians are called to respond to this differently from non-Christians. Non-Christians find themselves as "nomads", wandering the world with no sense of meaning or purpose, while Christians are "pilgrims", recognizing that our journey has a direction and that the trip itself is sacred. The pilgrim Christians of Waters's framework are residents of the earthly city, though they are citizens of the heavenly city ([18], p. 149). Christians, in this framework, recognize that their will is set right by grace toward the Parousia, while non-Christians variously try to navigate as nomads through private revelation, universal reason, casuistic readjustment or moral subjectivism ([18], pp. 148–52). Thus, Christians, as citizens of the heavenly city, are called to a different moral orientation from non-Christians who have no such awareness, despite the fact that our situation as homeless in the technological world is the same. The heavenly orientation of Christians makes our journey here one of pilgrimage, while the lack of such vision among non-Christians results in aimless nomadism. This heavenly orientation, Waters contends, allows the Christian to not fear death the way the transhumanist does; for while death is the enemy of both transhumanists and Christians, the transcendent focus on Christ's resurrection changes the meaning of death for the Christian pilgrim [19].

Celia Deane-Drummond writes much on Thomistic and Aristotelian implications of new scientific advances and technological developments. Deane-Drummond's approach is interesting in that she combines both a strong natural scientific perspective and a strong Thomistic perspective into one. She concedes, for example, an evolutionary understanding of humanity: we are a species in continuum with other living species and not necessarily morphologically distinct from extinct hominids [20,21]. She likewise takes seriously the promises offered by transhumanist technologies, including human gene editing. Nonetheless, she holds this in tension with a strong theological view. She champions, for example, the centrality of virtue for moral decision-making, especially Aquinas's four cardinal moral virtues and the three theological virtues [22,23]. She argues virtue is a necessary moral orientation for us to have because of the centrality of grace for Christian anthropology. Our transformation through grace is a transformation of both our moral orientation and our being, and so a perspective that admits for moral growth is necessary. Furthermore, she contends that humans are not distinct from other animals by virtue of our rationality alone, but more significantly, through God's transformative grace our animal nature is uplifted to one imprinted by the divine [20]. Thus, human beings are simultaneously natural, rational *animals* and *imago Dei* transformed through God's grace [20,21]. Therefore, accounts of the person which either denigrate the natural and animal elements of being human or which ignore the divine spark within us fail to do justice to theological accounts of personhood. Technological projects that seek to "take leave of the animal" by evacuating soul from body or control our future and thus obviate grace are immoral [21,22].

Francis Fukuyama is a secular philosopher who sat as a member of George W. Bush's President's Council on Bioethics. He is strongly influenced by both Nietzsche and Aristotle, but his anthropological orientation centers around the concept of human dignity separate from any theological underpinnings. Fukuyama defines human dignity as "Factor X" which is "some essential human quality underneath [all contingent characteristics] that is worthy of a certain minimal level of respect" ([24], p. 149). Lest we attribute this to some central aspect of our being human, such as rationality, Fukuyama assures us that Factor X "cannot be reduced to the possession of moral choice, or reason, or language, or sociability, or sentience, or emotions, or consciousness, or any other quality that has been put forth as a ground for human dignity. It is all of these qualities coming together in a human whole that make up Factor X" ([24], p. 171). He does not provide greater explanation to this; he simply contends that the Gestalt of Factor X is worthy of moral respect. Fukuyama goes on to suggest this entails a need to preserve what is biologically natural and to ensure the "genetic endowment" of all of humanity for future generations ([24], p. 171). In terms of transhumanism, this means any morphological change that directly violates Factor X or affects our genetic endowment would be a violation of human dignity. Thus, uploading, which renders the genetic endowment obsolete and would likely alter or distort elements of being human like emotion and sociability, would violate human dignity in a profound way. The uploaded mind is a natural transgression and thus a trespass against human dignity.

The above should not be taken to be any sort of exhaustive look at the various anthropologies offered to reflect on transhumanism, nor is this a thorough examination of even these three thinkers' positions. My intention here is simply to note that there are, in fact, various philosophical and theological positions raised against transhumanism, coming from diverse viewpoints and contending in favor of certain traditional understandings of the person. This selection could have been substituted for others, including non-Augustinian patristic thinkers like Todd T. W. Daly or other humanists like Michael Sandel. However, I believe the selection above provides a diverse-enough sampling to understand what people are saying about transhumanism and why there is resistance to it. In all three above cases, the patternists' anthropology is seen as dangerous because it violates key components of what it means to be human.

2. Hearing amid the Noise

If one browses through such volumes as Mercer and Trothen's *Religion and Transhumanism: The Unknown Future of Human Enhancement*, Mercer and Maher's *Transhumanism and the Body: The World Religions Speak* or Hansell and Grassie's *H±: Transhumanism and Its Critics*, she may believe that there are many more arguments against uploading than there are in favor of it. Indeed, the positions outlined above suggest this is the case: uploading is primarily supported by a very particular humanist perspective based on the thought of figures like Bacon and informed by an uncertain amount of Cartesian dualism. However, many authors, from various traditions, contend that the pro-uploaders are wrong, and, worse still, that their project is dangerous. One might dream this agreement would solve the problem once and for all, but transhumanism remains still popular. Moreover, a further moral challenge arises due to the diversity represented in anti-uploading views; while transhumanism itself may be widely opposed, the reasons why authors oppose it are diverse and sometimes incompatible.

We may see a preliminary problem in this challenge by noting that while Waters, Deane-Drummond and Fukuyama agree that uploading is morally irresponsible, they come to this consideration from rather different standpoints. Waters, a Protestant theologian, follows Augustine and Arendt (who also follows Augustine to a certain extent) in his thought. Deane-Drummond, a Catholic theologian, follows Aquinas and Aristotle in her thought. Fukuyama, a secular philosopher, nominally follows Aristotle and Nietzsche, though his thinking looks unlike either of theirs and is more informed by a rich Enlightenment humanism. These three thinkers do depart from their point of origin—it would be hard to *really* apply Augustine, Aquinas or Nietzsche to the problem of uploading—but they also do take their cues from these sources. More importantly, while Augustine, Aquinas and Nietzsche can all be broadly categorized under the rubric of the Western philosophical canon, they occupied very different social locations, with very different interests and had very different understandings of the world. Augustine's Roman Christian concerns are different from Aquinas's scholastic concerns, and neither are strictly relevant to Nietzsche's Wilhelmian Germany. These differences are not irrelevant, so we should be careful in relativizing all philosophical perspectives that share some modicum of agreement too quickly.

Secondly, and more to the point, our three authors' views are not all the way consonant. Augustinian "earthly city" language does not flatter Aquinas's natural law position favoring the "natural", nor does it favor Fukuyama's deference to secular philosophers. Similarly, Fukuyama's view of the unassailability of the "genetic endowment" of humanity seems at odds with Waters's favored perspective of our alienation on this earth, and more so to Deane-Drummond's recognition that human uniqueness goes beyond genetics. Thus, a challenge in reading these arguments is deciding which has the most merit. A clever uploader could "cherry pick" elements from each anthropology to support his own: the dualism characteristic of Augustine's view, the transformative aspect of the Thomistic vision, and the secularism of Fukuyama all resonate with patternism, though they do not resonate across the boundaries of our three authors. Indeed, the discordance of these thinkers functions to the advantage of patternists and it becomes easy (and perhaps prudent) for transhumanists to dismiss the other positions as merely differences of opinion.

The conclusion we are left with after surveying and analyzing these positions is that from an outside position, the disagreements boil down to differences in philosophy. Those who uphold a patristic or patristic inspired worldview are not likely to share the same values or understandings as those who uphold a scholastic or neo-scholastic worldview nor those who favor a humanistic worldview. In other words, if Deane-Drummond's account of the human is right, then Fukuyama's, Waters's, and the transhumanists' cannot be. But transhumanists have no vested interest in accepting either theological or non-theological philosophies that contradict their own. It is in their best interest to allow the challenge of their opponents to reduce to qualms about philosophy. Thus, the obstacle remaining is to somehow overcome these intractable philosophical anthropological differences.

3. STS: A Way Out?

At the risk of pursuing a seeming non-sequitur, I wish to suggest that a solution to this problem may arrive from Science, Technology and Society (STS) studies. STS combines approaches from the social sciences of anthropology, sociology and history. The work done in STS over the past eighty years has yielded new insights into the way that scientific knowledge is produced (Sociology of Scientific Knowledge), the historical development of scientific theories and technologies (History of Science and History of Technology), the way that technologies are created in social circumstances (Social Construction of Technology) and even multi-disciplinary approaches that appreciate the interconnected networky nature of scientific work and technological progress (Actor-Network Theory or ANT). While philosophers and theologians of technology going back to Heidegger and Ellul have been engaged in debates about the development of technologies, the best models to oppose certain developments, the dangers present and the way out, STS folk have been happy to examine primarily how things came to be the way they are.

Among STS insights that are helpful here, the ANT work of Bruno Latour is perhaps the most pertinent. In his landmark *We Have Never Been Modern*, Latour suggests that the "modern constitution" consists of two important tenets. First, "it is not [human beings] who make Nature; Nature has always existed and has always already been there; we are only discovering its secrets". Second, "human beings, and only human beings, are the ones who construct society and freely determine their own destiny" ([25], p. 30). In other words, we traditionally believe that the world of human commerce and interaction (including politics, sociology, and, dare I say, philosophy and theology) is necessarily separate from the world of "science" (the things of nature); the elements pertaining to the former are contingent and made by human minds for human beings while elements pertaining to the latter are intrinsic to the world and only involve us in the "discovery" of their secrets. Latour argues that the modern constitution is not true: the propositions for the human world and those for the natural world are not held separate but are all "mixed" together and so that all forms of knowledge are "hybrid" knowledge ([25], p. 41). We thus never fully achieved the "modern" separation of these two spheres: our science of Nature is tainted by our human biases and our society is affected by natural relations. Humans and non-humans interplay in entangled networks that ground our mode of being in the world. In other words, just as the clever anthropologist notes the cosmological unity of "pre-modern" peoples' views of nature and society, Latour argues that our society is likewise cosmologically unified and has never truly been modern ([25], p. 46).

This insight helps us understand the epistemological heritage of the uploaders. As Hubert Dreyfus notes in *What Computers* Still *Can't Do*, the assumption that computers emulate human thought is itself based on ancient Greek perspectives of human cognition as calculation ([26], p. 67). The image of a calculating machine influences Alan Turing, whose work in computing and hypothesis of a "Turing Machine" become the basis for artificial intelligence work ([26], p. 74). The possibility of a Turing machine in turn underlies much of the theory informing the uploaders. This Plato-Turing lineage finds its expression in patternist philosophy in the following manner: the mind operates on a set of instructions like a computer, and so a sufficient calculating machine (perhaps one running numerous parallel processes and operating with formidable processing power) will accomplish what the human brain accomplishes and therefore be able to run the same program as a brain ([9], ch. 1). Assuming Dreyfus is correct, this means that the viability of uploading relies, not on a thoroughly "modern" natural science worldview, but rather on Socratic theories of epistemology, the same epistemology that contends all knowledge is intrinsic and simply in need of being brought forth by the right stimulus rather than learned. The patternists, however scientific they may seem, are not "postmodern" or even "modern"; they are, in fact, pre-modern.

STS reveals, therefore, three crucial dangers about the uploading project that are otherwise obscured by arguments from various philosophical anthropologies. The first problem is that the patternist philosophy of the transhumanists is just that—a philosophy and not a science. Thomas Kuhn notes that science is singular among all disciplines of knowledge in that it does not allow for competing schools to emerge ([27], p. 162). The scientific paradigm that admits of oxygen as a chemical element utterly replaces the paradigm that understands dephlogisticated air. Newtonian theory replaces Aristotelian physics and becomes hegemonic—one cannot be a scientist and now hold that fire is attracted to the sun. This is not the case, however, with philosophy or theology (barring, notes Kuhn, dogmatic theology). The diversity of thought detailed above is proof of this. The rigor and policing that keeps science from admitting "junk science" (when done properly) is not relevant to systems like philosophy where plural views are held within the same discipline. This is why the modern constitution is held—science is practiced with much greater scrutiny and authoritarianism than any other field, and so is held to be unbiased and unaffected. Any given philosophical view, therefore, should not be treated as though it were a scientific principle.

The second danger is that modern theories are constantly in flux. Braden Allenby warns that our constructions of technological versions of humanity will be based on our current mental models, models which are subject to destabilization with new discoveries [28]. Each of the authors mentioned above represents a different perspective of what it means to be human, and each importantly represents an evolution of earlier ideas as well. Waters is not *fully* Augustinian; he is also informed by twentieth and twenty-first century science and philosophy. Deane-Drummond is not *fully* Thomistic; she synthesizes the Angelic Doctor with evolutionary theory. Scientific models evolve and, hopefully, are perfected over time. The scientific perspectives of patternism are yet untested, and a failure on this front will be fatal ("suicidal"). Human lives should not be staked on unstable scientific claims. This principle holds true across moral traditions and one does not need to hold a strong "precautionary" view to support it.

The final danger, a sort of synthesis of the first two, is that contingent philosophical views are being taken to have the same certainty as scientific ones. Transhumanists, in taking their philosophical view to be scientific, risk great danger because patternist philosophy is not subject to the same rigor or trials of strength as scientific theories ([29], pp. 74–79). One cannot prove theories about human consciousness or identity in a laboratory, just as one cannot prove moral propositions, literary theories or the existence of God. These are positions held as a matter of worldview, not as scientific principles. To treat them as scientific theories, as the uploaders do, is dangerous first and foremost because the "patternist" theory is not subject to proof or disproof the way that the vacuum of Robert Boyle's air pump was subject to proof [30]. Consciousness and identity are held as philosophical propositions—there is no "proof" of a human soul or any given person's persistent mind. These are rather universally held philosophical and theological positions. Indeed, the belief in a self that persists over time chafes against scientific findings that all somatic cells are replaced every seven years, leading to a veritable "Ship of Theseus" paradox for human identity ([31], p. 260). To treat philosophical tenets as scientific views, therefore, is a category mistake, and misunderstands both the nature of the philosophical claims of human identity and what pertains to the domain of science.

4. Conclusions: Complicating Anthropologies

The discussion above may lead one to conclude that there is no solution to the problem at hand. The uploaders will do as they please, and the anti-uploaders will do as they please, and neither side will convince the other. Perhaps, for example, a sufficient program can be uploaded that passes the "Kurzweil Turing Test", convincingly responding to any given stimulus the way that a given person (e.g., Ray Kurzweil) would ([31], p. 257). Pro-uploaders will accept this as sufficient scientific evidence to validate their claims. Anti-uploaders, however, will see reason to dispute this—perhaps the immaterial soul was lost, or perhaps the program is merely a clever mimic (or perhaps demonic impersonation) of the uploaded person. Arguments grounded in older philosophical systems, whether in favor of or against uploading crash against the same obstacle, namely the non-scientific nature of claims of consciousness and identity.

STS illustrates not only the problem of this category mistake, but also suggests a solution. Our world is not yet modern, so Latour claims, though he offers us a way to accept this. Human beings are hybrid creatures—"quasi-subjects" creating "quasi-objects" ([25], p. 137). ANT theorists note that we live and operate in long "networks" of being, constituted by both human and non-human actors affecting and influencing each other. This offers two conclusions for the present discussion. The first is that our philosophical and theological arguments must take seriously the intermingling of fields. Theology has, in fact, influenced science, just as science fiction has influenced technological progress. There is no clean divide, and the uploader who believes his work is "pure science" is mistaken. Uploaders must be ready to see that their "patternist" philosophy is not more scientific than Thomistic theories about the self or Augustinian accounts of fallen nature. Anthropological accounts are and always have been informed by a series of discussions about the person that cross between "hard" scientific and "soft" philosophical and theological domains. Deane-Drummond's evolutionary Thomism is a wonderful example of this cross-disciplinary approach. The patternists' view is likewise a constructed philosophical vision, articulated through discussions about the nature of cognition reaching back as far as Socrates, and given further strength in twentieth-century computer science. All positions have genealogies, and none is "purified" from the messiness of disciplinary intermingling.

The second, more significant conclusion, is that human nature, whatever it is, is not "finished." Our accounts of humanity are continually evolving. One thinks of the anthropological "revolutions" associated with Copernicus, Darwin and Freud: heliocentricity, evolutionary theory and psychoanalysis have yielded ineradicable changes to our conception of what we are. We are, of course, not done yet either. The past several decades have seen the success of the Human Genome Project, discussions of nuclear cloning, and the discovery of CRISPR/Cas9 gene editing. Philosophical and theological accounts of humanity may be struggling harder to keep up with these changes than are popular understandings (or, worse yet, "scientistic" understandings like that of the uploaders), but this only underscores the need for caution. There may never be a "finalized" concept of the human person—new discoveries about the mind, about evolution, about genetics and epigenetic factors or even sociological data may yield unending knowledge. This instability, however, suggests the need for caution. A technological project that risks ending human lives deliberately should not be pursued based on highly contestable and overly confident scientifically-masked philosophies of what it means to be a person.

A final word must be said for theological accounts of being human. While it is reckless, and perhaps impossible, to try to utterly abandon ancient theological visions of the human being (e.g., those of Augustine, Aquinas, Luther and others), we should be cautious about holding too strictly to them as well. Augustine's theology was informed by his neo-Platonic understanding of the world, just as Aquinas's was shaped by his Aristotelian science. As new sciences and technologies emerge, we must be willing to rethink our anthropological models. A step in this direction is the recognition with ANT theorists that part of being human is being part of these entangled webs of relations. The twenty-first century Western Christian cannot be understood wholly apart from the Internet, smartphones, global positional satellites and worsening climate change. Developments in and toward transhumanist visions of the future may be misguided, but the Christian must also be ready to understand herself in new terms if a consciousness is "successfully" uploaded. The strength of Christian faith has been in its adaptation throughout the centuries to new sciences and philosophies. We may face another such task of adaptation in the "posthuman" future.

Conflicts of Interest: The author declares no conflict of interest.

References

1. Stock, Gregory. "The Battle for the Future." In *The Transhumanist Reader Classical and Contemporary Essays on the Science, Technology and Philosophy of the Human Future*. Edited by Max More and Natasha Vita-More. Malden: Wiley-Blackwell, 2013, pp. 302–16.
2. More, Max. "The Philosophy of Transhumanism." In *The Transhumanist Reader Classical and Contemporary Essays on the Science, Technology and Philosophy of the Human Future*. Edited by Max More and Natasha Vita-More. Malden: Wiley-Blackwell, 2013, pp. 3–17.
3. Kass, Leon. "Death with Dignity and the Sanctity of Life." In *Life, Liberty and the Defense of Dignity: The Challenge for Bioethics*. San Francisco: Encounter Books, 2002, pp. 231–56.
4. Kamm, Frances. "What Is and Is Not Wrong with Enhancement?" In *Human Enhancement*. Edited by Julian Savulescu and Nick Bostrom. Oxford: Oxford University Press, 2009, pp. 91–130.
5. Coady, C. A. J. "Playing God." In *Human Enhancement*. Edited by Julian Savulescu and Nick Bostrom. Oxford: Oxford University Press, 2009, pp. 155–80.
6. Bostrom, Nick. "In Favor of Posthuman Dignity." In *H±: Transhumanism and Its Critics*. Edited by Gregory Hansell and William Grassie. Philadelphia: Metanexus Institute, 2011, pp. 55–66.
7. Savulescu, Julian. "The Human Prejudice and the Moral Status of Enhanced Beings: What Do We Owe the Gods?" In *Human Enhancement*. Edited by Julian Savulescu and Nick Bostrom. Oxford: Oxford University Press, 2009, pp. 211–50.
8. "2045 Strategic Social Initiative." Available online: http://2045.com/ (accessed on 28 January 2017).
9. Moravec, Hans. *Mind Children: The Future of Robot and Human Intelligence*. Cambridge: Harvard University Press, 1988.
10. Lanier, Jaron. "One Half of a Manifesto." Available online: https://www.edge.org/documents/archive/edge74.html (accessed on 2 February 2017).
11. Koene, Randal. "Uploading to Substrate-Independent Minds." In *The Transhumanist Reader Classical and Contemporary Essays on the Science, Technology and Philosophy of the Human Future*. Edited by Max More and Natasha Vita-More. Malden: Wiley-Blackwell, 2013, pp. 146–56.

12. Agar, Nicholas. "Ray Kurzweil and Uploading: Just Say No! " *Journal of Evolution & Technology* 22 (2011): 23–36.
13. Hayles, N. Katherine. "Wrestling with Transhumanism." In *H±: Transhumanism and Its Critics*. Edited by Gregory Hansell and William Grassie. Philadelphia: Metanexus Institute, 2011, pp. 176–88.
14. Thweatt-Bates, J. *Cyborg Selves: A Theological Anthropology of the Posthuman*. Farnham: Ashgate, 2012.
15. Berdyaev, Nicholas. "Man and Machine." In *Philosophy and Technology: Readings in the Philosophical Problems of Technology*. Edited by Carl Mitcham and Robert Mackey. New York: The Free Press, 1972, pp. 203–13.
16. Ellul, Jacques. "Technique and the Opening Chapters of Genesis." In *Theology and Technology: Essays in Christian Analysis and Exegesis*. Edited by Carl Mitcham and Jim Grote. Lanham: University Press of America, 1984, pp. 123–38.
17. Clarke, W. Norris. "Technology and Man: A Christian View." In *Philosophy and Technology: Readings in the Philosophical Problems of Technology*. Edited by Carl Mitcham and Robert Mackey. New York: The Free Press, 1972, pp. 247–58.
18. Waters, Brent. *Christian Moral Theology in the Emerging Technoculture: From Posthuman Back to Human*. Farnham: Ashgate, 2014.
19. Waters, Brent. "Flesh Made Data: The Posthuman Project in Light of the Incarnation." In *Religion and Transhumanism: The Unknown Future of Human Enhancement*. Edited by Calvin Mercer and Tracy J. Trothen. Santa Barbara: Praeger, 2015, pp. 291–302.
20. Deane-Drummond, Celia. "God's Image and Likeness in Humans and Other Animals: Performative Soul-Making and Graced Nature." *Zygon* 47 (2012): 934–48. [CrossRef]
21. Deane-Drummond, Celia. "Taking Leave of the Animal? The Theological and Ethical Implications of the Transhuman Projects." In *Transhumanism and Transcendence: Christian Hope in an Age of Technological Enhancement*. Edited by Ronald Cole-Turner. Washington: Georgetown University Press, 2011, pp. 115–30.
22. Deane-Drummond, Celia. "How Might a Virtue Ethic Frame Debates in Human Genetics?" In *Brave New World? Theology, Ethics and the Human Genome*. Edited by Celia Deane-Drummond. London: T & T Clark, 2003, pp. 225–52.
23. Deane-Drummond, Celia. "Future Perfect? God, the Transhuman Future and the Quest for Immortality." In *Future Perfect? God, Medicine and Human Identity*. Edited by Celia Deane-Drummond and Peter M. Scott. London: T & T Clark, 2006, pp. 168–82.
24. Fukuyama, Francis. *Our Posthuman Future: Consequences of the Biotechnology Revolution*. New York: Farrar, Strauss and Giroux, 2002.
25. Latour, Bruno. *We Have Never Been Modern*. Translated by Catherine Porter. Cambridge: Harvard University Press, 1993.
26. Dreyfus, Hubert L. *What Computers Still Can't Do: A Critique of Artificial Reason*. Cambridge: MIT Press, 1994.
27. Kuhn, T. *The Structure of Scientific Revolutions*, 50th Anniversary ed. Chicago: University of Chicago Press, 2012.
28. Allenby, Braden. "Technology and Transhumanism: Unpredictability, Radical Contingency and Accelerating Change." In *Building Better Humans? Refocusing the Debate on Transhumanism*. Edited by Hava Tirosh-Samuelson and Kenneth L. Mossman. Frankfurt: Peter Lang Gmbh, 2012, pp. 441–63.
29. Latour, Bruno. *Science in Action: How to Follow Scientists and Engineers through Society*. Cambridge: Harvard University Press, 1987.
30. Shapin, Steven, and Simon Schaffer. *Leviathan and the Air-Pump: Hobbes, Boyle, and the Experimental Life*. Princeton: Princeton University Press, 1985.
31. Kurzweil, Ray. *The Singularity Is Near: When Humans Transcend Biology*. New York: Viking, 2005.

religions

MDPI

Article

Willful Control and Controlling the Will: Technology and Being Human

Brent Waters

Garrett-Evangelical Theological Seminary, Evanston 60201, USA; brent.waters@garrett.edu; Tel.: +1-847-866-3933

Academic Editor: Noreen Herzfeld
Received: 23 February 2017; Accepted: 8 May 2017; Published: 10 May 2017

Abstract: One purported benefit of technology is that it gives humans greater control over how they live their lives. Various technologies are used to protect humans from what are perceived to be the capricious whims of indifferent natural forces. Additionally, technology is used to create circumstances and opportunities that are believed to be preferable because they are more subject to human control. In large measure, the lives of late moderns are effectively constructed and asserted as artifacts of what they will themselves to be. This control is seen prominently at the beginning and end of life. Technology is employed to overcome infertility, prevent illness, disability, and undesirable traits, to select desirable traits and increasingly enhance them. At the end of life, late moderns have a far greater range of options at their disposal than past generations: they can choose to delay death, control pain, or end their lives at the time and with the means of their choosing. The greater control that technology offers helps humans to survive and even flourish, but it comes at a price. One such cost is that it tends to reduce humans to being little more than a will confined within a body. The body is thereby effectively perceived to be an impediment to the will that should be overcome. Is this troubling? Yes. I argue that the purported control technology offers often serves as a distraction or blind spot that may prevent humans from understanding and consenting to their good. In making this argument I draw upon the Christian doctrine of the incarnation as a way of disclosing the creaturely good of finitude against which the will should conform rather than attempting to overcome. I also draw upon Iris Murdoch's and Simone Weil's concept of "unselfing" as a way of conforming the will with this good. I revisit issues related to the beginning and end of life to draw-out some of the implications of my argument.

Keywords: technology; ontology; will; mastery; Hannah Arendt; George Grant; Iris Murdoch

---

The word "technology" engenders a range of responses. For some, it evokes a highly positive reaction. With the aid of various technologies humans can, over time, fashion for themselves a virtual heaven on earth. For others, technology conjures a grave threat. Devices are invading every aspect of life, collectively diminishing its quality and perhaps ending in the extinction of the human species. For most, however, technology is taken for granted. Ubiquitous gadgets are part of the fabric of everyday life, and the significant role they play in weaving that fabric is largely unnoticed, except on those relatively rare occasions when they fail to perform as expected. For example, who thinks about electricity until there is a power failure?

In this article, I focus on this latter group, who have easily embraced a manufactured habitat as their normal environment. What would have appeared to previous generations as a magical world is now commonplace. I assume that one of the primary reasons for this easy embrace is the functionality or utility that technology affords. Computers, mobile phones, dishwashers, cars, airplanes, and the countless other items that could be added to this list make our lives easier, productive, and more entertaining. And I have no quarrel with affirming these benefits. Yet what does this easy embrace disclose and occlude about what being human is coming to mean for late moderns? In the following inquiry, I offer some provisional thoughts about this question by concentrating on the relation between technology and asserting greater control, and assessing the some of the costs incurred in such an assertion in respect to human ontology.

Presumably one of the chief benefits of technology (referred to here as the collection of devices used to achieve various goals and objectives) is that it enables humans to assert greater control over the circumstances they encounter. Indeed, these circumstances are increasingly manufactured by humans. Many, if not most, late moderns live and work in environments of their own making, and are thereby also subject to their control. Presumably, this control improves the quality of being human. It is difficult to object to this presumption. Who would want to return to a status in which humans were largely at the mercy of natural processes that are indifferent to our survival, much less our flourishment? Technology is merely a tool that humankind, as homo faber, uses to fashion a hospitable habitat. Without tools, humans are something less than human. The world, then, into which people are born is not a given, but a human artifact. As Hannah Arendt recognized, the world "is the result of human productivity and human action" (Arendt 2005, p. 107). The world "is not identical with the earth or with nature", but a "human artifact, the fabrication of human hands" (Arendt 1998, p. 52).

As George Grant declares: "In each lived moment of our waking and sleeping, we are technological civilisation" (Grant 1986, p. 11). These waking and sleeping moments disclose an obsessive drive for asserting greater mastery over nature and human nature (Grant 1969; Grant 1995; Grant 1985). Grant's references to "nature" and "human nature" in the works cited are admittedly cryptic, but what he has in mind is the late modern project of creating a world more amenable to human purposes. In the "will to mastery", humans make things happen (Grant 1986, pp. 12–13). Through employing technology, humans transform nature into resources that both expand the range of available options, while diminishing the threat of chance or randomness. Asserting such mastery is thereby relentless and progressive, as reflected in the late modern belief that the chief accomplishments of a civilization are measured by its ability to predict, construct, and control the future. Moreover, technology is used to achieve a relative equality among people, compensating the disadvantages the natural lottery distributes to some unfortunate individuals. More just societies can be engineered, and unwanted outcomes of natural selection can be ameliorated. In short, it is through technology that humans create a world as their suitable habitat for being human.

Asserting such mastery, however, is not an extrinsic act, but reveals the will to mastery as intrinsic to being human, especially to late moderns. It is in this willing that humans free themselves from the constraints of nature and human nature to become more fully human (Arendt 1978, pp. 3–5). Consequently, nature and human nature are effectively transformed into artifacts of the human will. Nature is little more than raw material that may be used or abused, cherished or despised in accordance to its assigned valuation. Pristine wilderness may be farmed, mined, developed, or preserved, but each instance is the outcome of what is willed. Human nature as well is an artifact of the will. Behavior, for instance, is controlled through incentives and disincentives, therapy, drugs, and perhaps someday extensive genetic modification.

Even such universal natural events as birth and death are increasingly subjected to technological control. Fetal development is routinely monitored, and in some instances tested. Infertility can be overcome through drugs, gamete donation, artificial insemination, in vitro fertilization (IVF), and surrogacy. A variety of techniques—such as fetal screening and abortion, or IVF and preimplantation genetic diagnosis (PGD)—may be used to prevent the birth of children with severe illnesses or disabilities. More broadly, these same technologies may be employed to avoid undesirable traits or select desirable ones. Should safe and reliable technologies be developed, selected genetic traits may someday be enhanced. At the end of life, various drugs and medical procedures alleviate pain. Increasingly, death itself is becoming more a matter of choice than necessity. Patients can choose to prolong their lives, delay their deaths, or be assisted in dying at a time and means of their choosing. The beginning and end of life, as well as the time in between, are now more artifacts of the will than a natural unfolding of a human life.

Is it wrong or bad to assert greater mastery over nature and human nature? The answer for most late moderns is presumably no, for they turn to technology more and more in living out their lives. In many respects, the lives of late moderns are more akin to a project than an accident or gift. And projects must be managed, and such managing requires tools, and the more sophisticated and efficient tools are at hand, the better. Moreover, it is difficult to argue against asserting greater mastery given the obvious and expansive range of benefits it has provided. Late moderns are exceedingly healthier, richer, and more comfortable than their ancestors, and their descendants will be even better off, provided some foreseen calamities can be avoided or unforeseen disasters do not occur. Technology has not only assisted the survival of the human species in untold ways, but has also enabled human flourishing. Being in control enriches the human condition, so how can asserting greater mastery over nature and human be a problem, or even troubling?

Critics may be quick to complain that, to the contrary, there is much to worry about: examples such as ecological degradation, diminished privacy, weapons of mass destruction, hybrids and chimeras, robots and artificial intelligence enslaving or obliterating humankind come readily to mind. Every technology has the potential to be misused or go terribly awry in unexpected ways. In asserting greater mastery, humans are becoming mastered by their own technology, ultimately imperiling their wellbeing, and perhaps even their survival. These critics may be offered the rejoinder, however, that many problems have already been identified and are being addressed; have they not heard, for instance, of green technologies? Moreover, many of the concerns raised are potential rather than real and can be avoided. The tools used to assert mastery over nature and human nature are controlled by their users who determine how they shall and shall not be used. Since Hiroshima and Nagasaki, no atomic or nuclear weapons have been used in a war, and measures have been taken to limit their proliferation. Granted, unintended consequences cannot be predicted or always prevented, but no progress can be achieved without taking acceptable risks. The benefits incurred to date have far outpaced any problems encountered.

There is much truth in the proponents' question and rejoinder to skeptics. To have greater control over one's circumstances and destiny is not inevitably problematic or troubling. There is no compelling reason to question, much less deny, that technology has, over time, improved the human condition. But the question and rejoinder ignore an important follow-up question: what is the cost? Asserting greater control is not free. George Grant was fond of quoting a Spanish proverb: "Take what you want, said God—take it and pay for it" (Grant 1986, p. 9). Humans pay a price for asserting greater mastery, but has the cost been exorbitant or reasonable? I do not know the answer to this question, but in what follows I identify some of the costs without assigning a precise valuation to the price.

One cost is that human identity, both individually and collectively, is increasingly reduced to acts of the will. This is understandable, perhaps unavoidable in any attempt to master, for to master something requires willing its mastery; a will to mastery. To be in control is to also be more fully human, and this fulfilment is accomplished by imprinting the human will on the world, and on human lives within the world that they make. Late moderns cannot simply say "let it be", but must add the words "thus and so". To be fully human is to make and to master. To effectively reduce what being human means to willful mastery, however, is to render embodiment problematic. The body becomes a problem to be solved, because to be embodied constrains and frustrates the will. I cannot simply will myself to be an athlete, mathematical wizard, or live forever. Nonetheless, asserting greater mastery achieves small victories over finitude that accrue over time; increasingly, nature and human nature are becoming artifacts of the will.

As mentioned above, there is much to say in favor of asserting such mastery. Human flourishing is wider and deeper when humans are steadily less at the mercy of indifferent natural processes. But there is a price to be paid, particularly in "solving" the "problem" of embodiment. One possible cost is that being in control may serve to distract. Control is properly a means rather than an end. One controls A to achieve B. When control becomes effectively an end, then the resulting process of asserting control becomes circular. One controls A to achieve A. It is not clear what purposes late moderns are seeking in asserting greater control or mastery over nature and human nature. Apparently, mastery is often asserted for the sake of achieving greater mastery, but no explicit good is invoked that this mastery purportedly serves. Following Grant, late moderns are "resolute in their will to mastery, but they cannot know what that mastery is for" (Grant 1995, pp. 45–46). One practical consequence of this circular willing is that technological development becomes a default solution, thereby defining the problem a priori. Consequently, "when we are deliberating in any practical situation our judgment acts rather like a mirror which throws back the very metaphysic of the technology which we are supposed to be deliberating about in detail. The outcome is almost inevitably a decision for further technological development" (Grant 1986, p. 33). Once the relative safety of a proposed technological development can be demonstrated, the case is closed.

But why is a circular assertion of the will a distraction? It may, in part, prevent humans from discovering, understanding, and consenting to their good *as creatures*. To invoke the Christian doctrine of creation, humans are creatures created by God. They are willed into being by their creator. Being properly human is thereby to be more receptive than assertive. It is somewhat similar to Josef Pieper's notion of leisure as a "receptive attitude of mind, a contemplative attitude, and it is not only the occasion but also the capacity for steeping oneself in the whole of creation" (Pieper 2009, pp. 46–47). If humans are artifacts, they are divinely made rather than self-made; their being is more akin to a gift received than a construct or self-directed project. As creatures, however, humans are finite and mortal, and these qualities are part of what the good of being a creature entails. Embodiment, then, is not a problem to be solved, but the prerequisite of being creaturely; not an impediment against the will to be overcome, but a standard against which the will conforms. Human flourishing is predicated upon discovering, understanding, and consenting to the good of being *finite and mortal* creatures.

The doctrine of the incarnation affirms the creaturely goods of finitude and mortality. The Word became flesh; the creator became a creature. Jesus is constrained by the limits of his body—miracles notwithstanding—and he does not escape death. In the incarnation, the creaturely goods of finitude and mortality are confirmed by their created source. It is in and through their finitude and mortality that humans participate fully in the unfolding "drama of being" (Voegelin 1989, pp. 39–40). To experience being is to experience that which is lasting and that which is passing. To be an actor in the unfolding drama of being, humans must experience both life and death (Voegelin 1989, pp. 42–43). And it is in consenting to finitude and mortality that humans attune themselves to that which is genuinely lasting. This is why, in part, Christian hope is placed in death and resurrection into the eternal life of God rather than the technological transformation of human creatures into immortal beings of endless time; they look for signs of resurrection and new life rather than clutching to a life that can somehow cheat death.

To be clear, consenting to finitude and mortality does not require one to refuse ameliorating the ill effects entailed in these goods. There is nothing inherently wrong in employing technologies, especially those associated with medical care, to relieve the pain and suffering of injured or deteriorating bodies, or even to extend longevity. Nevertheless, when being human is effectively reduced to the will, to perceive embodiment, either wittingly or unwittingly, as a barrier to be overcome is a temptation difficult to resist. Rather than consenting to finitude and mortality as creaturely goods, they become enemies to be conquered. And herein lies the distraction. In fixating on the will as the paramount feature of their being, late moderns become self-absorbed. The drama of being becomes *my* drama. *My* survival, *my* flourishing commands one's attention. The passing is confused with the lasting, and in doing so one's life becomes discordant, for the expansive drama of being is displaced by autobiography. Rather than perceiving ourselves as participating in an unfolding saga greater and outlasting ourselves, we fixate on bit parts, and resent the prospect of being removed from the stage. In brief, to make oneself the centerpiece of the drama of being is to also remove oneself from participating fully in being human. In addition technology is proficient at reinforcing this misperceived centering.

There is no reason to deny that willful control is required in making a world suitable for human flourishing. This requires, however, that the will and what is willed must also be controlled to ensure that humans participate fully in the unfolding drama of being as finite and mortal creatures; that they avoid the distraction of self-absorption. But how? An extensive survey of how various philosophical and theological accounts of virtues and practices might help to remain properly focused on the passing and the lasting is beyond the scope of this article. Examining briefly Iris Murdoch's notion of "unselfing" (Antonaccio 2012; Gordon 1995; Widdows 2005), however, suggests one way for how controlling the will might be undertaken.

According to Murdoch, freedom does not consist of an isolated individual leaping "in and out of an impersonal logical complex, it is a function of the progressive attempt to see a particular object clearly" (Murdoch 2001, p. 23). Love is central to the process of gaining such clarity. It is in loving the world in general, and individuals in particular, that we come to see both more clearly in their own respective right, for in so doing we "apprehend" their related goodness that "belong(s) to a continuous fabric of being" (Murdoch 2001, p. 29). Following Simone Weil, we must cast a loving and just gaze upon the reality of the other in order to be genuinely attentive to its own good. This attentive love "can prompt a process of unselfing wherein the lover learns to see, and cherish and respect, what is not himself" (Murdoch 1993, p. 17). "If I attend properly I will have no choice and this is the ultimate condition to be aimed at" (Murdoch 2001, p. 38). The ideal situation is similar to that of a kind of necessity. Freedom is not unimpeded movement, but is more akin to the notion of obedience. "I can only choose within the world I can *see*, in the moral sense of 'see' which implies that clear vision is a result of moral imagination and moral effort" (Murdoch 2001, pp. 25–26). Freedom is the result of attention and not action. Consequently, the moral life is something that is formed continually, and not just confined to relatively few moments of decisions or choices.

How might unselfing help avoid the distraction of willful control or mastery? Murdoch contends: "We need a moral philosophy in which the concept of love, so rarely mentioned now by philosophers, can once again be made central" (Murdoch 2001, p. 45). When love is properly ordered, it is directed outwardly, allowing the other to be, whereas mastery is directed inwardly, controlling the other to be what is willed. To oversimplify, the will to mastery is disordered love. The consequence of this disordered love is significant. "In the moral life the enemy is the fat relentless ego" (Murdoch 2001, p. 51). The will to mastery feeds this ego relentlessly, diminishing the center of reality to the one willing and controlling. Mastery is asserted for the sake of the one asserting it. This centering of the ego is, of course, illusory, and such a fantasy, according to Murdoch, is the nemesis of moral excellence. Why? A fantasized self is incapable of attending to the other, and thereby cannot know the good of the other. The other is good only in so far as the value it is assigned by the one seeking to master and control for its own sake. This lack of loving, unselfed attention exposes the fallacy of mastery, in that the freedom purportedly offered in mastering is counterfeit. "The freedom which is a proper human goal is the freedom from fantasy" (Murdoch 2001, p. 65). Fantasy is rooted in self-centeredness, whereas attending to reality is derived from love. True freedom is more akin to proper vision than an assertive will. Reality, one that is given and engaged in rather than constructed and manipulated, is the proper object of love, and knowledge of that object is freeing. It is in this knowledge that we can will to love the neighbor as an other with its own inherent good. Moreover, it is only as finite and mortal beings that we can perceive and attend to the good of other finite and mortal beings (Murdoch 2001, pp. 96–97).

Admittedly, unselfing alone can neither prevent nor resolve the problem of mastery as a distraction. Yet it offers a promising starting point by reorienting attention, at least initially, from the will and what is willed toward encountering an external reality. Borrowing from H. Richard Niebuhr, it entails first asking the question: what is going on? as opposed to asserting what I will to do or to make (Niebuhr 1963). Asking what is going on does not negate the will or willing, for when some determination about what is occurring is made a response must be willed, nor does starting with this question necessarily preclude willful mastery. However, it serves to help shape, and thereby control, what is willed by recasting attention away from the self to the other. To respond to the good of the other, especially through the lens of Murdoch's loving and just gaze, is in large measure to let the other be rather than something to be mastered.

What difference this change in orientation might entail can be illustrated by briefly revisiting the perceptions of birth and death noted earlier in this article. Late moderns increasingly perceive birth as the successfully willed outcome of a reproductive project (Robertson 1994). Hence, the greater recourse to technology in selecting the biological material, testing, and monitoring fetal development for obtaining a desirable child. The child so conceived is effectively an artifact of its progenitor's will. This perception corrodes the traditional parent-child relationship, for begetting is not synonymous with making (O'Donovan 1984). In begetting, there is a fundamental equality of being that is shared by parent and child in a mode of receptivity; a baby is received by her parents. Whereas in making, there is a distinct inequality between maker and made that is inherent in any mode of mastery; a baby is created by the overseer of a reproductive project. To perceive a baby, either wittingly or unwittingly, as an artifact is to also to strip the accompany symbolism of its moral and political import. In Arendt's account of natality (Arendt 1998), she contends that the "law of mortality" is the only certainty of human life (Arendt 1998, p. 246). Humans, however, are not born to die, but are born to begin. It is natality that rescues humans from their natural mortality. But such rescue is not achieved by attempting to overcome mortality, but receiving the future through regeneration. To control the outcome of a reproductive project is in effect to deny the future by extending and instantiating a willed present in which nothing new can be received. The possibility of new and unanticipated beginnings, a possibility symbolized in begetting a child, is what gives men and women their faith and hope. It is the hope that is expressed in the Christian "glad tidings" of Jesus' birth: "A child has been born unto us" (Arendt 1998, p. 247).

Likewise, when death is perceived as more a matter of choice than a necessity, it ceases to be a fitting end to one's role in the unfolding drama of being. To play this role requires the actor to both live and die, and to play it well entails consenting to these necessities. Choosing the time and means of one's death is simply a final, defiant, and futile act of will; one last, empty attempt to protect the present from the future. In waging a lifelong war against finitude and mortality, the only end to be imagined is to control one's demise. This is tantamount to refusing to participate in the drama of being, because one never consents to the prerequisites of finitude and mortality; one cannot be unless one foresees and accepts ceasing to be. Moreover, refusing to participate is to essentially commit the deadly sin of acedia—a fundamental boredom and indifference to being itself. Ironically, the will to mastery is a denial of being, for humans were created to be recipients of life rather than its makers. The will to mastery is ultimately deadly.

To reiterate, unselfing alone cannot control what is willed in our inevitable acts of asserting willful control, but it does serve to remind that no one is at the center of being; the drama of the passing and the lasting is far larger. Unselfing may also serve to remind that humans should endeavor to remain creaturely for that is what they were created to be. Consequently, technology should be used in ways that assist humans to consent to their creaturely finitude and mortality rather than attempting to vanquish them through their mastery. Perhaps in reinforcing such unselfed consent, we might also gain some greater insight into what being human and human being might mean.

Conflicts of Interest: The author declares no conflict of interest.

References

Antonaccio, Maria. 2012. *A Philosophy to Live By: Engaging Iris Murdoch*. Oxford and New York: Oxford University Press.
Arendt, Hannah. 1978. *The Life of the Mind: Two, Willing*. San Diego and London: Harcourt.
Arendt, Hannah. 1998. *The Human Condition*. Chicago and London: University of Chicago Press.
Arendt, Hannah. 2005. *The Promise of Politics*. New York: Shocken Books.
Gordon, David J. 1995. *Iris Murdoch's Fables of Unselfing*. Columbia: University of Missouri Press.

Grant, George. 1969. *Technology and Empire: Perspectives on North America*. Toronto: House of Anansi.

Grant, George Parkin. 1985. *English-Speaking Justice*. Notre Dame: University of Notre Dame Press.

Grant, George Parkin. 1986. *Technology and Justice*. Notre Dame: Notre Dame University Press.

Grant, George. 1995. *Time as History*. Toronto and London: University of Toronto Press.

Murdoch, Iris. 1993. *Metaphysics as a Guide to Morals*. London and New York: Penguin Books.

Murdoch, Iris. 2001. *The Sovereignty of Good*. London and New York: Routledge.

Niebuhr, H. Richard. 1963. *The Responsible Self: An Essay in Christian Moral Philosophy*. New York and London: Harper and Row.

O'Donovan, Oliver. 1984. *Begotten or Made?* Oxford: Oxford University Press.

Pieper, Josef. 2009. *Leisure the Basis of Culture and the Philosophical Act*. San Francisco: Ignatius Press.

Robertson, John A. 1994. *Children of Choice: Freedom and the New Reproductive Technologies*. Princeton: Princeton University Press.

Voegelin, Eric. 1989. *Collected Works, Vol. 14: Order and History, Vol. 1: Israel and Revelation*. Baton Rouge: Louisiana State University Press.

Widdows, Heather. 2005. *The Moral Vision of Iris Murdoch*. Aldershot and Burlington: Ashgate.

MDPI

Article
Resurrection of the Body and Cryonics

Calvin Mercer

Religious Studies Program, East Carolina University, Greenville, NC 27858, USA; mercerc@ecu.edu

Academic Editor: Noreen Herzfeld
Received: 2 February 2017; Accepted: 14 May 2017; Published: 18 May 2017

Abstract: The Christian doctrine of resurrection of the body is employed to interpret the cryonics program of preserving legally dead people with the plan to restore them when future medicine can effectively address the cause of death. Cryonics is not accepted by mainstream science, and even if the vision is never realized, it is worth the effort to use it as a thought experiment to test the capability of the Christian theological system to address this issue in the unfolding new world of human enhancement. Drawing on the apostle Paul, whose view was based in the Jewish notion of psychosomatic unity, Christian resurrection includes emphases on physicality, radical transformation, and continuity of personal identity. Successful cryonics scenarios can include restoring a person to more or less the same life they had before or, more likely, utilize robotics, tissue regeneration, and other future advances in human enhancement technology to restore one to an enhanced state. Christian resurrection and the more likely cryonics scenario both entail physicality, radical transformation, and continuity of personal identity and, as such, can be understood to be technological expressions of Christian resurrection.

Keywords: body; Christian theology; cryonics; dualism; immortality of the soul; personal identity; resurrection; superintelligence; uploading; whole brain emulation

1. Introduction

Interest in the promising gene editing technique, known as clustered regularly interspaced short palindromic repeats (CRISPR), is just one indicator that we are recognizing, albeit slowly, the dawning of a human enhancement revolution. CRISPR allows scientists to modify DNA in organisms, and in addition to its use in fighting diseases, it may allow for old cells to regain youthful function (Achenbach 2015). A variety of other physical, cognitive, affective, moral, and even spiritual enhancements are unfolding. In this article I use enhancement to refer to radical transformation as opposed to therapy/healing. Many of the extreme enhancements being considered are unlikely to materialize. However, some of them likely will, and it is incumbent on religions (if they are to be relevant), in their theological and ethical fields, to examine the moral and metaphysical implications of human enhancement in light of their theologies. Resurrection of the body is a Christian doctrine that has emerged as potentially providing a valuable theological framework for understanding some human enhancement technologies (Peters et al. 2002; Mercer 2017; Peters 2006, pp. 28–46, 148–50; Steinhart 2014, pp. 84–87, 90–91, 98–100).

Perhaps due, at least in part, to the will to live, radical life extension has long been a central goal of transhumanists and other proponents of human enhancement. Biological, genetic, and digital scenarios have been proposed to defeat aging. The use of cognitive enhancement technologies may speed up the development of other life-extending technologies. However, until these extreme longevity technologies are available, some prolongevity advocates think we need stop-gap measures. Cryonics is a program for using very low temperatures and chemical processes to preserve human life beyond legal death with the plan to bring the person back when medical science has developed the necessary means to effectively address the cause of death. In this article, I consider the doctrine of resurrection as it could relate to cryonics.

My specific evaluation of cryonics in this article is framed by a general assessment of technology as potentially reflecting God's work in the world. Our abilities are God-given, nature is a domain of God's grace, and God can work though radical technologies just like God can work through the hands of the traditional oncologist. In this respect we are created co-creators with God (Hefner 1993).[1] God declared, following the sixth day of creation, that everything, including human beings and their cognitive capabilities, is "very good"—with not one hint of evil or fallenness (Genesis 1:31, *NRSV*). Radical transformation, indeed, transhumanism properly framed, is Christian (Cole-Turner 2017). That said, the biblical story continues in Genesis, chapter 3, with the appearance of evil and suffering. Transformation can also be for evil (Peters 2011); with our increasingly potent technologies we can create enormous Towers of Babel (Genesis 11:1–9) that bring confusion, or worse. Therefore, an appreciation of science and technology as yielding graceful divine actions must also be tempered by the recognition that selfish or otherwise damaged motivations can purpose capabilities to dreadful ends. The challenge is to make sure we responsibly and in community manage our God-given abilities and opportunities and, in the process, participate in God's transformation of all creation. Determining if a particular technology can be consistent with Christian theology is a good place to start that process, and that is what this article intends to do with regard to cryonics.

2. Christian Resurrection of the Body

The apostle Paul is the primary source in the early church for the notion of bodily resurrection, although he did not invent the doctrine. His understanding is grounded in Jewish anthropology, which stressed the psychosomatic unity of the person. Resurrection, then, for Paul, as well as for ancient Judaism, is resurrection of the whole person, which entails all dimensions of being, including physicality, i.e., resurrection of the body. In Paul's main reflection on resurrection (1 Corinthians 15), he affirms that resurrection of the believer will be modeled after the resurrected Christ, the "first fruits" of those who have died (1 Corinthians 15:20–23).

Paul's term for a resurrected person is "spiritual body" (*soma pneumatikon*, 1 Corinthians 15:44), an idea that is, arguably, incoherent. How can two forms—material and spiritual—interact? That said, we can grant Paul a measure of grace. He was a missionary, and his writings were occasional letters generally designed to speak to specific situations in the churches he had organized. To say it another way, he was not a systematic theologian who can be held to the professional norms of today's scholars. He did provide, however, theological building blocks that constitute some of the basic contours of a resurrection doctrine.

2.1. Bodily Resurrection

The Greek word *anastasis* (resurrection) is composed of two words, the preposition *ana*, "up", and *stasis*, the word for "stand". The word *anastasis* is distinct from *athanasia*, usually translated "immortality" and literally meaning "not death". In Paul's day *anastasis* (resurrection) had shades of meaning, for example, raise up, awaken, recover. Early Christian authors spoke of several kinds of raisings. Jesus raised Lazarus from the dead. In other words, he resuscitated the man's dead body and, presumably, except for the remarkable experience of being raised from the dead, Lazarus continued life pretty much as before he died.

Paul's "spiritual body", however, results from being raised to new and transformed life after the fashion of Jesus' resurrection. Paul explicitly models the resurrection of the believer on Jesus' resurrection (1 Corinthians 15; Romans 8:11). In this eschatological resurrection, the raised person, however personhood is defined, entails a bodily dimension. This somatic aspect is consistent with

---

[1] With regard to the "new creation" that resurrection provides, although it is a bit awkwardly termed, we can think of resurrection in the new world of enhancement as "created co-new-creators".

and framed by the importance of physicality in other key doctrines, such as creation, incarnation, and eschatology (i.e., a new heaven and a new earth) (Mercer 2014; 2015a).

While we have had detractors throughout Christian history and today, in general, in affirming the psychosomatic unity of the person, there is a rejection of a Gnostic-like sentiment that yields an afterlife based in immortality of the soul, a view that minimizes the importance of the body. That persons are embodied is the consensus of academic theology and definitely of Christian thinkers addressing transhumanist enhancement concerns (Peters 2006, pp. 119, 130; Cole-Turner 2009; Labrecque 2015; Herzfeld 2012; Moltmann-Wendel 1995; Mercer 2015b).

2.2. Transformation

As distinguished from resuscitation of a dead body to normal life, the believer's resurrection, modeled after Jesus' resurrection, is transformative, resulting in a changed body that is qualitatively different from the body before the resurrection. New possibilities abound. In his newly transformed body, Jesus appeared and disappeared before witnesses (Luke 24:13–43), moved through doors (John 20:26), and made himself invisible (Acts 9:1–9). The relationship between Jesus' raised body and his ascended/glorified body is an open question (Gulley 1992).[2] While the resurrection clearly entailed transformation, if there is a difference between the resurrected and ascended body, then the transformation continued in a process that culminated in the glorified body.[3]

Paul appreciated the existence of different kinds of bodies. The resurrected body is imperishable, glorious, and powerful, as compared to the "flesh and blood" perishable, dishonoring, and weak body (1 Corinthians 15:42–43). Transformation of the believer is not isolated speculation among early Christians. It can be framed in the anticipated and hoped for cosmic transformation of a "new heaven and a new earth" (Revelation 21:1, *NRSV*).

Indeed, Ron Cole-Turner argues that because transformation is at the core of the religion, transhumanism is a Christian concept, and he traces the origin of the word back to Dante. "Dante's *trasumanar* has now morphed into transhumanism ... But because this word is invented to describe the transformation that constitutes the very heart of the Christian gospel, Christians must claim it and own it as their own" (Cole-Turner 2015, p. 151). In an article titled "Christian Transhumanism", he writes that "Christian transhumanism is not an accommodation to our age. It is instead an affirmation of the radically transformative nature of the hope that lies at the heart of a Christian view of humanity and the cosmos" (Cole-Turner 2017).

2.3. Continuity of Personal Identity

Although he was radically transformed, the personal identity of Jesus continued in the resurrected Lord. Disciples who knew him before his death recognized him and interacted with him in conversation following the resurrection.

Paul affirms that Jesus resurrected was the same person with the same body, albeit transformed. In other accounts, the disciples were "startled and frightened, and supposed that they saw a spirit" (Luke 24:37, *NRSV*). Jesus responded: "See my hands and my feet, that it is I myself; handle me, and see; for a spirit has not flesh and bones as you see that I have" (Luke 24:39, *NRSV*). Doubting Thomas said he would not believe, "Unless I see in his hands the print of the nails and, and place my finger in the mark of the nails, and place my hand in his side ... " (John 20:25, *NRSV*). Jesus appeared and told Thomas: "Put your finger here, and see my hands; and put out your hand, and place it in my side" (John 20:27, *NRSV*).

---

2 For the diverse Greek terms referring to the ascension and a brief review of the history of the doctrine, see (Gulley 1992).
3 Theological reflection on the ascended/glorified body as it relates to the resurrected body, with regard to human enhancement, merits further treatment.

Paul's reflection on the continuity between pre- and post-death utilizes the analogy of a seed and the resulting plant. The kernel is sown into the ground, and it grows into a body consistent with the kind of seed sown (1 Corinthians 15:35–41).

3. Cryonics

According to the Alcor Life Extension Foundation, arguably the leading cryonics organization, "Cryonics is an effort to save lives by using temperatures so cold that a person beyond help by today's medicine can be preserved for decades or centuries until a future medical technology can restore that person to full health" (Alcor Life Extension Foundation 2017a). The contemporary focus of cryonics research is on achieving a high-fidelity preservation of the body, and especially the brain, viewed by advocates as containing memory and personality information. "If a brain can be preserved well enough to retain the memory and personality within it, then restoring health to the whole person is viewed as a long-term engineering problem" (Alcor Life Extension Foundation 2017b).

Cryonics has progressed considerably from the days of placing bodies in a deep freeze, hoping for the best. In a process called vitrification (ice-free preservation), a cryoprotectant solution is used to enable structural preservation of the brain. My purpose here is not to defend the legitimacy of cryonics nor assess the prospects of its success. Although not accepted by mainstream science, cryonics does seem to have enough support to merit theological reflection, if only in the form of a thought experiment. The Alcor website provides "Selected Journal Articles Supporting the Scientific Basis of Cryonics" (Alcor Life Extension Foundation 2017c) and presents the following "Scientists' Open Letter on Cryonics", with 69 signatories:

> *The signatories, speaking for themselves, include leading scientists from institutes such as MIT, Harvard, NASA and Cambridge University to name a few:* Cryonics is a legitimate science-based endeavor that seeks to preserve human beings, especially the human brain, by the best technology available. Future technologies for resuscitation can be envisioned that involve molecular repair by nanomedicine, highly advanced computation, detailed control of cell growth, and tissue regeneration. With a view toward these developments, there is a credible possibility that cryonics performed under the best conditions achievable today can preserve sufficient neurological information to permit eventual restoration of a person to full health. The rights of people who choose cryonics are important, and should be respected (Evidence-Based Cryonics 2011).

4. Cryonics and Resurrection

Alcor and other cryonics organizations view their legally dead members as "patients". From a Christian perspective, there are three ways cryonics can be interpreted. First, a cryopreserved person can be regarded in a way similar to how a coma patient, who eventually revives, is viewed. The person is in some sort of deep unconsciousness until they come back—or are brought back—to consciousness. From this first perspective, cryonics is simply a significant extension of always advancing medical technology. This is the way Alcor prefers cryonics to be viewed. From their perspective, death is not an event but a process, and cryonics is interrupting that process so critical information in the brain can be preserved for future restoration. They contend that cryopreservation is a form of suspended animation in a fashion similar to procedures already used in medicine and point out that human embryos, for example, are routinely cryopreserved and revived.

Because of the radical nature of cryonics, not to mention the social and legal issues involved, cryonics is probably never going to be seen, by the general public at least, as a normal medical procedure. Likewise, Christianity will also sharply differentiate between mainstream medical procedures and cryonics. While some Christians may see cryonics as a significant medical advance, that is not going to be the prevailing view.

The second way cryonics can be interpreted is as a resurrection in the sense of resuscitation of the dead. Just as Jesus miraculously raised Lazarus from the dead to continue living pretty much as before he died, so God uses cryonics to bring people back from dead. In this scenario, to play on the Greek word, we "stand up" (*anastasis*) the same kind of body the person had before, except that, for example, the "terminal" cancer is now cured (Mercer 2008).

However, a successfully cryopreserved patient can be maintained for an indefinite period of time before being restored, a situation that opens up the third and most likely way successful cryonics would be interpreted. This indefinite period would most definitely be a very long time, compared to the length of a coma, because we are not close to having the ability to restore a preserved person. Being unconscious, i.e., preserved, for hundreds and maybe thousands of years makes the difference between a coma and cryopreservation significant enough that they are best addressed in different ways. Also, if cryonics ever works, it will be so far into the future that restoration of a cryonics patient could involve significant use of advanced enhancement technologies, such as robotics, artificial intelligence, tissue regeneration, and nanotechnology.

As we saw earlier, Christian resurrection of the dead entails at least three aspects: embodiment, transformation, and continuity of personal identity. Cryonics, if it is ever successful, is likely to also entail these three aspects.

4.1. Embodiment

With regard to embodiment, in their facility in Scottsdale, Arizona, Alcor keeps the preserved *patients* in a controlled environment and awaiting developments in future medicine that can restore them. Some patients are preserve thed whole body. In these cases, if and when the preserved body is restored to proper functioning, any requirement that a person is embodied has is met.

Some cryonic patients, however, have opted for "neuropreservation" (head only). Many theologians, along with others, challenge the idea that who we are can be reduced to information in the brain. This is a complicated debate involving personhood, *imago Dei* (image of God), and other considerations. The contention that we have "body memory", apart from memory found in the brain, is relevant here (Swinton 2014). Alcor, however, resists the charge that in these cases the organization is preserving "heads only". The company insists that it preserves people, although with the understanding that the one organ essential to personhood is the brain. Preserving the memory and personality information in the brain with the highest possible fidelity is linked to an expectation that developments in biomedical technology will enable medicine of the future to regrow a body.

Some theologians might object that a newly newly-grown body, or one utilizing robotics, is not made of the same type of material constituting the person's body prior to legal death. But However, Paul asserts a resurrected "spiritual body" that, for him, satisfies the physicality requirement of psychosomatic unity. However, Paul's "spiritual body" clearly has a different composition. It moves through doors and so is not the same kind of body as in Jesus' life pre-death. Theologians objecting that a restored, even robotic, body is not theologically acceptable would need to explain how they can accept Paul's "spiritual body", which also has a different composition.

Moving to another issue, resurrection, admittedly, is post-death and cryopreservation, as depicted by the industry, is pre-death, that is, death is being intercepted and put on hold to await complete reversal in the future. However, cryonics is not generally accepted by the scientific community nor the general public. Currently, the legal and social understanding is that cryonics patients are dead. So if restoration is ever accomplished, it will be viewed as bringing back to life someone who was dead, which allows for interpreting that restoration as resurrection.

As we have seen, Christian resurrection is holistic, inclusive of the body in some sense of that word. Restoration of a cryopreserved person would also entail physicality, whether the patient has their whole body cryopreserved or the head only. The latter is done, as noted above, with the expectation of using robotics, tissue regeneration, and other technologies to provide the person's somatic dimension.

Although I will not pursue it at length here, Christianity's intermediate state between death and the "last day", when the resurrection of the believer occurs, may merit further examination. Could the deep unconsciousness or coma period in cryonics between cryopreservation and restoration be associated with the intermediate state? The Bible and the Apocryphal (2 Maccabees 12:39–45) speak very little about this interim state, but it was developed among early church fathers (e.g., Clement of Alexandria, Origen, and Augustine) as a notion of purgatory and affirmed as a doctrine by the Roman Catholic Church. The purpose of purgatory is purification to ready one for the bliss of the age to come and, in this sense, it fits well with the transhumanist project of enhancing us for a sustainable life into the future.

4.2. Transformation

Since restoration, if it comes, is likely to occur far in the future, other human enhancement technologies will certainly have developed and be available as part of the restoration process. Embodiment options possibly will include robotics, tissue regeneration, and as yet unknown biomedical and other technologies. While we are unable to depict what the restored body might look like far into the future, I think we can safely say that, compared to the bodies we now have, future bodies will be worthy of the adjective "transformed".

The resurrected and transformed body of Jesus was able to materialize through doors and appear on remote roads. I am certainly not suggesting that these first-century depictions of resurrection are literally relevant for our modern, scientific age. They are not. They do indicate, however, that Paul and the other Christian writers were creative in reaching for the eschatological vision. Paul called the believer's eschatological body imperishable, glorious, and powerful (1 Corinthians 15:42–43). While these are rather imprecise descriptions, again, they can serve to inspire modern theology as it works to understand rapidly advancing human enhancement technology in light of Christian doctrine.

The transformation entailed in cryonics restoration, if far enough into the future, may not be limited to new and improved bodies. If mind uploading—technically termed whole brain emulation—capability is available when the preserved person is restored, that will open up a whole new avenue of cognitive enhancement possibility. Experts tell us that mind uploading is likely the surest path to superintelligence, intelligence that greatly surpasses general human intelligence (Bostrom 2014, p. 50). If uploading is an option when the person is restored, then any discussion about cryonics will bleed into a discussion about mind uploading and possibly superintelligence (Mercer 2017).

4.3. Continuity of Personal Identity

Cryonics, in its most straightforward form—as restoring to health a cryopreserved patient—is clearly about continuation of the individual person being preserved. Alcor's goals and the legal contracts signed by those intending to be cryopreserved all are predicated on continuity of personal identity following restoration. Using the same body and restoring it to health need not raise questions about this being the same person.

Some transhumanist projects, such as whole brain emulation, could raise difficult questions about the continuation of personal identity (Mercer 2017). Issues about whether personal identity is continued after the person is brought back can arise, but only if the restoration uses radical techniques, such as mind uploading, that raise questions about whether identity has been replaced.

With respect to resurrection, regardless of how remarkable and extensive the transformation, this Christian doctrine is predicated on the resurrected person being a continuation of same person. That is clearly Paul's view, and it is also clear that how this might actually be implemented remains a mystery.

5. Concluding Summary

The cryonics' vision of preserving our memory and personality and restoring them in the future may never be realized. Even if the vision is never achieved, it is worth the effort to use it as a thought experiment to test the capability of the Christian theological system to address the unfolding new world of human enhancement and in particular the role of cryonics in that world.

I have provided a favorable, though qualified, theological assessment of cryonics. I can anticipate at least several critiques and will mention three and provide brief responses. Firstly, resurrection as I have framed it, and cryonics as envisioned, are focused on the life of the individual. Preservation and transformation of the individual can be seen as leaving unattended an important communal focus that Christianity affirms. In response, resurrection of a community is predicated on resurrection of individuals in the community. I have tried to begin a conversation that might establish that cryonic restoration of the individual can be assimilated into a theological vision. Depending on the degree of success, it lays the groundwork for placing this eschatological or salvific event into a larger communal framework of an eschatological heaven on earth. Although he may not agree with the thrust of this article, I think Ted Peters' comment, in the context of his commentary on Wolfhart Pannenberg and John Polkinghorne, is apt here: "The Easter resurrection of Jesus was more than a nice thing that happened to this one person one day in Jerusalem. Built right into the meaning of the Easter event is God's promise to establish the divine kingdom, to renew all creation" (Peters 2006, p. 33).

A second possible critique is that the new creation resulting from the resurrection will be ordered according to God's perfect will, free from sin. There is no compelling reason to think that the cryogenic and enhanced community will be so characterized. In fact, there is considerable concern that enhanced humanity will create more mischief than we are presently capable of managing (Juengst and Moseley 2015).[4] Indeed, this is a potential significant inconsistency between the Christian vision of resurrection and a possible hellish transhumanist future. That said, moral bioenhancement is an emerging category in the enhancement debate, and the theoretical possibility exists that success on this front could bring about a sinless future. However, I admit that depending upon moral bioenhancement, a most controversial and debated topic, to save us from our fallen nature, is something of a reach.

Thirdly, someone may say that resurrection is traditionally understood as a resurrection for judgment, and enhancement does not include that aspect. Admittedly, the traditional "day" of judgment does not cohere well with a new creation, technologically transformed. The key word here is "traditional". Nothing about the unfolding world of radical human enhancement is going to fit cleanly into biblical or systematic theology, traditionally interpreted. Extreme enhancement is going to stretch doctrines if Christianity proves capable of embracing the developments.

Finally, the objection could be made that resurrection is to eternal life, and cryonics restores one to a biological body still subject to decay. That deterioration, however, at least in the transhumanist vision, will be reversed in an ongoing manner by new technologies. Indeed, the entire cryonics program is predicated on the belief that cryonics is available whenever the body is in need of preservation in order to await whatever restorative technology is needed. Death, then, is reinterpreted as the "passing" of the frail body, paving the way for the new creation.

In conclusion, there are understandable differences of opinion about the compatibility of Christian theology and radical human enhancement programs. Cryonics, too, will elicit a variety of views. This article attempts to initiate a theological appreciation of cryonics, and hopefully the conversation will continue. In the meantime, I suggest we consider that, at the very least, cryonics and resurrection might agree on the following, articulated by the apostle Paul:

> When the perishable puts on the imperishability, and the mortal puts on immortality, then shall come to pass the saying that is written: "Death is swallowed up in victory." "O death, where is thy victory? O death, where is thy sting?" (1 Corinthians 15:54–55, *NRSV*).

Conflicts of Interest: The author declares no conflict of interest.

---

[4] This article provides an overview of concerns voiced about various ypes of human enhancement. Ray Kurzweil is perhaps the most well-known transhumanist with an optimistic vision of an enhanced future. See, e.g., (Kurzweil 2005).

References

Achenbach, Joel. 2015. A Harvard Professor Says He Can Cure Aging, But Is That a Good Idea? *Washington Post*. December 2. Available online: https://www.washingtonpost.com/news/achenblog/wp/2015/12/02//professor-george-church-says-he-can-reverse-the-aging-process/ (accessed on 5 May 2017).

Alcor Life Extension Foundation. 2017a. What is Cryonics? Available online: http://www.alcor.org/AboutCryonics/index.html (accessed on 21 January 2017).

Alcor Life Extension Foundation. 2017b. Scientists' Cryonics FAQ. Available online: http://www.alcor.org/sciencefaq.htm (accessed on 21 January 2017).

Alcor Life Extension Foundation. 2017c. Selected Journal Articles Supporting the Scientific Basis of Cryonics. Available online: http://www.alcor.org/sciencerefs.html (accessed on 21 January 2017).

Bostrom, Nick. 2014. *Superintelligence: Paths, Dangers, Strategies*. Oxford: Oxford University Press.

Cole-Turner, Ronald. 2009. Extreme Longevity Research: A Progressive Protestant Perspective. In *Religion and the Implications of Radical Life Extension*. Edited by Derek F. Maher and Calvin Mercer. New York: Palgrave Macmillan, pp. 51–61.

Cole-Turner, Ron. 2015. Going beyond the Human: Christians and Other Transhumanists. *Theology and Science* 13: 150–61. [CrossRef]

Cole-Turner, Ron. 2017. Christian Transhumanism. In *Religion and Human Enhancement: Death, Values, and Morality*. Edited by Tracy Trothen and Calvin Mercer. In *Palgrave Studies in the Future of Humanity and Its Successors*. Edited by Steve Fuller and Calvin Mercer. New York: Palgrave Macmillan.

Evidence-Based Cryonics. 2011. Scientists' Open Letter on Cryonics. Available online: http://www.evidencebasedcryonics.org/scientists-open-letter-on-cryonics/ (accessed on 21 January 2017).

Gulley, Norman R. 1992. Ascension of Christ. In *The Anchor Bible Dictionary*. New York: Doubleday, vol. 1, pp. 472–74.

Hefner, Philip. 1993. *The Human Factor: Evolution, Culture, and Religion*. Minneapolis: Fortress Press.

Herzfeld, Noreen. 2012. Human-Directed Evolution: A Christian Perspective. In *The Routledge Companion to Religion and Science*. Edited by James W. Haag, Gregory R. Peterson and Michael L. Spezio. New York: Routledge, pp. 591–601.

Juengst, Eric, and Daniel Moseley. 2015. Human Enhancement. *Stanford Encyclopedia of Philosophy*, April 7. Available online: https://plato.stanford.edu/entries/enhancement/ (accessed on 5 May 2017).

Kurzweil, Ray. 2005. *The Singularity is Near: When Humans Transcend Biology*. New York: Viking.

Labrecque, Cory Andrew. 2015. Morphological Freedom and the Rebellion against Human Bodiliness: Notes from the Roman Catholic Tradition. In *Religion and Transhumanism: The Unknown Future of Human Enhancement*. Edited by Calvin Mercer and Tracy J. Trothen. Santa Barbara: Praeger, pp. 303–14.

Mercer, Calvin. 2008. Cryonics and Religion: Friends or Foes? *Cryonics* 29: 10–21.

Mercer, Calvin. 2014. Sorting out *Soma* in the Debate about Transhumanism: One Protestant's Perspective. In *Transhumanism and the Body: The World Religions Speak*. Edited by Calvin Mercer and Derek F. Maher. In *Palgrave Studies in the Future of Humanity and Its Successors*. Edited by Steve Fuller and Calvin Mercer. New York: Palgrave Macmillan, pp. 137–54.

Mercer, Calvin. 2015a. Whole Brain Emulation Requires Enhanced Theology, and a 'Handmaiden'. *Theology and Science* 13: 175–86. [CrossRef]

Mercer, Calvin. 2015b. Bodies and Persons: Theological Reflections on Transhumanism. *Dialog: A Journal of Theology* 54: 27–33. [CrossRef]

Mercer, Calvin. 2017. A Theological Assessment of Whole Brain Emulation: On the Path to Superintelligence. In *Religion and Human Enhancement: Death, Values, and Morality*. Edited by Tracy Trothen and Calvin Mercer. In *Palgrave Studies in the Future of Humanity and Its Successors*. Edited by Steve Fuller and Calvin Mercer. New York: Palgrave Macmillan.

Moltmann-Wendel, Elisabeth. 1995. *I Am My Body: A Theology of Engagement*. New York: Continuum.

Ted Peters, Robert John Russell, and Michael Walker, eds. 2002. *Resurrection: Theological and Scientific Assessments*. Grand Rapids: Eerdmans.

Peters, Ted. 2006. *Anticipating Omega: Science, Faith, and Our Ultimate Future*. Religion, Theology and Natural Science 7. Göttingen: Vandenhoeck & Ruprecht.

Peters, Ted. 2011. Progress and Provolution: Will Transhumanism Leave Sin Behind? In *Transhumanism and Transcendence: Christian Hope in an Age of Technological Enhancement*. Edited by Ronald Cole-Turner. Washington: Georgetown University Press, pp. 63–86.

Steinhart, Eric Charles. 2014. *Your Digital Afterlives: Computational Theories of Life after Death*. Palgrave Frontiers in Philosophy of Religion; New York: Palgrave Macmillan.

Swinton, John. 2014. What the Body Remembers: Theological Reflections on Dementia. *Journal of Religion, Spirituality and Aging* 26: 160–72. [CrossRef]

religions   **MDPI**

Article

Big Data, Ethics and Religion: New Questions from a New Science

Michael Fuller

School of Divinity, University of Edinburgh, Mound Place, Edinburgh EH1 2LX, UK; Michael.Fuller@ed.ac.uk;
Tel.: +44-131-650-8963

Academic Editor: Noreen Herzfeld
Received: 30 January 2017; Accepted: 3 May 2017; Published: 10 May 2017

Abstract: Hopes, fears, and ethical concerns relating to technology are as old as technology itself. When considering the increase in the power of computers, and their ever-more widespread use over recent decades, concerns have been raised about the social impact of computers and about practical issues arising from their use: the manner in which data is harvested, the preservation of confidentiality where people's personal information is concerned, the security of systems in which such data is stored, and so on. With the arrival of "big data" new ethical concerns surrounding computer-based technology arise—concerns connected not only with social issues, and with the generation of data and its security, but also with its interpretation by data scientists, and with the burgeoning trade in personal data. The first aim of this paper is to introduce some of these ethical issues, and the second is to suggest some possible ways in which they might be addressed. The latter includes some explorations of the ways in which insights from religious and theological perspectives might be valuable. It is urged that theology and data science might engage in mutually-beneficial dialogue.

Keywords: big data; computing; consent; ethics; hermeneutics; hippocratic oath; interpretation; privacy

1. Introduction

As any technology develops it might be expected that its increasing capabilities give rise to a succession of ethical issues, and computer technology is certainly no exception to this (Tavani 2013a, pp. 6 ff.). Concerns which have been raised in the past include the deskilling of the workforce, increased unemployment, and the health, stress, and isolation of workers, together with issues relating to the storage of personal data in the form of databases (Barbour 1992, pp. 146 ff.). A further concern is the implication of computers in broadening divisions between rich and poor, through the opening up of imbalances between those who have access to computer facilities and the benefits which they bring, and those who do not (Tavani 2013a, p. 305; Barbour 1992, p. 156). All of these concerns are ongoing.

In recent years the increasingly widespread use of computers in all walks of life, from the PCs and smartphones that many consumers use on a daily basis to the supercomputers used in research programmes in astronomy, physics, and medicine, has generated the phenomenon that has become known as "big data":[1] extremely large, often highly heterogeneous, datasets that require novel techniques and new sets of skills to interrogate them. In turn, this has led to a new set of ethical issues surrounding big data. The aim of this paper is to identify, describe, and evaluate some of these ethical

---

[1]   Not least of the issues surrounding big data are linguistic: should these words should be capitalised or not, and should this term should be treated as singular or plural? This paper uses the lower case (except when quoting sources which use the upper), and it follows the convention (given some justification in (Rosenberg 2013, p. 18)) of treating "big data" as a singular form.

issues, and to suggest ways in which some of them may be addressed. It further suggests that insights from the religious domain might be of considerable value in developing these new approaches to big data.

2. Big Data and Data Science

Before going further, it is worth exploring exactly what big data is understood to mean. Although the term is widely used, there is little agreement around a definition, in part because what counts as "big" in this context is changing so rapidly. The description by Laney (2001) in terms of the "three Vs" (volume, variety, and velocity) has been widely quoted: on this understanding, big data is characterised as being concerned with very large quantities of data, which is highly heterogeneous, and which is generated at enormous speed. (Kitchin 2014, p. 68) comments that, in addition to this, big data is exhaustive in scope, fine-grained in resolution, relational in nature (enabling different datasets to be linked), and both flexible and scalable (enabling new fields to be added to it, and the rapid extension of the size of the dataset). Other, broader, definitions have been offered (e.g., (boyd and Crawford 2012, p. 663)).

The distinctiveness of big data goes beyond straightforward issues of size. Mayer-Schönberger and Cukier point out that with the accumulation of so much data, "something new and special is taking place. Not only is the world awash with more information than ever before, but that information is growing faster. The change of scale has led to a change of state. *The quantitative change has led to a qualitative one*" ((Mayer-Schönberger and Cukier 2013, p. 6), my emphasis). Similarly, Kitchin notes that "It is becoming clear that big data have a number of inherent characteristics that make them qualitatively different to previous forms of data" (Kitchin 2014, p. 79). Extremely large datasets are not simply quantitatively different to smaller ones: their sheer scale brings about a "step change", making them qualitatively distinct, too. This means that different tools and different models are required for their handling and analysis.

This, in turn, means that such analysis amounts to a new kind of practice. The development of practices appropriate to the handling of very large datasets has led to the coining of the terms "data science" and "data scientist" (cf. (O'Neil and Schutt 2014, p. 8)) to describe the new techniques which are required, and the practitioners of those techniques. The capabilities required of these practitioners are considerable: according to (Mayer-Schönberger and Cukier 2013, p. 125), the data scientist must combine "the skills of the statistician, software programmer, infographics designer, and storyteller".

These new approaches in turn bring new sets of questions. As boyd and Crawford note, "The age of Big Data has only just begun, but it is important that we start questioning the assumptions, values, and biases of this new wave of research" (boyd and Crawford 2012, p. 675). This is an urgent task, as such assumptions, values and biases may be unhelpful or erroneous, and may have the potential to cause considerable harm.

3. Some Examples of Ethical Concerns Arising from Big Data

There is already a significant literature regarding ethical concerns in information and communication technology (cf. (Tavani 2013b)). What concerns are specific to the big data context? We may immediately note that anyone who engages with services which make use of computers surrenders data to those who run those computers—whether they are consciously aware of it or not. This surrendering of data may occur through engagement with retail or professional services, or through engaging with particular institutions which involve the gathering, analysis, and retention of personal data (e.g., hospitals), or simply through surfing the Internet, or using a mobile phone. A range of issues may then emerge.

3.1. Privacy and Consent

It is standard practice to obtain the informed consent of any party whose data is to be harvested and stored. In practice, consent has generally been obtained through giving information to the individual concerned, usually in the form of a written text, and by that individual signing a form or ticking a box to confirm that they have understood and accept the terms which have been given to them. When using an Internet-based service, such consent is regularly sought by the service providers. In practice, however, it has been observed that this is a process which is geared more towards limiting the liabilities of those harvesting the data rather than genuinely informing the data subjects: "the parties gathering the data typically attempt to minimize the ability of the person about whom the data is being gathered to comprehend the scope of data, and its usage, through a mixture of sharp design and obscure legal jargon" (Wilbanks 2014, p. 235). The practical difficulties of managing privacy and generating informed consent have been summed up as:

> (1) people do not read privacy policies; (2) if people read them, they do not understand them; (3) if people read and understand them, they often lack enough background knowledge to make an informed choice; and (4) if people read them, understand them, and can make an informed choice, their choice may be skewed by various decision-making difficulties (Solove 2013, p. 1888).

Moreover, "little bits of innocuous data can say a lot in combination [...] it is virtually impossible for a person to make meaningful judgments about the costs and benefits of revealing certain data" (Solove 2013, p. 1890). This leads to situations in which "people consent to the collection, use, and disclosure of their personal data when it is not in their self-interest to do so" (Solove 2013, p. 1895).

Not only this: the long-term storage of big data means that situations may arise in which there is a desire to use it for purposes that may not be remotely connected to those for which it was gathered (and for which consent was given) in the first place. What alternative measures might be taken to ensure that *genuinely* informed consent is obtained from those who give up their data *for all the purposes to which it might be subsequently put*? Or are Barocas and Nissenbaum correct in their assertion that "it is impossible, even absurd to believe that notice and consent can fully specify the terms of interaction between data collector and data subject" (Barocas and Nissenbaum 2014, p. 66)?

Further issues surround the practice of anonymizing data in order to preserve the privacy of those who have supplied it. Preserving that anonymity turns out to be deeply problematic. In practice, when data has been anonymized (or "de-identified") it may well be possible to break that anonymity by triangulating between multiple datasets. For example, in the American context "knowing an individual's ZIP code localises that person to one in 30,000 (the average population of a ZIP code). Linking a ZIP code with a birthdate reduces the pool to approximately one in 80, while further connecting gender and year-of-birth are sufficient, on average, to uniquely specify an individual" (Koonin and Holland 2014, p. 146). In other words, if different anonymized databases which contain my ZIP code, birthday, gender and year of birth are linked, it is highly likely that I can be identified (for further examples of the ways in which data can be de-anonymized see (Porter 2008)). The ease with which de-anonymisation may be carried out leads Raley to observe that "anonymisation cannot and should not be considered a means of privacy protection" (Raley 2013, p. 128). It is hard to resist the conclusion of Barocas and Nissenbaum that "[p]rivacy and big data are simply incompatible" (Barocas and Nissenbaum 2014, p. 63).

3.2. Security

How is data to be kept intact, and safe from accidental or malicious threats? Strategies for dealing with such threats typically take the form "prevent, detect, respond, recover" (Landwehr 2014, p. 214). It is incumbent upon data handlers to use whatever technologies are feasible to prevent the exposure of data to degradation or cyber-attack. However, given that not every disaster may be foreseen, and that those with nefarious purposes will always be seeking new ways in which to circumvent security measures, it is equally important to have robust systems in place to detect such attacks when they are made, respond appropriately to them, and ensure that the system which has been attacked is restored to its pre-attack state—with, if necessary, appropriate new safeguards in place.

Whatever measures are taken, the frequent occurrence of news headlines concerning the hacking of computers and publication of confidential material suggests that the possibility of security breaches will always be a problem. If this is so, then we might wish to ask: to what extent are those whose personal data might be compromised by such breaches made aware of the risks to which they are exposing themselves?

3.3. Ownership

Are data property? If so, who owns data? Should it be the person to whom it relates, or the organisation which has gathered it? Should something akin to copyright protection apply to data, to prohibit its use or reproduction by parties who infringe ownership, and maximise the opportunity for those who own data to extract profit from it? It has been observed that "the prime driver of big data is not technological; it is financial and the promises of greater efficiencies and profits" (Kitchin 2014, p. 119). Is this inevitable? Or should data be part of an "information commons", which might be understood as "a body of knowledge and information that is available to anyone to use without the need to ask for or receive permission from another, providing any conditions placed on its use are respected" (cf. (Tavani 2013a, p. 256))?

To illustrate this, consider the data which is routinely stored whenever individuals give samples as part of a medical procedure. That data may be enormously important for the conduct of research into the aetiology and treatment of diseases, and it might be urged that it should be freely available to medical researchers for that purpose. However, it might also be possible to mine that information for data which is of great commercial significance, in the development of new drugs, for example, or in the provision of health insurance. Should the data be freely available, to assist the researchers? Or should it be treated as a commercially-sensitive asset, with restrictions placed on accessing it?

3.4. Regulating Commercial Use of Personal Data

This brings us to another important set of issues. If big data might be used in such a way as to turn a profit, then what regulation should exist around its use, in terms both of its commercial exploitation, and of trade in the data itself? Data may be commercially useful in a number of ways, in addition to those already mentioned. Information about a person's past purchases, recorded by a website which they use, or through their use of a store card, can be used to target advertising and encourage further expenditure by that person. Many people will doubtless find it helpful to be alerted to products which they might like, regarding which they might otherwise have been unaware.

However, given the potential for deriving financial gain from people's data, a whole industry has sprung up around the generation of data products which can be sold for profit. As Kitchin explains it:

> Data brokers (sometimes called data aggregators, consolidators or resellers) capture, gather together and repackage data into privately held data infrastructures for rent (for one-time use or use under licensing conditions) or re-sale on a for-profit basis [...] Data consolidation and re-sale, and associated data analysis and value-added services, are a multi-billion dollar industry, with vast quantities of data and derived information being rented, bought and sold daily across a variety of markets—retail, financial, health, tourism, logistics, business intelligence, real estate, private security, political polling, and so on (Kitchin 2014, p. 42).

Kitchin further notes that "At present, data brokers are generally largely unregulated and are not required by law to provide individuals access to the data held by them, nor are they obliged to correct errors relating to those individuals" (Kitchin 2014, p. 44). A report by the Canadian Internet Policy and Public Interest Clinic (CIPPIC) on the Canadian data brokerage industry makes the sobering judgment that "the increasing accumulation of personal data and consolidation of databases leaves individuals vulnerable to abuses by those with access to the data. Once released into the marketplace, personal data cannot be retrieved. Potential uses of this data are limited only by law and ethics" (CIPPIC 2006, p. 47).

The financially-motivated phenomenon of data brokerage has developed swiftly in response to market demands. It has yet to be properly held to account by either ethicists or legislators, and it would appear that the longer this situation continues, the more this business is likely to mushroom, and the harder it is likely to become to impose ethical or legal restrictions upon it. This is an area where the need for concerted action is becoming more acute by the day.

3.5. Surveillance

The possibility exists of forming detailed pictures of an individual around that person's digital footprint: not only their purchases of goods and services, but also their communications via phone and email, and their physical movements (if they carry a device which has Global Positioning System (GPS) enabled). This has been termed "dataveillance" (Raley 2013). There may be justification for such activity, in terms of monitoring the activities of individuals who may be thought to be terrorists or security risks: this thinking lies behind the UK's Investigatory Powers Act 2016 (widely dubbed the "snooper's charter"), which "requires web and phone companies to store everyone's web browsing histories for 12 months and give the police, security services, and official agencies unprecedented access to the data" (Travis 2016). However, such dataveillance may also be seen as an infringement of privacy and, as such, it raises the same suite of ethical problems identified under Sections 3.1–3.3 above.

3.6. Entrenching Unfairness

In the United States in particular, big data has found widespread use in such fields as policing, assessing people's suitability for loans or for jobs, and targeted advertising aimed at everything from selling products to enrolling people in university courses. As O'Neil has pointed out in a thought-provoking analysis (O'Neil 2016), this frequently has the net effect of reinforcing existing social inequalities. For example, if a person's poor credit record and home address in a poor neighbourhood are judged to make them unsuitable candidates for a job which they are seeking, or are used as justification for charging them higher insurance premiums, this has the net effect of denying them opportunities and reinforcing their existing poverty. It has long been recognised that access (or lack of it) to the benefits brought by computers has the potential to deepen social inequality: the application of big data to categorising and sorting people has the capacity to take unfairness to entirely new levels. As O'Neil puts it, "The poor are expected to remain poor forever and are treated accordingly—denied opportunities, jailed more often, and gouged for service and loans. It's inexorable, often hidden and beyond appeal, and unfair" (O'Neil 2016, p. 155).

3.7. Generation and Analysis of Data

A raft of issues exists around the gathering of data, its treatment and analysis, and the presentation of the results of such analysis by experts to those who have little understanding of the way those results have been obtained, but who may be making potentially far-reaching decisions based on them (recall that one task of the data scientist is to be a storyteller: that is, to formulate persuasive narratives accounting for the results of data analyses).

It might be thought that a big dataset just "is". However, consider the following ways in which it embodies particular values and biases. (a) Data do not just happen: they are generated by one process, and captured or selected for retention by another. A variety of factors may introduce bias into these processes. (b) "Raw" data is routinely "cleaned" prior to detailed analysis, and it has been noted that "decisions about how to handle missing data, impute missing values, remove outliers, transform variables, and perform other common data cleaning and analysis steps may be minimally documented. These decisions have a profound impact on findings, interpretation, reuse, and replication" (Borgman 2015, p. 27). (c) The particular tools used to analyse "cleaned" datasets may, themselves, have preconceptions embedded within them: "the algorithms used to process the data are imbued with particular values and contextualised within a particular scientific approach" (Kitchin 2014, p. 136). (d) Biases in the interpretation of data may lie not only in the tools analysts use, but in the analysts themselves. boyd and Crawford note that "researchers must be able to account for the biases in their interpretation of the data. To do so requires recognizing that one's identity and perspective informs one's analysis" (boyd and Crawford 2012, p. 668). (e) Additionally, Rosenberg observes that such individual bias is, itself, shaped by the context in which the individual is located: "from the beginning, data was a rhetorical concept [. . .] As a consequence, the meaning of data must always shift with argumentative strategy and context—and with the history of both" (Rosenberg 2013, p. 36).

It is crucial, then, to understand the biases built into the ways in which data are generated, the tools used to "clean" and analyse them, the influences acting on those undertaking the analysis, and the context in which the analysis in undertaken. As O'Neil and Schutt warn, "it is wrong to believe either that data is objective or that 'data speaks', and beware of people who say otherwise" (O'Neil and Schutt 2014, p. 25). However, to what extent is this kind of nuanced understanding pursued in practice? Commenting on a study of those engaged in data analytics, Kitchin notes: "Worryingly, those who 'let the data speak for themselves' [...] outnumber those best able to make sense of big data" (Kitchin 2014, p. 161). It would appear that the subtle and nuanced approach required of data scientists in practising their craft is still at an early stage of development.

Attention needs to be paid not only to the analysis of data, but to the presentation of the fruits of that analysis. This will frequently involve the production of visualisations of the data and of what it is telling us, through graphs, charts, diagrams, and so on; and these visualisations may, themselves, incorporate conscious or unconscious bias in those who have prepared them, which might encourage those to whom the data is being presented to read it in particular ways. As Gitelman and Jackson put it, "Data visualisation amplifies the rhetorical function of data, since different visualizations are differently effective, well or poorly designed, and all data sets can be multiply visualised and thereby differentially persuasive" (Gitelman and Jackson 2013, p. 12). Given that decisions affecting the lives of thousands of people may rest on such visualisations, it is crucial that those who devise them clearly understand their impact.

3.8. The End of Science?

A sensationalist response to the arrival of big data analysis has been to see it as effectively replacing science, as it has been practiced hitherto, with an entirely new approach to generating information about the world. In an article titled *"The End of Theory: Will the Data Deluge Makes the Scientific Method Obsolete?"*, Anderson has written that:

> This is a world where massive amounts of data and applied mathematics replace every other tool that might be brought to bear. Out with every theory of human behaviour, from linguistics to sociology. Forget taxonomy, ontology, and psychology. Who knows why people do what they do? The point is they do it, and we can track and measure it with unprecedented fidelity. With enough data, the numbers speak for themselves (Anderson 2008).

This kind of rhetoric strikes the present writer as both alarming and dangerous since, as we have seen, numbers emphatically do not "speak for themselves", but rather require careful explication and acknowledgment of the complexities and biases present in their collection, analysis, and presentation. It is to be hoped that more cautious voices will rapidly come to prevail when thinking about what big data can, in practice, achieve.

Even if that is so, however, data science may still present challenges to science as it has traditionally been understood. As an example of this, consider the much-discussed Google Flu Trends (GFT) project, which attempted to use data input to the Google search engine in order to predict outbreaks of flu in the United States (cf. (Fuller 2015)). Traditionally, scientific results are published in such a way that they are (at least in principle) reproducible; however, it was pointed out that publications relating to the GFT project withheld data and did not disclose the particular search terms on which the project was based. Presumably, commercial reasons lay behind this withholding of information. It, nevertheless, represents an approach to the publication of scientific research which is incompatible with traditional understandings of scientific practice.

4. Addressing the Issues

The issues identified here are complex and overlapping. How might they best be addressed? I suggest that there are, broadly, four ways in which this might happen, and I would urge that at least some of these ways of addressing the complex issues raised by big data can be informed by thinking, and by practical activity, which may come from theological and religious communities.

4.1. Technical Responses

Some of the concerns raised above may be addressed through technological development and innovation—that is, through the upgrading of hardware and software systems used to store and process big data. For example, as suggested earlier, some of the issues relating to security can best be dealt with by constant monitoring and development of infrastructure and of protocols designed to prevent accidental or malicious contamination of data, or the release of personal information. Since data science is a rapidly-changing and advancing field, it is likely that techniques for improving security will similarly change and develop—and it is equally likely that those who wish to counter that security will also change and develop their methods for doing so. Insofar as these technical responses are responses to unforeseen events, it is difficult, if not impossible, to plan ahead regarding them. Ultimately, though, those whose lives may be affected by technical failures and security breaches should, at the very least, be informed of the risks they are undertaking, and consent to those risks.

4.2. Legal Responses

A number of matters might be dealt with by legal and regulatory means. However, there are significant difficulties here, of which we may note three which are particularly acute. First, the rapidity with which big data, its analysis, and its commodification are developing means that action is required urgently if legislation is not always going to be several steps behind current practices, with the risk of its becoming obsolete at the moment it hits the statute-books. Second, there may be circumstances in which legislation already exists, but in practice it is either unfit for purpose or routinely ignored (or both). In such cases, the adaptation or enforcement of laws needs to be made a priority (cf. (O'Neil 2016, pp. 212 ff.)). Third, there is the problem of making legislation universally applicable. Data is not restricted by borders, but laws are enacted by nation-states which may vary greatly in the ideals which they wish to enshrine in those laws. Much of the discussion around the regulation of big data thus far has focussed on the U.S. context, but it should be noted that other, well-developed legal frameworks are operative elsewhere, such as those set out in the UK's Data Protection Act 1998 and the European Union's General Data Protection Regulation of 2016 (see, e.g., (Elias 2014)). Ideally, international regulation of big data gathering, usage, and trade is surely desirable. It may be possible for some international standards to be agreed, but it is likely that there will be a continuing need for coordination and cooperation between countries in producing arrangements for the cross-border policing of such issues. These may be significant (and significantly expensive) undertakings, but they are surely crucial.

4.3. Ethical Responses

The tools used by data scientists have not tended to prioritize ethical considerations. O'Neil has urged that "we have to explicitly embed better values into our algorithms, creating Big Data models that follow our ethical lead. Sometimes that will mean putting fairness ahead of profit"

(O'Neil 2016, p. 204). Since much work with big data is profit-driven, ethical frameworks are required that can override financial considerations. How might these be generated?

Tavani has noted that many professional societies—including some related to the computing profession—have adopted codes of conduct governing the behaviour expected of their members (Tavani 2013a, p. 106 ff.). In the data science context, we may note that the Association of Internet Researchers has produced recommendations on ethical decision-making and internet research for its members (Association of Internet Researchers 2012). Guidelines and recommendations are a good start, but more is surely required to ensure that all data science practitioners act in ethically responsible ways.

Now, although a science based on the manipulation of data might appear "objective" to an outsider, we have seen that this is, in fact, very far from being the case, and that data scientists are required to use considerable personal skill and judgment in their work. This, perhaps, makes data science more akin to the practice of medicine than to that of a "hard science", like physics. This, in turn, suggests a possible way of addressing those issues noted above which relate specifically to the practice of data analysis. Doctors have a touchstone for ethical behaviour in the Hippocratic Oath (cf. (British Medical Association 2012, p. 887)), and it has been suggested that data scientists, too, might undertake a similar oath, holding them to particular ethical standards in the practice of their craft (O'Neil 2016, pp. 205–206; Fuller 2015, p. 581). This might involve an undertaking to ensure that their work is conducted with fairness to all the parties on whom it impacts, and that it is used to ends which promote human flourishing, rather than otherwise. Were such an oath to be devised, it might be an occasion for collaboration between data scientists, ethicists, and those from religious traditions in shaping the form it might take. Paul Ohm (Ohm 2014, pp. 108–9) has averred that "as we expand the reach and power and influence of data science, we must take steps to prevent harm, to ensure that this remains always a humanistic endeavour, and to help people preserve their power and autonomy". That might not be a bad set of objectives from which to start.

The adoption of a binding oath by data scientists might be thought of as a way in which many ethical concerns might be addressed. However, for this to be effective (a) the oath would have to be obligatory for all data science practitioners, and (b) sanctions or penalties would need to be applied to any practitioners found to be in it to be in breach of it. There are no indications at present that this is a likely scenario. If self-policing is ruled out, how else might issues raised by data science be addressed? What other bodies are in a position to raise and discuss them?

Many of the concerns raised by big data are fuelled by the ignorance of the general public regarding the ways in which data are used, stored, and traded. Given the many vested interests involved in the ownership and trading of data, and the likelihood that these will lobby against measures which would see a diminution of their profits (both real and potential), the addressing of this ignorance is a matter of some urgency. Education—making people more aware of the consequences of their giving away information about themselves—is clearly important. So, too, is counter-lobbying, which is likely to be required if legal measures are to be put in place around big data issues. What fora exist which might address these educational and lobbying tasks? Dedicated pressure groups, such as those concerned with the privacy of citizens, will have an important part to play in addressing these issues, but these tend to involve relatively few people. How might more citizens become engaged with the new problems raised by big data?

4.4. Religious, Theological, and Hermeneutical Responses

Religious communities, such as churches, are surely in a position to play a significant part in raising awareness and encouraging discussion of these matters. Christianity, in common with many other faith traditions, places a high value on notions of accountability and fairness. Where such values are seen to be being flouted—for example, through keeping people ignorant of the consequences of their giving up data, or through the use of big data to reinforce social inequalities, or through the gathering, storage, and trade of personal data without effective consent, by unaccountable commercial organisations—the churches might speak out against such practices, and lobby for their restriction.

Such church involvement need not be solely concerned with restrictions. There are very large benefits which the application of big data may bring to society, and the churches might, therefore, also lobby to ensure that such benefits are distributed amongst all citizens (cf. (Fuller 2016)). To give an example of such engagement in a different context: the Church of Scotland, through its Society, Religion, and Technology Project, addressed issues of public concern raised by the cloning of Dolly the sheep through setting up a group of academics from the biological, agricultural, and social sciences, together with theologians and ethicists, to explore bioethical questions raised by this advance. A subsequent publication made the fruits of their discussions widely available to the lay public (Bruce and Bruce 1998).

Such practical actions as these are likely to come from the organisational leadership of religious organisations like churches, but such bodies have further roles to play in that they are communities which allow issues to be discussed and "owned" by a broader public than that which is likely to engage with issues when they are presented in purely ethical terms. They can also constitute fora which enable an engagement with these important issues through both "head" and "heart". Ethical matters can elicit visceral, as well as intellectual, responses, and churches offer areas of engagement where both may be engaged effectively. Churches and other religious groupings can, thus, offer a "safe space" in which people's enthusiasms, hopes, and fears regarding big data might be discussed, and openness with regard to big data might be encouraged. As awareness of the questions surrounding big data increases, the need for such a space will inevitably become more and more acute.

In parallel with public action of this kind, religious engagement with issues raised by big data can also take place through raising theological concerns at a more academic level. It is important not to lose sight of the fact that data constitute just one part of a much greater picture. Individuals focussed on particular data-analytical tasks may lose sight of the human stories which lie behind their data, and of their work as anything other than the application of mathematical processes, directed towards abstract ends. Effectively, human beings are reduced to numbers, patterns, and trends. Here, insights from theological anthropology might offer a helpful corrective. It might be urged that every person is unique, complex, and formed by their relationships with others and with God. Moreover, people are intrinsically valuable, rather than having a value conferred upon them through the measurable parameters that can contribute to a large dataset. Theological insights such as these have a part to play alongside purely ethical critiques of big data. Both, alike, can serve the purpose of constantly reminding data scientists and data subjects alike of the "big picture" within which all of our endeavours are set, and by insisting that the goal of those endeavours should be the promotion of human flourishing. Both can also give voice to the imperative that big data be used justly, so that the gains which might be made through its use are shared as widely as possible, and benefit as many people as possible.

There is a further, very particular, skill which the theological community can offer to the practice of data science. It has been observed that "when the amount of data is sufficiently large, you can find almost anything you seek lurking somewhere within" (Berman 2013, p. 145). As noted above, data scientists are engaged in a complex interpretative exercise which involves recognition of the history and context of the data which they are analysing, the biases contained both in it and in the analytical techniques which are being used to explore it, their own inbuilt biases, both conscious and unconscious, and the complexities of the (quite possibly, commercial) context in which their work is being carried out. Complex interpretative exercises of this kind are familiar to those theologians who deal with the interpretation of texts, and they have developed a suite of hermeneutical skills to assist them in engaging with such interpretation. A dialogue between data scientists and theologians concerning hermeneutical practices could be an important way in which skills developed in the service of a religious tradition might also valuably inform practices within this developing new science—an idea I have developed more fully elsewhere (Fuller 2015, pp. 577–80), and such a dialogue is likely to be of considerable benefit to theologians, too (Fuller forthcoming).

5. Conclusions

The arrival of big data has already brought with it numerous questions that have yet to be properly addressed, and others will doubtless emerge as data science develops further. These questions are methodological, epistemological, and ethical, and they concern (inter alia) the ways in which data are collected, stored, interpreted, re-presented, and traded. A further complication is the speed with which data science is advancing, which means that (for example) the application of legal and ethical restrictions to the practice of that science will always risk being several steps behind the point that it has currently reached. There are indications that we are currently sleepwalking towards a situation in which the commercial exploitation of big data routinely increases social division, and renders privacy a thing of the past.

Many of the issues highlighted in this paper are complex, and may appear intractable. Addressing them will certainly involve the engagement of many parties—data scientists, lawyers, ethicists, politicians, and representatives of the business community and of the general public. There will also need to be an engagement of different jurisdictions, as solutions are sought which will command general consent, and which will have legally-binding international validity.

In addition to a purely "secular" treatment of these ethical issues, this paper argues that the engagement of religious communities and theologians has an important part to play. Religious communities may offer critiques based on particular sets of values which treat human beings as more than simply data points, and they may offer fora for discussions which may aid in the dissemination of information about data science, as well as an opportunity to critique it. In addition, there is enormous potential to be harnessed in bringing data scientists into dialogue with theologians, since the hermeneutical skills developed by the latter may have much to offer to the former.

The arrival of big data has brought with it concerns which are only starting to be appreciated and discussed. All resources—including those of religious communities—which can enable such appreciation and discussion are to be welcomed.

Conflicts of Interest: The authors declare no conflict of interest

References

Anderson, Chris. 2008. The End of Theory: Will the data deluge make the scientific method obsolete? *Edge*. June 30. Available online: https://www.edge.org/3rd_culture/anderson08/anderson08_index.html (accessed on 11 January 2017).

Association of Internet Researchers. 2012. Ethical Decision-Making and Internet Research. Available online: https://aoir.org/reports/ethics2.pdf (accessed on 17 January 2017).

Barbour, Ian G. 1992. *Ethics in an Age of Technology*. London: SCM Press.

Barocas, Solon, and Helen Nissenbaum. 2014. Big Data's End Run Around Anonymity and Consent. In *Privacy, Big Data and the Public Good: Frameworks for Engagement*. Edited by Julia Lane, Victoria Stodden, Stefan Bender and Helen Nissenbaum. New York: Cambridge University Press, pp. 44–75.

Berman, Jules J. 2013. *Principles of Big Data*. Amsterdam: Elsevier.

Borgman, Christine L. 2015. *Big Data, Little Data, No Data: Scholarship in the Networked World*. Cambridge: MIT Press.

boyd, danah, and Kate Crawford. 2012. Critical Questions for Big Data. *Information, Communication and Society* 15: 662–75. [CrossRef]

British Medical Association. 2012. *Medical Ethics Today: The BMA's Handbook of Ethics and Law*. Oxford: Wiley-Blackwell.

Donald Bruce, and Ann Bruce, eds. 1998. *Engineering Genesis: The Ethics of Genetic Engineering in Non-Human Species*. London: Earthscan Publications Ltd.

Canadian Internet Policy, Public Interest Clinic (CIPPIC). 2006. On the Data Trail: How detailed information about you gets into the hands of organisations with whom you have no relationship. A Report on the Canadian Data Brokerage Industry. Available online: https://cippic.ca/sites/default/files/May1-06/DatabrokerReport.pdf (accessed on 11 January 2017).

Elias, Peter. 2014. A European Perspective on Research and Big Data Analysis. In *Privacy, Big Data and the Public Good: Frameworks for Engagement*. Edited by Julia Lane, Victoria Stodden, Stefan Bender and Helen Nissenbaum. New York: Cambridge University Press, pp. 173–91.

Fuller, Michael. 2015. Big Data: New science, new challenges, new dialogical opportunities. *Zygon* 50: 569–82. [CrossRef]

Fuller, Michael. 2016. Some Practical and Ethical Challenges Posed by Big Data. In *Embracing the Ivory Tower and Stained Glass Window: A Festschrift in Honor of Archbishop Antje Jackelen*. Edited by Jennifer Baldwin. Heidelberg: Springer International Publishing, pp. 119–27.

Fuller, Michael. Forthcoming; Boundless riches: Big Data, the Bible and Human Distinctiveness. In *Issues in Science and Theology: Are we special?* Edited by Dirk Evers, Michael Fuller, Anne Runehov and Knut-Willy Saether. Heidelberg: Springer International Publishing.

Gitelman, Lisa, and Virginia Jackson. 2013. Introduction. In *"Raw Data" is an Oxymoron*. Edited by Lisa Gitelman. Cambridge: MIT Press, pp. 1–14.

Kitchin, Rob. 2014. *The Data Revolution: Big Data, Open Data, Data Infrastructures and Their Consequences*. London: Sage Publications.

Koonin, Steven E., and Michael J. Holland. 2014. The Value of Big Data for Urban Science. In *Privacy, Big Data and the Public Good: Frameworks for Engagement*. Edited by Julia Lane, Victoria Stodden, Stefan Bender and Helen Nissenbaum. New York: Cambridge University Press, pp. 137–52.

Landwehr, Carl. 2014. Engineering Controls for Dealing with Big Data. In *Privacy, Big Data and the Public Good: Frameworks for Engagement*. Edited by Julia Lane, Victoria Stodden, Stefan Bender and Helen Nissenbaum. New York: Cambridge University Press, pp. 211–33.

Laney, Doug. 2001. 3D Data Management: Controlling Data Volume, Velocity, and Variety. META Group Report. Available online: http://blogs.gartner.com/doug-laney/files/2012/01/ad949-3D-Data-Management-Controlling-Data-Volume-Velocity-and-Variety.pdf (accessed on 20 July 2016).

Mayer-Schönberger, Viktor, and Kenneth Cukier. 2013. *Big Data: A Revolution That Will Transform How We Live, Work and Think*. London: John Murray.

O'Neil, Cathy. 2016. *Weapons of Math Destruction: How Big Data Increases Inequality and Threatens Democracy*. London: Allen Lane.

O'Neil, Cathy, and Rachel Schutt. 2014. *Doing Data Science*. Sebastopol: O'Reilly.

Ohm, Paul. 2014. General Principles for Data Use and Analysis. In *Privacy, Big Data and the Public Good: Frameworks for Engagement*. Edited by Julia Lane, Victoria Stodden, Stefan Bender and Helen Nissenbaum. New York: Cambridge University Press, pp. 96–111.

Porter, C. Christine. 2008. De-Identified Data and Third Party Data Mining: The risk of re-identification of personal information. *Shidler Journal of Law, Commerce and Technology* 5: 1–8.

Raley, Rita. 2013. Dataveillance and Countervaillance. In *"Raw Data" is an Oxymoron*. Edited by Lisa Gitelman. Cambridge: MIT Press, pp. 121–45.

Rosenberg, Daniel. 2013. Data before the Fact. In *"Raw Data" is an Oxymoron*. Edited by Lisa Gitelman. Cambridge: MIT Press, pp. 15–40.

Solove, Daniel J. 2013. Privacy management and the consent dilemma. *Harvard Law Review* 126: 1880–903.

Tavani, Herman T. 2013a. *Ethics and Technology: Controversies, Questions and Strategies for Ethical Computing*. Hoboken: Wiley.

Tavani, Herman T. 2013b. ICT Ethics bibliography 2012–2014: A select list of recent books. *Ethics and Information Technology* 15: 243–47. [CrossRef]

Travis, Alan. 2016. 'Snooper's Charter´ bill becomes law, extending UK state surveillance. *The Guardian*. November 29. Available online: https://www.theguardian.com/world/2016/nov/29/snoopers-charter-bill-becomes-law-extending-uk-state-surveillance (accessed on 11 January 2017).

Wilbanks, John. 2014. Portable Approaches to Informed Consent and Open Data. In *Privacy, Big Data and the Public Good: Frameworks for Engagement*. Edited by Julia Lane, Victoria Stodden, Stefan Bender and Helen Nissenbaum. New York: Cambridge University Press, pp. 234–52.

religions

MDPI

Article

The Limits of Machine Ethics

Sara Lumbreras

Institute for Research in Technology, Universidad Pontificia Comillas, Madrid 28001, Spain;
slumbreras@comillas.edu

Academic Editor: Noreen Herzfeld
Received: 17 March 2017; Accepted: 17 May 2017; Published: 19 May 2017

Abstract: Machine Ethics has established itself as a new discipline that studies how to endow autonomous devices with ethical behavior. This paper provides a general framework for classifying the different approaches that are currently being explored in the field of machine ethics and introduces considerations that are missing from the current debate. In particular, law-based codes implemented as external filters for action—which we have named *filtered decision making*—are proposed as the basis for future developments. The emergence of values as guides for action is discussed, and personal language –together with subjectivity- are indicated as necessary conditions for this development. Last, utilitarian approaches are studied and the importance of objective expression as a requisite for their implementation is stressed. Only values expressed by the programmer in a public language—that is, separate of subjective considerations—can be evolved in a learning machine, therefore establishing the limits of present-day machine ethics.

Keywords: ethics of machines; theory of mind; values; learning automata

1. Machine Ethics: The Rise of a New Field

Robots are growing in importance; they are assuming more roles in the industry and are expected to be an expanding factor in the future economy (International Federation of Robotics IFR 2016). In addition, the interactions between robots and humans are increasingly intense, even appearing in some sensitive fields such as military activities or medical caregiving. This has led some authors to describe the next century as the *age of robots* (Veruggio et al. 2016, pp. 2135–60). These human–machine interactions are already reshaping the way we relate to each other and process information, in some favorable as well as detrimental ways (Head 2014).

This has motivated the emergence of *roboethics*, which deals with the issues derived from the diverse applications of robots understood as particular devices[1] and of *machine ethics*, which studies how to endow self-regulated machines with ethical behavior. It should be noted that there is no consensus yet about the scope of these two fields, and the previously presented definitions have been chosen because of their usefulness and are being accepted by a seemingly increasing group of scholars (Veruggio et al. 2016, pp. 2135–60). There have been myriad works dealing with roboethics and exploring the implications of the use of robots in particular activities (Luxton 2014, pp. 1–10), such as their implications for employment, but the contributions to the ethics of machines are still taking shape. The first efforts focused on the ethics of automatic machines insofar as their actions impacted human beings. With this aim, some authors have classified the interactions into mere observation, interference, interaction, or advice (Van de Voort et al. 2015, pp. 41–56). However, there have been some voices

---

[1] An autonomous device is understood as a machine that receives some sensory *inputs* from the environment and, using some specific rules, reaches an *action* that can have an impact on the environment. The term *autonomous device* (or, *device*, for short) is used in this text interchangeably with *robot*, *machine*, *autonomous machine*, or *automaton*. A *learning* automaton would be the automaton where these rules are not static but rather change to adapt to achieve a given defined goal.

claiming for the dignity of the machines in themselves rather than just objects having an impact on humans, such as the *ontocentric* ethics proposed by Floridi (Floridi 2005, p. 3).

This paper attempts to provide a comprehensive framework for the different proposals that have appeared in the context of machine ethics and discusses their relative worth. Its main contributions are as follows:

Providing a comprehensive framework for analyzing the different proposals within machine ethics. This framework is based in the existing double dichotomy negative vs. positive and top-down vs. bottom-up. The paper studies their relative strengths and disadvantages.

Proposing a mechanism to ensure compliance in evolving, interconnected devices, which has been named *filtered decision making*.

Identifying subjectivity (understood as *being a subject, an individual which possesses conscious experiences, such as perspectives, feelings, beliefs and desires* (Honderich 2005)) as the final frontier of machine ethics. Approaches that require it should not be considered implementable with present-day technology, as there is no basis to suppose that subjectivity and consciousness will emerge from it.

Analyzing the conditions for the implementation of utilitarian approaches, which establish a further limit for machine ethics: the objective function of the automaton should be expressed in a public language in order to be implementable.

The rest of this paper is organized as follows. First, the main existing proposals for machine ethics are classified into a double categorization of *negative* vs. *positive* or *bottom-up* vs. *top-down*. This is briefly presented in Section 2. Then, negative approaches are discussed in depth in Section 3, with Section 4 focusing on filtered decision making, one of the main contributions of this paper. Sections 5 and 6 deal with positive approaches and present our conditions for the development of utilitarian approaches. Finally, Section 7 extracts conclusions.

2. A Wide Spectrum of Proposals

The proposals that have been put forward in the context of machine ethics—that is, the diverse procedures that have been proposed for endowing machines with ethical behavior—reflect, quite naturally, the different existing understandings about ethics as a whole.

It is particularly interesting for our purposes to work with the following double dichotomy, which classifies approaches to ethics based on their object:

Negative ethics is concerned with preventing harm to other beings. In general, they can be expressed as moral codes composed of actions that should be avoided (such as killing, stealing, or lying (Howard and Korver 2008; Lichtenberg 2010, pp. 557–78)).

Positive ethics focuses on creating the largest good instead of avoiding harm. They are usually consequentialist approaches, where the good associated to a given decision determines if it is the best course of action or not (Handelsman et al. 2009, pp. 105–13; Jackson 1991, pp. 461–82; Slote 1985).

In addition, it is useful to distinguish the way in which these perspectives are developed (Allen et al. 2005, pp. 149–55):

Top-down ethics conceive the moral rules or the definition of ethical good as something objective that is accepted by the agent. Kantian ethics would be an example of this kind of approach (Allen et al. 2005, pp. 149–55; Powers 2006, pp. 46–51; Kant and Abbott 2004).

Bottom-up ethics consider that it is the subject who selects the values that guide her behavior, progressively refining them in a learning process that depends on experience.

An example of this is the plastic definition of values that appears in the work of Campbell (Campbell et al. 2002, pp. 795–823) and in the basis of social cognitive theory (Martin 2004, pp. 135–45) as well as some approaches to morality and identity development in child psychology (Lapsley and Narvaez 2006; Hardy and Carlo 2011, pp. 212–18).

These two dichotomies can be combined with the aim of framing a particular approach to ethics. *Top-down negative ethics* would describe settings where moral rules are externally imposed and determine behaviors that should be avoided. *Top-down positive ethics* present a framework where a desirable output must be maximized but where the definition of what is desirable or not has been externally given. Complementarily, *bottom-up negative ethics* would describe a scheme where the definition of harmful actions to avoid emerges from the experience of the moral subject, while *bottom-up positive ethics* would maximize goodness and discover the meaning of goodness itself.

The following sections make use of these definitions as a way of structuring the approaches that have been proposed in the context of machine ethics[2].

3. Negative Approaches

Negative approaches are undoubtedly appealing as they have been the fundamental approach to ethics until the past century. However, as stated by several authors (Veruggio et al. 2016, pp. 2135–2160), any approach based on rules can result in conflicts (i.e., situations where complying with one rule implies breaking another). This problem was overcome by Asimov by establishing priorities among rules in his rules of robotics (Asimov 1950). For illustration, the first text where the rules appeared is reproduced below:

1. A robot may not injure a human being or, through inaction, allow a human being to come to harm.
2. A robot must obey orders given by human beings except where such orders would conflict with the First Law.
3. A robot must protect its own existence as long as such protection does not conflict with the First or Second Law.

It should be noted that establishing priorities does not necessarily solve any conflict generated in rule-based approaches. In some cases, meta-priorities or the random selection of an action (known as *dice throwing*) might be necessary.

Rules can correspond to the expression of a moral duty (such as the categorical imperative in Kant), which implies a considerable difficulty in expressing them in a simple action approval/dismissal framework. In addition, rules can be the reflection of a social contract, of abiding the explicit norms (law and regulations) or implicit rules (customs) of behavior. The second type is more easily amenable to objective expression, which would have considerable advantages when considering implementation into a self-regulating, evolving machine.

It should be noted that opting for a law-based approach does not necessarily entail a modest view of the question of machine ethics. In many fields, unfortunately just abiding the law would result in

---

2   Dual process theory has been successfully used to explain some of the characteristics of ethical reasoning, and it is worth discussing its merits. The main idea of its proponents is that ethical reasoning happens through two distinct mechanisms: emotion-based, intuitive judgment (1), and rationality-based judgments (2). Greene linked them to deontological ethics and consequentialism, respectively (Greene et al. 2001, pp. 2105–8). The two types of thought according to Kahneman (Kahneman 2011) have been linked to these two mechanisms, with System 1 ("thinking fast") corresponding to emotion-based judgments and System 2 ("thinking slow") describing rationality-based ethical reasoning. Although it might be tempting to identify this dichotomy with top-down vs. bottom-up ethics, they are not exactly equivalent. The main difference is that rationality-based judgment, which as discussed would be related to consequentialism, should be identified with positive ethics in the sense of choosing the action that delivers the largest good. By contrast, bottom-up ethics refers to the emergence of values. Values are implicit in the consequentialist evaluation (which, for instance, in the trolley problem could be expressed as the number of people that remain alive). Consequentialism takes this definition of "goodness of an outcome" as a given rather than provide it as an output as would be the case with the emergence of values in bottom-up ethics. However, the point of combining two different modes of ethical reasoning is extremely powerful and is also one of the features of the framework for machine ethics provided in this paper.

more ethical behavior than the one commonly displayed by human beings. This would be the case, for instance, in war operations, where environmental conditions mean that it is relatively difficult to respect the established rules of behavior.

There have already been some authors, such as Casey (Casey 2017), that claim that law-based approaches are sufficient to tackle the question of machine ethics. This is not the position defended in this paper; however, law-based approaches can be a good starting point for more sophisticated systems and, in any case, a necessary step to ensure safety for human beings in their ever increasing interaction with the automata. The power of the approach proposed would be to combine a negative and a positive approach to ethics of machines as will be described in the rest of the paper.

It should not be forgotten that it is necessary to question our ability to ensure compliance in evolving, learning automata. Safety engineering is, in this context, a growing concern, as robots can easily learn to circumvent the rules if that leads to a more beneficial result (Yampolskiy and Fox 2013, pp. 217–26). A particularly clear example of this is anti-discrimination laws in insurance. While regulations require companies to offer equal treatment to their customers regardless of sex or race, as stated by Ronen, "(insurance companies) are in the business of discriminating" (Avraham et al. 2012). Learning algorithms that have been trained to predict default rates without being given sex or race as an input are able to build proxies of these attributes and use them in their internal calculations, so that their output is more accurate—albeit discriminatory. Knowledge extraction and ex-post testing can be used for this purpose.

4. Within the Limits of What is Possible: Filtered Decision-Making and Transparency

The issue with learning automata is fundamentally a conflict between the top-down nature of law-based ethics with the underlying constructivist mechanics of learning, evolving algorithms. This paper distinguishes two different types of problems related to this conflict:

> It is not obvious to determine whether a learning automaton complies necessarily with some given rules, given that their behavior can be unpredictable even for their programmer.

> In addition, learning-based algorithms are not necessarily based on clearly understandable strategies. This might lead to situations where it is unclear whether they comply with top-down ethics or not. For instance, an algorithm might be designed to give quotes for insurance. It is in principle possible for it to evolve towards giving worse quotes to a racial minority, for example, which would violate anti-discrimination laws as explained above. However, if the algorithm is designed in a nontransparent way (for instance, using deep learning[3]), it can be challenging to detect whether this will occur.

I would like to propose *filtered decision making* as a possible solution. This idea consists in designing the learning-based automaton in such a way that it can obtain inputs from the external world and process them to get a decision, but not activate that decision by itself. Instead of determining the output of the process directly, the learning automaton would send the preliminary output to an external, objective module, which would be accessed online. This objective module would assess, in an independent way, whether the action selected by the automaton complies with the established rules. If it does, then the decision is sent back to the action module of the automaton. If it does not, then the automaton goes to its *default action* (determined as the safest by the same committee that designed the top-down rules). In addition, a flag is raised so that the programmer can inspect the issue.

This filtered decision making ensures that the robot will comply with the rules, and eliminates some of the problems that make for tedious implementation in an actual context. General learning machines can be divided into categories depending on their function, for which different sets of rules can be enacted (for instance, trading machines, war automata, and caregiver automata).

---

[3] It should be noted that the particular learning algorithm that is implemented in each case is not relevant, but only the fact that it is not transparent. Any non-transparent machine learning algorithm could have been used in this example.

Moreover, it would be automatic to update these codes when necessary—avoiding the need for updating the programming of the full array of devices in operation. In addition, the filtering module should not be capable of learning, which would ensure it will function correctly in the future.

Filtered decision making draws on the idea of a moral governor that was proposed by Arkin to control lethal behavior in the particular case of war operations (Arkin 2009), which as explained above is a particularly relevant research field within machine ethics and roboethics. The external module proposed in this paper would incorporate additional characteristics to Arkin's moral governor, such as evolving to incorporate any updates, exceptions, or patches that might be deemed necessary given the ever-evolving experience, not only with a particular device but also with all devices belonging to the same class. Another difference is that Arkin proposes that there can be overriding on the ethical control, albeit "with upmost certainty on the part of the operator". The external module in this paper could contemplate overriding as a "big-red-button" decision, but only before the external module, so that it should not be possible to override the top-down rules in any context. The behavior of the device should be constrained by the external module regardless of the circumstances. The external module must be separate from the machine so that it can remain unaffected by the specific users or programmers of the autonomous device. This requires all autonomous devices to be connected to the external module (e.g., via Wi-Fi) to function and calls for immediate pause of all actions in the event that this connection is lost.

It should be noted that building such an external module is plausible in principle, but it would be by no means an easy task; implementing such a system entails two main risks:

Defining the set of agreed rules in an objective and transparent way, as well as the possible outcomes of any action belonging to the space of decisions.

Establishing the consequences of actions in complex or uncertain settings. One example tool that could be applied for this is inference engines, which would be able to test whether any undesired consequence arises from the knowledge base of the device or the intended action. In addition, fuzzy logic can be used to deal with the degree of ambiguity that is usually present in real-world decisions.

The insurance problem manifests a *need for transparency* in the decision making of automata. Given that the strategy developed by the robot should ultimately be understandable by human beings, not all algorithms should be valid to develop automata, regardless of their good performance. For instance, approaches based on artificial neural networks should be examined carefully, as they commonly lead to black-box solutions where the logic underlying the decision is not easily identifiable. On the contrary, approaches such as size-constrained decision trees would be extremely useful, as they can, in small cases, be understandable in terms of human behavior. Along the same lines, knowledge extraction techniques can effectively clarify the results of complex optimized algorithms. These methods should be used extensively as the need for transparency grows larger.

Last, even if knowledge extraction is not practical in a particular instance, law-enforcement can rely on test cases (in the example, feed several profiles to the algorithm and assess whether decisions are discriminatory up to a given percentage). That is, if it is not possible to establish a priori if the rule is followed, it can always be tested ex-post. This last-resort option should be avoided if possible.

With these two proposals in mind (filtered decision making and a restriction on suitable algorithms for the sake of transparency), it should be reasonable to establish behavior codes to be abided by self-evolving machines in a safe and transparent way. These codes should be updated regularly as more information is known about the possible courses of action for the automata. Filtered decision making would avoid scenarios where machines get out of control.

5. The Appeal of Positive Ethics and Subjectivity as a Hard Limit

The approaches based on top-down, negative ethics seem to be far from the complete experience of morality in human beings. The rationale of decision making by seeking the best consequence in terms of a given objective (such as a common good or maximizing a given definition of utility) is undoubtedly appealing.

These utilitarian or consequentialist approaches have been criticized in the past because of the computational problems that might arise when calculating the consequences of any given action. Calculating first-order effects might be difficult, but even in the simplest of circumstances, calculating all cascade of effects quickly becomes an unmanageable task.

However, there is a more problematic issue underlying utilitarian approaches: the definition of the utility function is not always obvious. In order to be implementable, it must be expressed in the programming language the machine is built on. This might not seem like a restrictive condition: it is easy to build a trading automata dealing in a stock exchange to maximize profit, or profit for a given risk. The utility function that guides the trading automaton is purely beneficial, which can be expressed as the amount of money made in the trades it closes in the market. Similarly, a robot with a higher human interaction such as a robotic hotel receptionist might have its utility function defined as being agreeable to customers. In order to give a numerical value to this, we might ask clients to fill a quick survey about their satisfaction. The receptionist robot will try different strategies and select the ones that please customers the most as revealed in the surveys.

The past examples are easily understandable and immediately implementable. However, the proponents of bottom-up machine ethics go far beyond this conception. For instance, Kurzweil as a representative of the most extreme versions of technooptimism, believes that machines will not only behave in a way consistent with values, but experience these values themselves and become, in his words, *spiritual machines* where, from an artificial intelligence basis, consciousness and authentic ethics will *emerge* (Kurzweil 2012).

There have been very compelling proposals dealing with bottom-up values in other sciences, particularly with respect to the plasticity of values, which are understood as inherently subjective but built in cooperation with other human beings. Some authors, such as E.O. Wilson, have long ago discussed the emergence of values in societies (Wilson 1975). Interestingly, values such as cooperation for a common good have been explained in an evolutionary framework as a survival-optimizing strategy, as in the works of Danielson, (Danielson 1998). Evolutionary game theory (EGT) is extremely interesting in this context. However, I would argue that the behaviors that emerge in EGT and that we categorize as "ethical" are not guided by moral values themselves (such as helping the weak) but are rather the result of adapting to a very different goal (survival of the individual, the family or the community). Some of the strategies that emerge seem to have a moral component to it (such as helping the weak) and result in eusocial behavior in general, while some others exemplify selfish behavior (e.g., cuckoo-like strategies). I would argue that these behaviors are guided by survival and not by any moral values, even if a human observer could interpret them as being moral or immoral depending on the case. This categorization might be interesting and useful, but giving a useful description should not be confused with guiding behavior itself.

The thinkers that defend emergence in machines stay silent about the possible mechanisms that can give origin to this phenomenon. For instance, Kurzweil states that a complete, functioning mind can be created by adding a *value module* to a brain based on pattern recognition (Kurzweil 2012), but does not give any details on how this module should be created or how it can be coded. All these bottom-up proposals have in common this lack of theoretical support at this point. It should be noted that the three concepts are usually understood to be related: values emerge within consciousness, and consciousness is one of the main properties of subjectivity. The emergence of values presupposes the emergence of subjectivity and consciousness. There have been some attempts at studying the characteristics of current AI in relation to the properties of consciousness, such as the interesting work of Kuipers (Kuipers 2008, pp. 155–70). However, these descriptive studies do not provide any proof of the existence of subjectivity in the machines.

Very importantly, the emergence of values should not be confused with the emergence of a function to fit externally defined values. An objective function defining a value can effectively emerge (e.g., via reinforcement learning, where the output of a given function could be adjusted to the value given by a user – for instance, evaluating whether a decision is fair or not). In this case, *the function to evaluate fairness* emerges, rather than the *concept of fairness itself*. This distinction is very important, as fitting a function does not require any subjective experience and can effectively be accomplished—even if the task at hand is difficult. This would be an example of possible "positive ethics", as an automaton can be designed to maximize fairness as long as it is given an input including this evaluation (in this case, this could be expressed as a fairness evaluation coming from an external judge. This fairness evaluation would be used as the desired output for supervised learning). Once again, in this case, a fitness function emerges, but the concept of justice comes from the outside in the form of the outputs for supervised learning. However, because the concept of fairness, rather than emerging within the learning automaton, is received by it, this does not constitute an example of bottom-up ethics. The strategy to optimize the objective function emerges bottom-up, but the objective function itself comes from the outside. This is discussed further in the next section.

6. Language as a Limit

It has been said that living beings are the only *beings with a purpose* (Rosenbrock 1990). However, machines can undoubtedly have a purpose as well, as long as it is given to them by the programmer. This purpose is, in the case of machines, the objective function that is optimized[4] by the learning algorithm implemented in their software. Utilitarian approaches to machine ethics take this as their starting point.

There are two elements that seem to be missing from the public debate. First, in order to be programmed, the objective function that will guide the machine's actions needs to be expressed in the same programming language used by the machine. By nature, this programming language must be a *public* one in the sense of being understandable by all the users of the language in the same way (Leach 2011). It is useful to remember the distinction proposed by Javier Leach between public languages (objective and understood by all users in the same way) and *personal* ones, which include all the concepts in the public ones and expand them to include subjective information and experience. Mathematics or programming code would be examples of public languages, while concepts referring to emotions (such as anger or disgust) or values (such as justice or beauty) would clearly belong to the personal sphere. It should be noted that the degree of subjectivity of a term varies widely, with "chair" being less exposed to subjectivity than "non-combatant" in war operations terminology, and values such as "fairness" being arguably the most subjective of them all.

It should be understood that the public domain includes only completely objective concepts, qualities, and magnitudes that can be impartially determined or measured. The public domain is the realm of the sciences and of programming. "Length", "weight" or "wavelength" belong to thepublic domain.

Any personal concept can be projected into the public domain at the expense of losing some of its nuances. If the degree of subjectivity is small, the projection will be relatively faithful to the personal concept. This would be the case if we project "color", for instance, as a table from wavelengths, which can be measured objectively, to words such as "red" or "blue". If the automaton has a very specific purpose and a narrow set of possible interactions with human beings, these projections can be defined in a relatively straightforward way. For instance, we could project the concept "avoiding harm", for a self-driving car, as "avoiding collision with another car or a human being". However, this should not distract from the fact that the value has not been represented in full.

If we project "distributive fairness" into "distributing wealth into equal portions" (assuming we have previously defined terms such as "wealth" and "portions"), we might incur a larger error and will probably have considerable trouble agreeing on a definition. While we can build attempts to

---

4   I include, within the broad term "optimization", approaches such as constraint satisfaction, which can be used to describe any general decision problem.

express a concept from the personal languages in a public way, this attempt can never capture the true essence of the concept.

We can train a robot that distributes food to calculate equal portions by measuring the weight of the trays it serves. However, that is far from understanding the concept of justice. In order to be able to program a given purpose in an automaton, this purpose must be amenable to expression in the programming language. Surprisingly, these considerations are missing from the current discussion, which seems to disregard the different types of language. It is dangerous to assume that the two spheres of language (public and personal) are the same, because it gives us the false notion that robots can act ethically by their own means and have authentic moral judgments, when they can only operate based on approximations expressed in a public language. In addition, this takes away the focus from the imminent task of the programmer: providing an objective function that is as similar as possible to the concept, which is not expressible in those terms. Happiness and justice belong to the personal sphere, so they cannot be used to define an automaton's purpose. However, profit and loss can be easily expressed as a number, so it can indeed be used to guide a robot's actions.

Nothing suggests that automata based on current technology will ever be able to deal with personal language (which seems to be linked to subjectivity) or have a subjective experience of their purpose—at the very least, there is nothing to make us think otherwise. Some authors seem to believe that there will be some emergence of subjectivity that could explain how automata would be able to deal with values and spirituality. The proponents of an emergence of subjectivity, as expressed in the previous section, have not been able to provide any proof or clues on what might underlie this phenomenon. Their purpose is not in themselves, but is rather given to them by the programmer; it comes from the outside. This means that this purpose will always be defined in terms of their relationship to human beings or the environment.

The responsibility of defining this objective function will always be the programmer's. In addition, assigning a good purpose definition is not enough. In the example of the robotic hotel receptionist, the purpose of the automaton was clear: improve client surveys. The robot could learn strategies to make clients more satisfied by trial and error. However, it could also learn to tamper with survey data, which could also lead to better results, albeit in a non-desired way. This sort of behavior can happen because the expression of value in that case—i.e., client satisfaction—in a public language—i.e., survey numbers—is not perfect. This example also shows the need for negative ethics as proposed in Section 4. Any learning, self-evolving robot should be subject to filtered decision making, where any unacceptable action should be detected and prevented before it happens. What is more, this example shows the importance of building the filtering module online: a priori, the tampering behavior probably was not anticipated. Once it has happened, however, a new rule can be added to the code abided by receptionist machines. This could be made effective immediately to prevent any future instances of the problem.

In short, negative approaches will always be necessary, while positive ethics can be implemented in some instances. The basic requirement for the latter is expression in a public language. This definition will be carried out by the programmer and will correspond to a projection of values into the public language, and should not be confused with the bottom-up emergence of values themselves.

The automaton can then develop, bottom-up, a strategy to optimize an objective function, but it is not able to learn or derive values themselves, which belong to the personal sphere and which the machine does not comprehend, as it only grasps approximate depictions expressed in a public language—the only one it understands. This rules out the possibility of spiritual machines that develop their own transcendent values, at least with current technology based on public languages. In addition, this stresses the responsibility of the programmer when creating the value approximations that will guide the machine's actions.

7. Conclusions

The growing field of machine ethics has proposed several strategies for endowing machines with ethical behavior. This paper has presented a classification that organizes these proposals around a double dichotomy. Negative ethics is concerned with preventing harm to other beings, while positive ethics focuses on creating the largest good. Top-down ethics conceive the moral rules or the definition of ethical good as something external that is adopted by the subject, which contrasts with bottom-up ethics, which considers that it is the subject who builds the values that guide her actions. All approaches to machine ethics can be classified using these categories.

Within negative ethics, ethics based on moral duty are difficult to implement. Law-based approaches have the advantage of being more easily implementable as they are objective. This paper proposes *filtered decision-making* as a framework, where the decisions of the automata should be approved by an external objective module. This filter checks that the robot's decision complies with the set of rules it is ascribed to and, in the event that the decision is noncompliant, prevents it from being enacted. This approach also has the benefit of providing an easy way of updating the legal codes for all automata at the same time.

Within the context of positive ethics, some authors have envisioned robots that evolve their own sense of moral consciousness in a bottom-up manner. However, they do not provide any ideas for explaining how this could happen. This paper has emphasized that current technology is based on public languages, so that values can only be projected from the public sphere in an approximate way. Machines can take their objective function from the programmer and develop bottom-up strategies to optimize it. However, they cannot emerge, bottom up, this objective function or the values that originated it. This discards the possibility of spiritual machines that develop their own transcendent values, at least with current technology. Language and subjectivity are, therefore, a limit for machine ethics.

Although machines cannot have a purpose in themselves, they can indeed have *a purpose*, as long as it is given to them by the programmer (in a top-down instance of ethics), so it would be a purpose *outside of themselves*. This must be expressed in a public language—which means, in other words, that it must be amenable to be written in a programming code. In addition, given that evolving machines can have unexpected behaviors, additional negative ethics in the form of filtered decision-making is still necessary. Only by combining a law-based approach with a well-understood definition of purpose (outside themselves and expressed through a public language)—that is, understanding the limits of present-day machine ethics—will we be able to tackle the challenges that lay in the future field of robotics.

Conflicts of Interest: The author declares no conflict of interest.

References

Allen, Colin, Iva Smit, and Wendell Wallach. 2005. Artificial morality: Top-down, bottom-up, and hybrid approaches. *Ethics and Information Technology* 7: 149–55. [CrossRef]

Arkin, Ronald. 2009. *Governing Lethal Behavior in Autonomous Robots*. Boca Raton: CRC Press.

Asimov, Isaac. 1950. *I, Robot*. New York: Gnome Press.

Avraham, Ronen, Kyle D. Logue, and Daniel Schwarcz. 2012. Understanding Insurance Anti-Discrimination Laws. Available online: http://repository.law.umich.edu/cgi/viewcontent.cgi?article=1163&context=law_econ_current (accessed on 19 May 2017).

Campbell, Robert L., John Chambers Christopher, and Mark H. Bickhard. 2002. Self and values: An interactivist foundation for moral development. *Theory & Psychology* 12: 795–823.

Casey, Bryan James. 2017. Amoral machines, or: How roboticists can learn to stop worrying and love the law. Available online: https://ssrn.com/abstract=2923040 (accessed on 1 May 2017).

Danielson, Peter. 1998. *Modeling Rationality, Morality, and Evolution*. Oxford: Oxford University Press on Demand.

Floridi, Luciano. 2005. Information ethics, its nature and scope. *ACM SIGCAS Computers and Society* 35: 3. [CrossRef]

Greene, J.D., R.B. Sommerville, L.E. Nystrom, J.M. Darley, and J.D. Cohen. 2001. An fMRI investigation of emotional engagement in moral judgment. *Science Magazine* 293: 2105–8. [CrossRef] [PubMed]

Handelsman, Mitchell M., Samuel Knapp, and Michael C. Gottlieb. 2009. Positive ethics: Themes and variations. In *Oxford Handbook of Positive Psychology*. Oxford: Oxford University Press, pp. 105–13.

Hardy, Sam A., and Gustavo Carlo. 2011. Moral identity: What is it, how does it develop, and is it linked to moral action? *Child Development Perspectives* 5: 212–18. [CrossRef]

Head, Simon. 2014. Mindless: Why Smarter Machines are Making Dumber Humans. New York: Basic Books.

Honderich, Ted. 2005. The Oxford Companion to Philosophy. Oxford: Oxford University Press.

Howard, Ronald Arthur, and Clinton D. Korver. 2008. Ethics for the Real World: Creating a Personal Code to Guide Decisions in Work and Life. Cambridge: Harvard Business Press.

International Federation of Robotics (IFR). 2016. *World Robotics 2016*. Frankfurt: International Federation of Robotics.

Jackson, Frank. 1991. Decision-theoretic consequentialism and the nearest and dearest objection. *Ethics* 101: 461–82. [CrossRef]

Kahneman, Daniel. 2011. Thinking, Fast and Slow. New York: Macmillan.

Kant, Immanuel, and Thomas Kingsmill Abbott. 2004. Critique of Practical Reason. Miami: Courier Corporation.

Kuipers, Benjamin. 2008. Drinking from the firehose of experience. *Artificial Intelligence in Medicine* 44: 155–70. [CrossRef] [PubMed]

Kurzweil, Ray. 2012. How to Create a Mind: The Secret of Human Thought Revealed. London: Penguin.

Lapsley, Daniel K., and Darcia Narvaez. 2006. Character education. In *Handbook of Child Psychology*. New York: John Wiley & Sons.

Leach, Javier. 2011. Mathematics and Religion: Our Languages of Sign and Symbol. West Conshohocken Templeton Foundation Press.

Lichtenberg, Judith. 2010. Negative duties, positive duties, and the "new harms". *Ethics* 120: 557–78. [CrossRef]

Luxton, David D. 2014. Recommendations for the ethical use and design of artificial intelligent care providers. *Artificial Intelligence in Medicine* 62: 1–10. [CrossRef] [PubMed]

Martin, Jack. 2004. Self-regulated learning, social cognitive theory, and agency. *Educational Psychologist* 39: 135–45. [CrossRef]

Powers, Thomas M. 2006. Prospects for a kantian machine. *IEEE Intelligent Systems* 21: 46–51. [CrossRef]

Rosenbrock, Howard H. 1990. *Machines with a Purpose*. Oxford: Oxford University Press.

Slote, Michael A. 1985. *Common-Sense Morality and Consequentialism*. Abingdon-on-Thames: Routledge & Kegan.

Van de Voort, Marlies, Wolter Pieters, and Luca Consoli. 2015. Refining the ethics of computer-made decisions: A classification of moral mediation by ubiquitous machines. *Ethics and Information Technology* 17: 41–56. [CrossRef]

Veruggio, Gianmarco, Fiorella Operto, and George Bekey. 2016. Roboethics: Social and ethical implications. In *Springer Handbook of Robotics*. Berlin and Heidelberg: Springer, pp. 2135–60.

Wilson, Edward O. 1975. Sociology: New Synthesis. Cambridge: Belknap Press.

Yampolskiy, Roman, and Joshua Fox. 2013. Safety engineering for artificial general intelligence. *Topoi* 32: 217–26. [CrossRef]

MDPI

Article

Moral Bioenhancement through An Intersectional Theo-Ethical Lens: Refocusing on Divine Image-Bearing and Interdependence

Tracy J. Trothen

School of Religion, Queen's University, Kingston, ON K7L 2N6, Canada;
trothent@queensu.ca; Tel.: +1-613-533-6000 (ext. 74319)

Academic Editor: Noreen Herzfeld
Received: 5 February 2017; Accepted: 26 April 2017; Published: 8 May 2017

Abstract: This article begins with a brief interrogation of the meanings of moral and virtue. Next, an intersectional Christian theo-ethical lens focusing on humans as divine image-bearers is used to generate critical insights regarding the influence of extreme individualism on approaches to moral bioenhancement. This alternative lens emphasizes the interdependence of life, and the contextual character of moral dispositions. The question of what it means to be creatures bearing the *imago dei* and making moral choices, is at the center of this exploration. The author concludes that while there may be justifiable exceptions, for now moral bioenhancements are unwarranted. Moral improvement will be better achieved through more effective educational strategies, and possibly spiritual enhancements, that are geared toward appreciation for the interdependence of all life.

Keywords: choice; Christian theology; intersectional theology; justice; moral bioenhancement; theological anthropology; virtue

1. Introduction and Preliminary Considerations

Enhancement technologies are being developed and applied to several domains of human being: the physical, the affective, the cognitive, the spiritual, and the moral. Moral bioenhancement is not mere science fiction. Pharmaceutical agents used primarily to treat other conditions also seem to affect morality. Ethical issues related to the development and use of moral bioenhancements must be probed from several perspectives. The lens we bring to the moral enhancement discussion shapes the questions that we ask and our understandings of key concepts, including the following topics that are explored in this article: morality, virtue, being human, and choice.

This article is an overview of some ethical issues raised through the application of an intersectional Christian theological lens to moral bioenhancement. An intersectional theology prioritizes and brings together justice concerns identified by several theologies that are written from the underside including but not limited to: liberation, queer, racial, womanist, feminist, and disability theologies. Intersectional theology emphasizes the complexity and impact of systemic privilege and power on experience and ways of seeing the world. As theologians Grace Ji-Sun Kim and Susan M. Shaw explain, "the further [one is] from the norm, the greater the marginalization. This marginalization, however, is not simply additive, but rather social categories of gender, race, class, and other forms of difference interact with and shape one another within interconnected systems of oppression. These systems of oppression—sexism, racism, colonialism, classism, ableism, nativism, and ageism—work within social institutions such as education, work, religion, and the family...to structure our experiences and relationships in such a way that we participate in reproducing dominance and subordination without even realizing it" (Kim and Shaw 2017).

I begin with attention to preliminary issues regarding the meanings of "moral" and "virtue". Next, I consider implications of humans as divine image-bearers to generate critical insights regarding the influence of extreme individualism on approaches to moral bioenhancement, emphasizing the interdependence of life and the contextual character of moral dispositions. The question of what it means to be creatures bearing the *imago dei* and making moral choices, is at the center of this exploration. I conclude that while there may be justifiable exceptions, for now moral bioenhancements are unwarranted. Moral improvement will be better achieved through more effective educational strategies, and possibly spiritual enhancements, that are geared toward appreciation for the interdependence of all life.

1.1. Moral Bioenhancement

Morality is a novel enhancement frontier. Proponents of moral bioenhancements hope that these biomedical technologies will better the world by improving moral reasoning, increasing prosocial behaviors, strengthening motivation to do good, and/or enhancing moral virtues. Well-known philosophers Ingmar Persson and Julian Savulescu advocate moral bioenhancement as a safeguard against the use of fast developing technologies that could be used to obliterate the planet. They reason that with the proliferation of technologies, and especially cognitive enhancements, we will have more opportunities and tools for inflicting mass destruction. Therefore, our collective sense of justice and inclination to care for each other need to be improved in order to minimize the possibility of such destruction. Certainly, if we consider war, genocide, and abuse to be moral failings, there is much room for moral improvement. The question is how best to do this.

Because moral enhancement interventions are biomedical, these enhancements are referred to as moral bioenhancements. Since morality is in part neurobiologically determined, morality can potentially be affected by pharmacological interventions. For example, there is behavioral, genetic, and neuroscientific evidence for the biological basis of aggression (Douglas 2008, p. 233). The drug Ritalin reduces impulsive aggression. Depending upon one's definition of morality, Ritalin can also contribute to moral enhancement by sharpening one's ability to focus and think more deliberately about problem-solving matters, including ethical analyses. The drug Modafinal may increase prosocial behaviors such as empathy, cooperation, trust, and concentration. The hormone serotonin increases aversion to harming others, as well as empathy. The hormone oxytocin increases prosocial behaviors such as empathy, cooperation, and trust.

Even if there was general agreement that aversion to aggression, and inclination to empathy, cooperation, and trust are desirable moral qualities, there are moral risks to these pharmacological agents. Oxytocin can make people more trusting, but it is not good to be more trusting in all situations (Jones 2013, p. 150). Oxytocin increases altruistic behavior and empathy but only towards in-group members (Jones 2013, p. 190; Persson and Savulescu 2015a, p. 338). As a result, their usage may increase global conflict by binding us closer to kin, possibly at the expense of appreciating others who are not kin.

There are also potential non-pharmacological moral bioenhancements. Deep brain stimulation (DBS), the less invasive transcranial magnetic stimulation (TMS), and transcranial direct current stimulation (tDCS) may increase cooperation (Piore 2015) and neuroplasticity, making it easier to learn prosocial behaviors. However, DBS, TMS, and tDCS may cause seizures or headaches, and may affect personal identity in unforeseen ways by changing thought patterns (Cabrera et al. 2014).

Although we use these biomedical technologies to treat various conditions, we lack consensus around how or if these technologies might improve morality. Morality is a very difficult concept to define. I am convinced that the main reason morality is difficult to define is its contextuality. For example, scholars including Inmaculada de Melo-Martin and Arleen Salles, and Michael Hauskeller (de Melo-Martin and Salles 2015; Hauskeller 2016) raise questions—as I will also discuss later in this article—concerning the desirability of "prosocial" qualities in all "moral" situations. As I will consider next, not all agree that morality is contextually driven to the degree that this contextuality presents a barrier to moral bioenhancement. For example, Persson and Savulescu, and James J. Hughes, emphasize a set of general virtues that they see as desirable, to some degree, across all, or almost all, contexts (Persson and Savulescu 2012; Hughes 2013).

1.2. How Do We Become More Moral? Problematizing the Conversation

The meaning of moral enhancement is debated. Some ethicists, including Persson and Savulescu, and Hughes, focus on dispositional traits with an emphasis on virtues and resulting prosocial behaviors, as being key to morality (de Melo-Martin and Salles 2015; Persson and Savulescu 2012; Hughes 2013). Philosopher Thomas Douglas focuses on increasing moral motivation, or the motivation to do good (Douglas 2008). Bioethicist John Harris emphasizes the cognitive capacity to engage in ethical analysis or moral reasoning (Douglas 2008; Harris 2011). Philosopher Michael Hauskeller is more concerned with increasing knowledge of what doing good means, and what are good actions in particular situations (Hauskeller 2016). There is no clear distinction between cognitive and moral enhancement. Insofar as improved cognitive abilities such as concentration and clear thinking affect one's ability to engage in ethical reasoning, cognition is related to decision-making regarding moral matters. In fact, Hughes names the "intellectual" (includes open-mindedness and curiosity) as one of the four moral virtues that he identifies for enhancement. However, a strong ability to engage in ethical reasoning does not necessarily imply adequate motivation, knowledge, virtues, and discernment needed for congruent, contextually appropriate and strategic moral responses. For example, simply because I see that someone is in pain and I can reason that she needs medical or psychological help, this does not mean that I will assist her in getting help. It may be that I decide instead to exploit her vulnerability for my own benefit. Even if we are able to enhance a set of virtues including intellectual virtue, as Hughes proposes, we may not have sufficient knowledge and insight to understand the moral relevance of a multi-layered context to doing "the right thing". I am more persuaded by Hauskeller's argument that we first need to examine and learn more about what doing good means. Persson, Savulescu, and Hughes make strong cases for bioenhancing moral dispositions but, as I will explain, I am not persuaded that we have sufficient agreement or even awareness of the diversity of interpretations of the virtues.

Moral dispositions are comprised of qualities, virtues, and vices that form moral character, and that lead us to behave in certain ways given similar situations. For example, a person who is empathetic will usually be moved to care for a person who is in need across a variety of contexts such as work, home, or recreation. A person who is honest will be honest in most situations. On the plus side, virtues provide a general foundation for the development of particular responses to ethical situations. However, the enhancement of a virtue does not necessarily imply well-informed or well thought-out responses to a given situation. This limitation raises important questions: Can we ensure that virtue-enhancement will be paired with education regarding the unjust distribution of global resources and power? In other words, will we assist people to connect an enhanced moral disposition to ethical behavior? And who decides what virtues are needed by whom? Will the marginalized be given priority? The ethical framework or lens that we use to approach the moral bioenhancement issue will shape the questions that are asked. Complicating the discussion further, is the relationship between virtues and values. What values (e.g., the things we consider to be important to us) are expected and desired—often implicitly—to arise out of these virtues? Feminist, relational, and intersectional theorists have established the complexity of social processes that shape normative values (Sherwin 2012). What we think we value and desire most, may be things that we have unconsciously internalized from our social context, but may not be the values and desires that we would embrace in the light of clear, explicit analysis. We need greater clarity around what values we might hope will arise out of the enhancement of virtues.

Philosophers including Marcuse, Habermas, and Foucault have argued persuasively that enhancement technologies, including moral bioenhancements, reflect and promote the values of utility and efficiency (Marcuse 1964; Habermas 1971; Foucault 1988). The more dishwashers, food processors, and specialty toasters we get, the more accustomed we become to expecting and wanting ourselves and others to get household tasks done quickly and efficiently, maximizing our time. This same technology-inspired expectation and desire can be applied to the workplace, sports (Trothen 2015), and other dimensions of our lives. Anyone or anything that fails to promote, or at least align with, the normative social values of utility and efficiency, is discarded. Philosophers Hubert Dreyfus and Sean Dorrance Kelly surmise that, paradoxically, in our drive to make life better by saving time and energy (not to mention making money), we have made it more difficult to find happiness and "shining moments" that inspire and uplift us (Dreyfus and Kelly 2011). Awareness of the social processes that have influenced these desires and values is necessary for critically determining the values that are consistent with adopted theological principles and related virtues.

The question of what makes one moral is foundational to what is morally enhancing. The social processes that shape desires, values, and virtues must be engaged critically if we are to understand the implications of increasing particular moral dispositions. Moral bioenhancements present possibilities for more caring and just global human communities, but only if we are cognizant of the power disparities and other contextual factors that impact the meanings of moral dispositions. Questions including how virtues are affected by context and by theoretical lens, must be probed and factored into the development and use of moral bioenhancements.

While there may be general agreement in principle on Hughes' distilled list of four virtues, which are based on contemporary neuroscience and psychological research, as well as several world religions and Plato and Aquinas' cardinal virtues—self-control, niceness (including empathy), intelligence, and positivity (Hughes 2015)—or on Persson and Savulescu's prioritizing of altruism and justice, the meanings of these virtues are ambiguous and driven, in part, by power and context. Many marginalized people, for example, likely need a form of niceness that includes more self-preservation, self-interest, pride, and capacity for indignation, whereas many privileged people would benefit from a form of niceness that includes more humility, self-sacrifice, and altruism. It is unclear as to whether science could develop sufficiently to account for this contextual diversity. To demonstrate the problems and contextual characters of virtues, I will briefly consider these examples from an intersectional theological perspective: pride, empathy, and self-sacrifice.

Pride is typically considered a vice, but if one is lacking pride or self-love, pride can be a virtue (Trothen 2015, pp. 55–58). Theologically, pride often has been understood as the quintessential sin and is cited in most theological analyses of human enhancement technologies. After all, hubris can stand behind the inclination to strive to become more than human—god-like. But the sin of pride is much more common to the privileged than the marginalized. The more privileged tend to be in greater need of humility than the less privileged who tend to suffer more from a lack of pride, confidence, self-love, and development of their own power (Saiving 1960). While the creators of enhancement technologies are generally more privileged, and therefore likely more inclined to excessive pride, those affected by these technologies are much more diverse. It can be difficult to hear the voices of the marginalized, since they are usually less prideful and more reluctant to express their own interests. The enhancement of pride as a moral disposition, in people who lack pride and confidence, could help people to promote justice by resisting marginalization and disempowerment. However, the enhancement of pride in the more privileged and confident could increase insensitivity and decrease humility in those who need to be made more accountable to others, and more open to seeing flaws and their potential to harm.

Similarly, empathy and the inclination to self-sacrifice—which Persson and Savulescu identify as conjoint virtues that could and should be enhanced (Persson and Savulescu 2012; Persson and Savulescu 2015b, p. 349)—are affected by social location. Persson and Savulescu make a strong case for the enhancement of altruism, which they understand as involving empathy, and the "setting aside of our own interests for the sake of others" (Persson and Savulescu 2015b, p. 349). Privileged people tend to have less empathy than the marginalized (Kraus et al. 2011). Psychologist Dacher Kraus and his colleagues have shown that empathy is affected by social class (Kraus et al. 2011). Wealth seems to reduce empathy; power and privilege lessens concern for others. Perhaps, the less aware we are of our true reliance on others, the less empathy we have (Kraus et al. 2011; Piff et al. 2012). On the other hand, less privileged people tend to have more empathy. For example, many elderly people may require less empathy enhancement and more assertiveness and confidence. Older adults can suffer from low self-esteem (Holstein et al. 2011) and be too ready to sacrifice their own needs, at least partially out of fear that they become a burden and are abandoned (Hardwig 2010).

The Christian tradition has too often perpetuated the message to accept undue self-sacrifice. Models of meek and mild Jesus turning the other cheek have been promoted at the expense of the Jesus who stood unflinchingly in solidarity with the oppressed, challenging the status quo and authority figures (Brown and Bohn 1989; Fortune 2005). While self-sacrifice for a greater good is very appropriate in some situations, people who endure abuse or exploitative conditions are usually not in need of more empathy and self-sacrifice. Rather, they are typically in need of enhanced assertiveness and more self-interest.[1]

These examples of vices and virtues—pride, empathy, and self-sacrifice—demonstrate the moral relevance of power and context to identifying and interpreting the virtues. Education regarding the moral relevance of context and power, and self-critical analysis are needed if we are to improve ourselves morally. At least for now, the development of appropriate virtues can best be addressed, not by moral bioenhancements, but by more and better educational strategies.

2. Dimensions of the Human Enhancement Debate

Human enhancement ethics can be broken down into three main, often overlapping, approaches. The first approach is, in my view, foundational to the other approaches, and centers on what it means to be human. From a theological perspective, the question is not whether or at what point we cease to be human due to enhancement technologies, but at what point do we cease to be creatures bearing the *imago dei*. This distinction has implications for ethical analyses that distinguish between therapy and enhancement, since this distinction depends on conceptions of "normal" ways of being human.

I suggest that the second approach to enhancement ethics which centers on choice, from a theological perspective, must be shaped by implications of the *imago dei*. This means that choice must be re-framed as extending beyond the individual, and the implications for other lives in addition to the self must be of central consideration. The third approach highlights distributive justice issues. Since social justice is germane to intersectional theory, justice concerns will be included in my examinations of the other approaches to the moral enhancement debate. I make the case that awareness and value for the interdependence of all life that comes with divine image-bearing, shifts the focus of the moral enhancement debate.

2.1. Being Human: Implications of the Imago Dei

What it means to be human, and to what degree we want to change what might be considered the defining markers of being human, are core questions in the human enhancement discussion. At what point, if any, do we recreate ourselves such that we are no longer "normal" humans or even human? From a theological perspective, the concern is not so much whether or not we remain human, but whether or not we cease to be creatures made in the image of God. An evolutionary understanding of the *imago dei* is based on the knowledge that humanity "is a relatively recent development within the 13.9 billion years of God's naturally evolving cosmic creation" (Fisher 2015, p. 29). Since humans as a species were not in existence at the time of Earth's creation, and since we still claim that humans are made in God's image, it follows that being a divine image-bearer is not contingent on being human per se, but depends on acceptance of God's grace to bear imperfectly an image of divine qualities.

---

[1]   Also, as other scholars have pointed out, empathy does not always lead to altruism (de Melo-Martin and Salles 2015, p. 226). And not all situations in which one may experience empathy warrant altruistic responses.

The *imago dei* doctrine has yielded a number of interpretations. Enlightenment approaches emphasize a Cartesian interpretation, seeing reason and rational thought as distinguishing and privileging humans in relation to other life. This reason-centered interpretation of what it means to be made in God's image is most congruent with the strain of transhumanist thinking that sees the brain and rational thought as fundamental to, and sometimes solely, representative of trans/human identity (Deane-Drummond and Scott 2006).

This emphasis on reason has been soundly critiqued for denying full personhood to the cognitively impaired, and to children.[2] As such, reason-centered interpretations of the *imago dei* fail to live up to Jesus' preferential option for the marginalized. Theologian John Swinton explores the meanings of memory and cognition as they relate to personhood in Christianity. He agrees that memory and rational thought are important to personhood, but enlarges our conception of memory beyond representational memory (e.g., cognitively recalled memories) to include "body memory" (Swinton 2014, pp. 166–67). In other words, we are more than rational cognition; we have intrinsic value. Memory and other forms of knowing are not confined to the brain and rational cognitive processes; other aspects of our embodied selves also remember and know. For example, people with moderate to severe dementia, who have lost most of or all of their short term, and much of their long-term memory, often remain responsive to rituals, such as saying the rosary and singing hymns. Our identities continue even when cognitive capacities are diminished. The concept of body memory challenges the sufficiency of an *imago dei* interpretation centered on reason and rational thought.

Another interpretation of the *imago dei* centers on self-determination (Migliore 2004, p. 141). This interpretation fits well with normative North American ideals of extreme independence and self-determination, but it emphasizes the individual at the expense of community, and the interrelationship of all life. It implicitly devalues dependence and interdependence as aspects of being creatures created in the image of God.

Alternative interpretations of the *imago dei* are relationally based (Migliore 2004, p. 141), emphasizing connection and interdependence as key to be being made in the image of God. The divine commandments to love one another, oneself, and God, and to care for creation (Labrecque 2015), are integral to the biblical story. The nature of God as trinitarian reflects relationality; God, within Godself, is relational. If, from a Christian perspective, God is trinitarian and if all people are made in God's image (e.g., the Christian doctrine of the *imago dei*), then relationality and interdependence are aspects of God-intended human identity. Furthermore, within the Christian narrative, Jesus as a full incarnation of God, expressed God's preferential option for the poor; the most vulnerable and marginalized are to be given preference.

Relationship includes mutual dependence; God needs humans to participate in the divine work in the world, and humans need each other, God and creation (Long 1993). From this theological perspective, interdependency and the attendant vulnerability are virtues. Theologian Mary Potter Engel takes this privileging of relationship and interdependence a step further and defines sin as a "lack of consent to the dependence and fragility of our lives to our vulnerabilities" (Engle 1998, pp. 170–71). If vulnerability and interdependence are recognized as virtues (and, conversely, the denial of vulnerability and interdependence as sins), community and mutual relationships would be prioritized in the moral bioenhancement conversation. This starting point would shift the moral bioenhancement conversation to a focus on the enhancement of communities rather than individuals, and to the needs of the most vulnerable first. This shift may even open up different possibilities for enhancement vehicles.

For example, consider the proposal to use oxytocin to enhance empathy and altruistic behavior. If responsibility for the well-being of people beyond, and including self and kin is prioritized, spiritual enhancement may be a more effective and safer way to enhance morality than oxytocin.

---

[2] Also, the assumption that only humans are created in God's image has also been debated vigorously (Moritz 2011; Deane-Drummond 2012).

Spirituality, as distinct from but possibly overlapping with religiosity, is associated with increased compassion and prosocial—including altruistic—behavior toward strangers (Saslow et al. 2013).[3] Oxytocin improves altruism, but only toward in-group members, not strangers. Spirituality can be enhanced via traditional methods such as spiritual practices and by psychedelics such as psilocybin, which research suggests is very promising for increasing openness, empathy, and altruistic behavior (Cole-Turner 2015; Tennison 2012).[4] If empathy, compassion, and altruism are critical to human morality, moral enhancement could possibly be achieved most successfully through spiritual practices and, potentially, psilocybin.

The enhancement of empathy, compassion, and altruism in the more privileged may help to generate a prioritization of resource sharing, and the creation of more strategies to empower and protect the marginalized. However, we do not yet have sufficient scientific evidence to support the use of medical technologies to enhance "moral" dispositions. Also, it is very unclear how we could sort out who needs these moral bioenhancements, and then convince these people to accept an intervention that may contravene their desires. (Now we are entering more into the issue of choice, which will be explored shortly.) Endeavors toward global social justice and the flourishing of all interdependent life will require not only moral bioenchancements (or even spiritual bioenhancements), but also education in various contextual studies including global dynamics, policy development, sociological analyses, economics, and political science. Additionally, self-reflexivity or "the process of reflecting on one's own story from multiple diverging standpoints in ways that try to take into account one's own experience of privilege and disadvantage within intersecting social systems like sexism, racism, heterosexism, and religious forms of oppression" (Doehring 2015, p. 191) is necessary to the enhancement of morality, if morality is understood to be linked with social justice.

Other approaches to enhancement ethics that center on being human, draw distinctions between therapeutic and enhancing interventions, with interventions that are clearly therapeutic being acceptable, while those that are clearly enhancing, being unacceptable. The dividing line between clearly therapeutic and clearly enhancing relies on the problematic concept of normal. The grey zone immediately surrounding "normal" is growing increasingly complex, with some ethicists seeing this unclear zone as including restorative therapies that bring recipients up to the standards of certain groups that exceed the average. For example, is 20/20 the accepted eyesight norm for everyone, or ought the norm be considered higher for major league baseball players, since average eyesight is sharper amongst pro-baseball players than the general population?

From a theological perspective, the question shifts and becomes: at what point do moral bioenhancement technologies cause us to cease being divine image-bearers? An intersectional and relational interpretation of the *imago dei* suggests that this dividing point comes when we cease to value the interdependence of life, and refuse our creaturely responsibilities to use our creative abilities (Hefner 1993) in order to enhance relationships and particularly the well-being of the marginalized.

Consider the example of an elderly person with dementia who exhibits violent behavior. Regarding moral bioenhancement, one approach would be to use pharmacological agents to minimize their impulsive aggression. This may or may not work for someone whose aggression is caused by dementia. The discussion may end there with a failure to flip around our thinking and reframe the issue as being about interdependence. Might it be more therapeutic to use a moral bioenhancement to induce greater empathy and compassion in clinical staff and managers of long-term care homes? How the standard for therapeutically normal levels of moral dispositions is determined will be affected by one's ethical framework.

---

[3] Saslow et al, the investigators of these studies, define compassion as including empathy (e.g., the ability to step into another's shoes) and the desire to help for the sake of helping without expecting other benefits.

[4] Michael N. Tennison has proposed that psilocybin would be appropriate as a moral bioenhancer, and Ron Cole-Turner has proposed that psilocybin would be appropriate as a spiritual enhancer (Cole-Turner 2015; Tennison 2012).

The question of whose virtues and values are promoted, is also of critical importance to approaches that hinge on assessments of what it means to be human. Context, power, and perspective will shape which moral dispositions are seen as most important for enhancement, and which behaviors are being sought as a result of enhancing these moral dispositions. These factors will also shape who is targeted to receive these enhancements.

From an intersectional theological perspective, limits are imposed by the interdependence and inherent value of all life, divine sovereignty, and the preferential option for the poor. The Christian belief that humans are created in God's image entails the understanding that the image of God is integral to identity, and confers unearned dignity on every person. The *imago dei* also confers the responsibility to create, as best we can, for the good of all life. The discernment of what is good involves spiritual practices, deference to God's wisdom through communal accountability, and the application of self-reflexivity and knowledge regarding diverse contexts and systemic power dynamics.

2.2. Choosing Morally

A second approach to enhancement ethics centers on choice, and more specifically the question of whether or not people ought to be free to choose enhancement technologies if they are judged medically safe.[5] Moral bioenhancements complicate choice. First, there is the question of who would choose moral bioenhancements, and whether these people would be likely to need these enhancements. Presumably if one lacks moral dispositions such as empathy and compassion, one may not feel motivated to acquire more of these moral dispositions, unless there is some other utility that fits with their interests. It is more likely that those who already have appreciable levels of empathy and compassion would be interested in increasing these moral dispositions. However, it is possible to become overly committed to the welfare of others to the neglect of one's own welfare. Second, are questions about the capacity to make authentic and free choices *after* one is morally bioenhanced. Will moral bioenhancements change us such that we are no longer able to make choices that are consistent with our identities? Will supposed "free choice" become a dated concept? Intersectional theological analyses of authenticity and choice shift this question by prioritizing community instead of the individual. I will first consider the issues regarding whether or not we should have the freedom to choose moral bioenhancements. In the subsequent section I will consider the concern about authentic choice post-moral-bioenhancement.

The desire to have "power over our fates" (Kurzweil 2005, p. 9) is fundamental to transhumanism and much of Western society. Self-governance is illusory if by self-governance we mean that individual choices affect only oneself, and that we never rely on anyone besides ourselves. For example, making breakfast may appear to be an independent task, informed only by free individual choice. But there are numerous people involved in getting that food to our kitchens, including farmers, those who transport the food to stores, and grocery stockers. Moreover, what we think of as appropriate breakfast food has been socially conditioned by many people and processes, including family, media, and government health policy makers. Our choices are not free if free means unfettered by contextual forces and unfettered by interdependence. What I choose has an impact on others, and others affect my options and choices. This interconnection needs to be considered in tandem with the choices we make, including choices regarding the design and use of moral bioenhancements.

As discussed earlier, technology is value-laden, as are other social processes that inform our choices. Self-reflexivity is important to autonomy, including choice, since this process helps us critically understand the layers of social forces that contribute to our formation and desires. Without a degree of critical understanding of the forces that shape us, many choices are driven by social norms and values

---

5   Ethicist Andy Miah is possibly the most well-known advocate of choice arguing that even professional athletes should be
     permitted to choose enhancement technologies for the purpose of improving athletic performance, so long as this use is
     overt and in continuity with their sense of authenticity.

without analysis of the desirability of these norms and values. Philosopher George J. Agich reframes the issue of choice in the context of what he calls actual autonomy: "the proper understanding of autonomy involves appreciating how individuals are interconnected and how persons develop in terms of historical and social circumstance" (Agich 2010, p. 608). There is a strong narrative dimension to autonomy and choice. Contextual factors including social privilege and barriers created by racism, ageism, sexism, classism, and numerous other systems of prejudice (Lebacqz 2012), impact our identities; we are connected to each other in both empowering and limiting ways.

An aversion to dependence in Western culture goes hand-in-hand with extreme individualism, and an illusion of self-governance that is independent of others (Holstein et al. 2011; Agich 2010, p. 605). These norms connect to the reduction of human worth to utility and efficiency; I am what I produce, and I am worth more if I produce things that are financially gainful. Theology promotes norms that are counter to these social norms, by affirming each person's intrinsic worth and dignity (regardless of utility) (Swinton 2014; Ryan et al. 2005; Perkins et al. 2015), and claiming interdependence as a virtuous dimension of being human. The reversal sayings of Jesus (e.g., the last shall be first) challenge normative Western values, including the emphasis on independence and utility. And, theologically, community is necessary for virtue: "on one's own, one cannot do the right things" (Swinton 2014, p. 164).

Should moral bioenhancement be a matter of individual choice? Persson and Savulescu, the best-known proponents of moral bioenhancements, argue that once these enhancements have been satisfactorily developed, individual choice should be overridden, and these enhancing agents should be given to all children much in the same way as we in the Western world have become mostly accustomed to childhood inoculations and fluoride in tap water. They argue that the risk of global harm or even destruction is very high, and justifies mandatory moral bioenhancement. Not only may catastrophic harm be obviated through the mandatory use of pharmaceutical moral bioenhancers, Persson and Savulescu argue, such mandatory usage would enhance and not limit individual autonomy. This is because a more altruistic and justice-centered world would increase individual moral agency and make us all freer (Persson and Savulescu 2008).

A relational theological approach to autonomy, however, would begin with and emphasize the implications of moral bioenhancement for all people, ecology and other creaturely life, and potentially the cosmos, rather than framing the issue in terms of individual choice. While individual well-being and desires would be factors in choosing moral bioenhancements, the ethics conversation about morality would extend far beyond individuals. The starting point is not be a utilitarian prioritization of the well-being of the greatest number of people. Rather, the starting point is the well-being of all life since, as creatures created in God's image, we are interdependent. This starting point means primary attention must be given to the most marginalized, and entails careful scrutiny of the meanings of morality including the meanings of virtue and vice. It is possible that moral bioenhancement technologies could be developed that enhance virtues as understood from the diverse perspectives, and especially the less privileged, but we are a long way from that step.

If medically safe moral bioenhancements become available, the enhancement of virtues appropriate to the well-being of the marginalized—and therefore also to the well-being of all—could become very desirable, but only if these bioenhancements are combined with a contextual approach to morality, education about diverse contexts and people, self-reflexivity, and an appreciation of the interdependence of life. From an intersectional theological perspective, an individualistic notion of moral enhancement (centering on individual choice) is an oxymoron. If we begin with the premise that life is interdependent, the social implications of choice must be acknowledged. While the idea of making the more privileged among us more empathetic, altruistic, and justice oriented is attractive, an approach that centers on individual choice (either for or against), instead of a more in-depth exploration of what "we" mean by moral enhancement, is inadequate from an intersectional theological perspective. If the well-being of others and the planet are factored into decision-making processes, then the priority must be the most disadvantaged, and we must ask whether the pursuit of such enhancements is a just use of resources.

2.3. Choosing Authentically

The second concern regarding choice and moral bioenhancement is whether we would maintain the capacity to make choices authentic to ourselves post-bioenhancement. Will we be able to make choices that are consistent with who we are and want to be? Or will our very identities be altered in ways that prevent us from being true to our full range of being human? Proponents contend that moral bioenhancements have the potential to help us become more fully the people we wish to be (Douglas 2008; Jones 2013). Hughes sees moral bioenhancements as possibly addressing neurological limitations that stop us from realizing our moral aspirations, and perhaps our truer selves (Hughes 2017). In this way, moral bioenhancements may allow us to be more authentic to who we are, and better able to make choices congruent with who we are.

Others disagree, arguing that moral bioenhancements may well restrict our freedom to be who we are and who we want to be, including the capacity to choose to act in socially unacceptable ways. Harris and Hauskeller see the human freedom to, in Harris' words, "fall" or even to "choose to fall" as critical human capacities (Harris 2011, p. 103; Hauskeller 2016, p. 159). For Harris, moral choice and the "self-conscious examination" of choices are essential aspects of autonomy. As a result, he argues for the enhancement of moral reasoning abilities, and against the enhancement of moral dispositions.

If choice cannot be understood apart from relationships and life narratives, and if a capacity to choose is a desirable feature of being human, then questions regarding authenticity, and particularly authentic choice, are important to moral enhancement ethics. We need to ask to what extent do we choose "authentically"—apart from moral bioenhancements—given the power of social constructs and norms. Harris makes an important case regarding the freedom to make choices that are contrary to social norms, including the freedom to "fall", but our freedom to make choices is already somewhat curtailed, or at least strongly influenced, by social norms. However, the reality that freedom is limited by social factors does not justify the further limitation of that freedom through moral bioenhancements. It may be that science will eventually be able to give us more information about the effects of moral bioenhancements on selfhood. Such information may also affect our understanding of particular moral bioenhancements for particular people, as therapeutic or enhancing. If Hughes is correct in surmising that moral bioenhancements will allow some people to overcome life-inhibiting neurological limitations, then such interventions potentially would be therapeutic and desirable. However, how we decide, and who decides which physiological anomalies are limitations and which are fortunate happenstances, is unclear. Again, we have an unsurprising but problematic habit of conforming to current social norms and values.

The idea of changing people through moral bioenhancements may or may not be a significant departure from social attempts to influence people to develop what are widely considered to be good moral traits and behaviors. Change is a necessary part of being authentically human. There is no one steady state that defines each of our identities. We embrace educational strategies, for example, with the goal of changing and shaping us, including our moral selves. We are developing cutting-edge forms of moral bioenhancements, and we are also developing cutting-edge educational means of moral enhancement (Ançel 2006; Batt-Rawden et al. 2013; Kidd and Castano 2013). Both moral enhancement modes could potentially be used to help us to be who we want to be, and help improve the world. Most moral bioenhancements, as they are unfolding, would increase moral dispositions but would not prevent us from making moral mistakes and learning from these mistakes. An exception to this may be the electrical stimulation of the brain. There is some evidence to suggest that DBS, TMS, and tDCS may change our brains and thought patterns in unpredictable ways that impact identity (Cabrera et al. 2014), including the capacity to make choices that are in continuity with who we are and who we hope to become.

From an intersectional theological perspective, individual choices extend beyond the self. While, in order to safeguard individual choice and individual well-being, it is important that the use of moral bioenhancements preserve some continuity with one's personal narrative, and contribute to the person whom one desires to become, overall global well-being is, by extension, also important.

The question of authenticity must take into account the reality that each of us affects others; because of our interdependence, in some way, my authenticity or lack of authenticity is tied to your authenticity or lack of authenticity. Failure to recognize and appreciate the interdependence of life, reduces choice to individual interests alone, and reinforces unjust power distribution; in short, choice becomes immoral and inconsistent with a relational interpretation of what it means to be made in God's image. Assuming the value and interdependence of all life, and the prioritizing of the marginalized, individual choice must be reframed on the basis that my choices affect other lives, and this also affects me, and in the knowledge that social norms and values need to be approached contextually and critically.

3. Concluding Summary: Seeing Moral Bioenhancements from an Intersectional Theological Perspective

I began by considering what it means to make someone morally better. I identified some of the medical technologies that may have morally enhancing effects. The lack of consensus around what we need to target if we want to improve morality, is telling. Ought we to focus on improving the motivation to do moral good? Or should we enhance virtues? Or moral reasoning capacities? I favor the improvement of education and critical thinking regarding what a good or "right" thing to do might be in a given situation. I supported the claim that contextuality is critical to morality, through a brief intersectional theological exploration of pride, self-sacrifice, and empathy.

Next, I developed a central theological feature of Christianity—the *imago dei*—and began applying this, using an intersectional theological lens, to two common approaches to moral bioenhancement ethics. I suggested that a key question is: what does it mean to be creatures bearing the *imago dei*? Taking an intersectional perspective, I focused on relational interdependence as a core aspect of the meaning of being created in God's image. I proposed that changing the starting point from an individualistic focus to the *imago dei* and the interdependence of life, significantly influences the moral bioenhancement conversation. Interdependence refocuses the discussion on context, and especially systemic power imbalances and the marginalized.

Extreme individualism steers much of the moral bioenhancement discussion. What it means to be moral and virtuous takes on a distinctive shape when the conversation starts with an understanding of morality as contextual, and the theological claim that life is interdependent and has intrinsic value. Our North American normative valuing of extreme individualism is troubling, and mitigates against choices that are relationally based and intended for the betterment of all life, instead of only particular groups.

In an efficiency-oriented, quick-fix society, it is tempting to think that moral bioenhancements will be sufficient to improve ourselves morally. Traditional educational efforts may no longer be considered worthy of attention and resources. Current research into empirically supported strategies for teaching empathy, for example, might become less of a priority, or even abandoned (Ançel 2006; Batt-Rawden et al. 2013; Kidd and Castano 2013; Trothen 2016; Vanlaere et al. 2012). Moral bioenhancements may help motivate us to be more self-reflexive and altruistic. But there are too many questions regarding the science and the ethics of this topic. Not everyone would benefit from more empathy or compassion. Not everyone needs less pride. Not every virtue is a virtue for everyone.

The science is still in its early stages. I can imagine a persuasive argument for the use of medical technologies to enhance morality in people who show evidence of neurological barriers, as Hughes suggests. But even in these cases I am uneasy, since we tend to evaluate anomalies in accordance with current social norms.

For now, moral bioenhancements are unwarranted. More effective educational strategies, and possibly spiritual enhancement, can help us to enhance relationships and general moral well-being. This education must include diverse perspectives, including religious ones, if we are serious about moral enhancement.

Conflicts of Interest: The author declares no conflict of interest.

References

Agich, George J. 2010. Ethical Issues in Long Term Care. In *Bioethics in a Changing World*. Edited by Jennifer A. Parks and Victoria S. Wike. Toronto: Prentice Hall, pp. 604–11.

Ançel, Gülsüm. 2006. Developing Empathy in Nurses: An Inservice Training Program. *Archives of Psychiatric Nursing* 20: 249–57.

Batt-Rawden, Samantha A., Margaret S. Chisolm, Blair Anton, and Tabor E. Flickinger. 2013. Teaching Empathy to Medical Students: An Updates, Systematic Review. *Academic Medicine* 88: 1171–77. [CrossRef] [PubMed]

Joanne Carlson Brown, and Carole R. Bohn, eds. 1989. *Christianity, Patriarchy and Abuse: A Feminist Critique*. New York: Pilgrim Press.

Cabrera, Laura Y., Emily L. Evans, and Roy H. Hamilton. 2014. Ethics of the Electrified Mind: Defining Issues and Perspectives on the Principled Use of Brain Stimulation in Medical Research and Clinical Care. *Brain Topography* 27: 33–45. [CrossRef] [PubMed]

Cole-Turner, Ron. 2015. Spiritual Enhancement. In *Religion and Transhumanism: The Unknown Future of Human Enhancement*. Edited by Calvin Mercer and Tracy J. Trothen. Santa Barbara: Praeger, pp. 369–83.

De Melo-Martin, Inmaculada, and Arleen Salles. 2015. Moral Bioenhancement: Much Ado about Nothing? *Bioethics* 29: 223–32. [CrossRef] [PubMed]

Deane-Drummond, Celia. 2012. God's Image and Likeness in Humans and Other Animals: Performative Soul-Making and Graced Nature. *Zygon* 47: 934–48. [CrossRef]

Deane-Drummond, Celia, and Peter Manley Scott. 2006. Introduction. In *Future Perfect: God, Medicine and Human Identity*. Edited by Celia Deane-Drummond and Peter Manley Scott. London: T & T Clark International, p. 2.

Doehring, Carrie. 2015. *The Practice of Pastoral Care–A Postmodern Approach*, 2nd ed. Louisville: Westminster John Knox Press, p. 191.

Douglas, Thomas. 2008. Moral Enhancement. *Journal of Applied Philosophy* 25: 228–45. [CrossRef] [PubMed]

Dreyfus, Hubert, and Sean Dorrance Kelly. 2011. *All Things Shining: Reading the Western Classics to Find Meaning in a Secular Age*. New York: Free Press.

Engle, Mary Potter. 1998. Evil, Sin, and Violation of the Vulnerable. In *Lift Every Voice*, 2nd ed. New York: Orbis Books, pp. 170–71.

Fisher, Mathew Zaro. 2015. More Human than the Human? Toward a 'Transhumanist' Christian Theological Anthropology. In *Religion and Transhumanism: The Unknown Future of Human Enhancement*. Edited by Calvin Mercer and Tracy J. Trothen. Westport: Praeger, pp. 23–38.

Fortune, Marie. 2005. *Sexual Violence—The Sin Revisited*. Cleveland: The Pilgrim Press.

Foucault, Michel. 1988. *Technologies of the Self*. Boston: University of Massachusetts Press.

Habermas, Jürgen. 1971. *Knowledge and Human Interest*. Boston: Beacon Press.

Hardwig, John. 2010. Elder Abuse, Ethics, and Context. In *Bioethics in a Changing World*. Edited by Jennifer A. Parks and Victoria S. Wike. Upper Saddle River: Prentice Hall, pp. 627–33.

Harris, John. 2011. Moral Enhancement and Freedom. *Bioethics* 25: 102–11. [CrossRef] [PubMed]

Hauskeller, Michael. 2016. The Art of Misunderstanding Critics: The Case of Ingmar Persson and Julian Savulescu's Defense of Moral Bioenhancement. *Cambridge Quarterly of Healthcare Ethics* 25: 153–61. [CrossRef] [PubMed]

Hefner, Philip. 1993. *The Human Factor: Evolution, Culture, and Religion*. Minneapolis: Fortress Press.

Holstein, Martha B., Jennifer A. Parks, and Mark Waymack. 2011. *Ethics, Aging, & Society: The Critical Turn*. New York: Springer Publishing Company.

Hughes, James J. 2013. Using Neurotechnologies to Develop Virtues: A Buddhist Approach to Cognitive Enhancement. *Accountability in Research* 20: 24–41. [CrossRef] [PubMed]

Hughes, James J. 2015. How Moral is (Moral) Enhancement? Moral Enhancement Requires Multiple Virtues toward a Posthuman Model of Character Development. *Cambridge Quarterly of Healthcare Ethics* 24: 86–95. [CrossRef] [PubMed]

Hughes, James J. 2017. Ancient Aspirations Meet the Enlightenment. In *Religion and Human Enhancement: Death, Values, and Morality*. Edited by Tracy J. Trothen and Calvin Mercer. Hampshire: Palgrave MacMillan, forthcoming.

Jones, D. Gareth. 2013. Moral Enhancement as a Technological Imperative. *Perspectives on Science and Christian Faith* 65: 187–95.

Kidd, David C., and Emanuele Castano. 2013. Reading Literary Fiction Improves Theory of Mind. *Science* 342: 377–80. [CrossRef] [PubMed]

Kim, Grace Ji-Sun, and Susan M. Shaw. 2017. Intersectional Theology: A Prophetic Call for Change, March 31. Available online: http://www.huffingtonpost.com/entry/intersectional-theology-a-prophetic-call-for-change_us_58dd823de4b0fa4c09598794 (accessed on 6 May 2017).

Kraus, Michael, Paul Piff, and Dacher Keltner. 2011. Social Class as Culture: The Convergence of Resources and Rank in the Social Realm. *Current Directions in Psychological Science* 20: 246–50. [CrossRef]

Kurzweil, Ray. 2005. *The Singularity is Near: When Humans Transcend Biology*. New York: Viking Press.

Labrecque, Corey Andrew. 2015. Morphological Freedom and the Rebellion against Human Bodiliness: Notes from the Roman Catholic Tradition. In *Religion and Transhumanism: The Unknown Future of Human Enhancement*. Edited by Calvin Mercer and Tracy J. Trothen. Westport: Praeger, pp. 303–14.

Lebacqz, Karen. 2012. Empowerment in the Clinical Setting. In *On Moral Medicine: Theological Perspectives in Medical Ethics*, 3rd ed. Edited by M. Theresa Lysaught and Joseph J. Kotva. Grand Rapids: Wm B Eerdmans Publishing Co., pp. 312–19.

Long, Grace D. 1993. *Cumming Long. Passion and Reason–Womenviews of Christian Life*. Louisville: Westminster/John Knox Press.

Marcuse, Herbert. 1964. *One Dimensional Man: Studies in the Ideology of Advanced Industrial Society*. Boston: Beacon Press.

Migliore, Daniel. 2004. *Faith Seeking Understanding—An Introduction to Christian Theology*, 2nd ed. Grand Rapids: Wm. B. Eerdmans Publishing Co.

Moritz, Joshua M. 2011. Evolution, the End of Human Uniqueness, and the Election of the Imago Dei. *Theology and Science* 9: 307–39. [CrossRef]

Perkins, Christine, Richard Egan, Rebecca Llewellyn, and Bronwen Peterken. 2015. Still Living, Loving, and Laughing: Spiritual Life in the Dementia Unit. *Journal of Religion, Spirituality & Aging* 27: 270–87.

Persson, Ingmar, and Julian Savulescu. 2008. The Perils of Cognitive Enhancement and the Urgent Imperative to Enhance the Moral Character of Humanity. *Journal of Applied Philosophy* 25: 162–77. [CrossRef]

Persson, Ingmar, and Julian Savulescu. 2012. *Unfit for the Future: The Need for Moral Bioenhancement*. Oxford: Oxford University Press.

Persson, Ingmar, and Julian Savulescu. 2015. Summary of Unfit for the Future. *Journal of Medical Ethics* 41: 338–39. [CrossRef] [PubMed]

Persson, Ingmar, and Julian Savulescu. 2015. Reply to Commentators on Unfit for the Future. *Journal of Medical Ethics* 41: 348–52. [CrossRef] [PubMed]

Piff, Paul, Daniel M. Stancato, Stephane Cote, Rodolfo Mendoza-Denton, and Dacher Keltner. 2012. Higher Social Class Predicts Increased Unethical Behavior. *Psychological and Cognitive Sciences* 109: 4086–91. [CrossRef] [PubMed]

Piore, Adam. 2015. A Shocking Way to Fix the Brain. *MIT Technology Review*. Available online: https://www.technologyreview.com/s/542176/a-shocking-way-to-fix-the-brain/ (accessed on 3 February 2017).

Ryan, Ellen B., Lori Schindel Martin, and Amanda Beaman. 2005. Communication Strategies to Promote Spiritual Well-Being among People with Dementia. *The Journal of Pastoral Care & Counseling* 59: 43–55.

Saiving, Valerie. 1960. The Human Situation: A Feminine View. *Journal of Religion* 40: 100–12.

Saslow, Laura Rose, Oliver P. John, Paul K. Piff, Robb Willer, Esther Wong, Emily A. Impett, Aleksandr Kogan, Olga Antonenko, Katharine Clark, Matthew Feinberg, and et al. 2013. The Social Significance of Spirituality: New Perspectives on the Compassion–Altruism Relationship. *Psychology of Religion and Spirituality* 5: 201–18. [CrossRef]

Sherwin, Susan. 2012. A Relational Approach to Autonomy in Health Care. In *Health Care Ethics in Canada*, 3rd ed. Edited by Francoise Baylis, Jocelyn Downie, Barry Hoffmaster and Susan Sherwin. Toronto: Nelson, pp. 242–57.

Swinton, John. 2014. What the Body Remembers: Theological Reflections on Dementia. *Journal of Religion, Spirituality & Aging* 26: 160–72.

Tennison, Michael N. 2012. Moral Transhumanism: The Next Step. *Journal of Medicine and Philosophy* 37: 405–16. [CrossRef] [PubMed]

Trothen, Tracy J. 2015. *Winning the Race? Religion, Hope, and Reshaping the Sport Enhancement Debate*. Sport and Religion Series; Macon: Mercer University Press.

Trothen, Tracy J. 2016. Engaging the Borders: Empathy, Teaching Religious Studies, and Pre-Professional Fields. *Teaching Theology and Religion* 19: 245–63. [CrossRef]

Vanlaere, Linus, Madeleine Timmerman, Marleen Stevens, and Chris Gastmans. 2012. An Explorative Study of Experiences of Healthcare Providers Posing as Simulated Care Receivers in a 'Care-Ethical' Lab. *Nursing Ethics* 19: 68–79. [CrossRef] [PubMed]

![religions logo] *religions*

MDPI

Article
Awe and Artifacts: Religious and Scientific Endeavor

Ionut Untea

School of Humanities, Department of Philosophy and Science, Wenke Building A, Jiulonghu Campus, Southeast University, Nanjing 211189, China; untea_ionut@126.com or 108109055@seu.edu.cn

Academic Editor: Noreen Herzfeld
Received: 4 February 2017; Accepted: 30 April 2017; Published: 8 May 2017

Abstract: The article takes as its point of departure the reflections of Henry Adams and Jacques Ellul on the possible gradual replacement of objects used in religious worship with objects used in technological worship, and advances the hypothesis that such a substitution is unlikely. Using information from psychology, history of religions, and history of science, the perspective proposed is that of a parallel historical analogous development of both religious and scientific attitudes of awe by the use of artifacts carrying two functions: firstly, to coagulate social participation around questions dealing with humanity's destiny and interpersonal relationships across communities, and secondly to offer cultural coherence through a communal sense of social stability, comfort, and security. I argue that, though animated by attitudes of awe ("awefull"), both leading scientists and religious founders have encountered the difficulty in representing and introducing this awe to the large public via "awesome" artifacts. The failure to represent coherently the initial awe via artifacts may give rise to "anomalous awefullness": intolerance, persecutions, global conflicts.

Keywords: scientific and religious awe; the sacred; hierophany; icons and scientific images

1. Introduction

Paris World Fair 1900: *Palais des Machines*. Among the major attractions: huge dynamos generating electricity. The quiet spectacle attracts hundreds of men and women staring with a sense of awe at the amazing technology. The reactions on their faces are quietly observed by the American historian and journalist Henry Adams. These reactions are not new: Adams remembers having seen similar attitudes previously on the faces of the pilgrims frequenting the shrines of the Virgin Mary throughout Europe. This leads him to the expectation that the "cult of the dynamo" might one day supersede the "cult of the Virgin" (Götz 2001, p. 9). About ninety years later, a similar perspective is proposed by the French philosopher Jacques Ellul, who observes the "sacred awe that we experience face to face with nuclear fission" and the "religious complex" that strikes the human being when faced with items such as "television, computers, bikes, and rockets". In his opinion, the advent of the modern era has not radically changed the ways we interact with our environment, but has rather changed the environment itself. In this case, the modern environment, far from being the result of the "supposed dedivinisation of the world", becomes instead "a fictional world in which our religious sense incarnates itself" in physical objects that are no longer natural, but are still considered worthy of adoration if used with "joy and fear" (Ellul 1990, p. 121).

The following discussion is intended to argue, contrary to the views of Adams and Ellul, that there are no reasons to conceive of an actual replacement of religious objects with technological objects. As I will argue, there has been, at least in the Western mind, a perennial parallel cultivation of scientific awe on the one hand and religious awe on the other, since the awe of ancient man of science for scientific enquiry is similar to the awe of the contemporary scientist when making an unexpected discovery, and since the awe animating the religious founder or prophet still corresponds to the mystical experience of contemporary famous or secluded religious members, irrespective of the degree of development of science and technology. Although the awe of the scientist is in a way analogous to the awe of the religious founder, the two kinds of awe should not be interpreted as interchangeable. In this article I focus on the similarities of these two kinds of awe, but I do not intend to argue that they are identical, an opinion which will rather resonate with Adams's and Ellul's argument that, since they are almost identical, awe for scientific artifacts might someday replace the awe for religious artifacts. The opinions of Adams and Ellul are essential in bringing more attention to the role played by both religious and scientific artifacts in the human effort to attain or to make present the kind of awe a member of either a religious or a scientific community aspires to. Both scientific and religious artifacts have an undeniable, indeed central, role in promoting awe. In this paper I distance myself from Adams and Ellul by considering that, if the idea of a replacement should be admitted, it will not be a replacement of religious with scientific artifacts. As I will argue, since these phenomena (awe in religion and awe in science) reflect parallel historical developments, a replacement may occur separately within each field: the initial feelings of awe of the scientist when making a discovery (the awefull event), feelings that the scientist tries to make available to a wider audience, may be superseded by a qualitatively less powerful awe for technologically sophisticated items, in the same ways that the initial feelings of awe of the prophet in front of a revelatory (awefull) event may be superseded by the awe of the people in front of the majestic tokens of human skill intended initially to attract social participation around feelings similar to those experienced by the prophet.

In the first two parts of this article, I integrate elements from recent findings in psychology dedicated to the study of awe as a psychological phenomenon, from the theoretical view on the concept of the "sacred" developed by Rudolf Otto and Mircea Eliade, and from examples mainly from the history of the Judeo-Christian tradition, in order to argue that, since the ancient developments of the western scientific and religious mind, human beings have been animated by a feeling of both fear and fascination in front of extraordinary phenomena, a feeling that I characterize by the term "awefullness". It is this awefullness that constitutes the source of the endeavor that prompts both prophet and scientist to advance further in the understanding of the mystery of the world, and to view their breakthrough discoveries as experiences entitling them to a special vocation to make their discovery known as widely as possible, ideally to the whole of mankind.

In the third part I will show that there has been a certain parallel tension inherited within both religious or scientific artifacts due to their ambiguous status as both vehicles of induced awe and instruments of wellbeing. I argue that these artifacts are meant to be "awesome" in the sense that their function is to reconcile the ideals and values of communion with the mystery of existence and community among social members with the ideals and values of practical applicability aiming at strengthening social cohesion in everyday interactions, and generating social stability and a sense of social order and hierarchy. In the fourth part I argue that, given the human feeling of pride, together with the passion for myth and the marvelous shape of religious or technological items, the practical role of scientific or religious artifacts tends to disconnect individuals and societies from the pursuit of higher goals, having sprung from the original "awefull" experience of either the prophet or the scientist. Given the fact that human awe can be induced, the use of artifacts may also be intentionally manipulated in order to induce in human beings a special kind of awe, no less awefull than the original founding awe in science or religion, but which emphasizes only selected aspects of the original *mysterium tremendum et fascinans*. I call this kind of awe "anomalous", as it does not cultivate the harmonious mixture of a wish for knowledge and a tremendous respect for the mystery of existence, and so may easily engender social and political unrest.

2. The Founding Awefull Event

The attention given in psychology to the human reaction usually described as awe is very recent. The 2016 *Encyclopedia of Mental Health* defines awe as a "self-transcendent emotion" which "sits in the upper reaches of pleasure and on the boundary of fear", and admits that the more extensive studies focusing on awe as a psychological attitude have been published after 2003 and have only made visible "the tip of the iceberg" of this essentially human manifestation (Zhang and Keltner 2016, pp. 131, 134). Nevertheless, some of the studies reviewed have emphasized at least three points that I find important for the development of my argument.

Firstly, J. W. Zhang and D. Keltner (Zhang and Keltner 2016, p. 131) argue that awe is not only restricted to psychological manifestations by the human beings in the face of religious events, but can also be triggered by other elements, such as grandiose natural landscapes, powerful leaders, and cognitive elicitors. Secondly, as suggested in the short definition, the essential characteristics of awe are to include both positive (fascination, pleasure) and negative reactions (fear). This corresponds with Rudolf Otto's definition of the sacred as *mysterium tremendum et fascinans*, a phenomenon that triggers human awe, a feeling that makes the person tremble, but nevertheless brings them closer to the extraordinary event (Otto 1958, p. 140). Thirdly, the *Encyclopedia* mentions the findings of two recent surveys which show that awe is a feeling that may either arise spontaneously, or may be artificially induced during psychological experiments via specific tasks or visual content. The first survey, by V. Griskevicious, M. N. Shiota, and S. L. Neufeld (2010) showed that people induced to feel awe were more able to process information-rich stimuli, and the second survey, published in 2012, and led by J. Berge and K. L. Milkman, has found that the feeling of awe stimulates curiosity and interest (Zhang and Keltner 2016, p. 132). This is again compatible with Otto's view on the fascinating force of the sacred event on human psychology.

Here I would like to place more emphasis on the third point revealed by these recent psychological surveys: besides arriving at a definition of secular awe that is highly compatible with the classic description of the phenomenon of the sacred, recent findings in psychology also show that awe can be induced. I argue that this has also been the case with sacred awe throughout the history of religion and science. It can generally be asserted that virtually all founders of great religions have intended to induce in their fellows the kind of awe they themselves experienced during an unexpected encounter with the sacred. The historian of religions Mircea Eliade emphasizes that the response of Jacob, after experiencing awe in his dream at Haran at the sight of a supernatural ladder ascending into heaven, was twofold: firstly, to utter the words "How dreadful is this place...", and secondly, to set up a monument consecrating the spot as special. Eliade sees in the gesture of the Patriarch a merely symbolic act, since the place had been consecrated not by the human action, but by the very phenomenon of theophany, which opens this space "above", making it thus a "point of passage from one mode of being to another" (Eliade 1959, p. 26). Nevertheless, the very act of consecration both by words and deeds functions as a sign which, although highly symbolic, encourages subsequent searches for renewed contact with the divine, either personal, or collective: "He called the place Beth-el, that is, house of God (Genesis, 28, 12–19)" (Eliade 1959). A human being, in themselves incapable of directly consecrating the place or instituting a gate toward a new dimension, but merely of acknowledging such theophany, can only re-present the experienced awe to themself and to others through words and actions. It is these words and actions that have an impact on the human community (in this case, the followers), since the original awefull event has been revealed only to the one experiencing it. By following the path and reaching the place or situation indicated by the words and actions of the person having had the original theophany, others may hope to attain similar results, although this time not by accident or chance.

3. The Human Representational Effort of the Awefull in Science and Religion

The recent history of science abounds in examples of accomplished scientists having experienced a feeling of awe at the unexpected discoveries unfolding in front of their eyes. To give a few examples, one may consider the awe felt by Ernest Rutherford at the discovery of alpha particles; Arthur Eddington's amazement at the deflection of light by the sun's gravitational field; Karl Popper's repeated use of the term "miracle" while speaking about human evolution; Stephen Hawking's prediction of black hole radiation inviting him to meditate about the hidden realities of the universe

(Stanesby 1988, pp. 101, 128); Francis Collins's comparison of the human genome's chemical structure with a book of human nature that was, until the year 2000, known only to God (Smith 2005, p. 10); Fritjof Capra's comparison of the "cosmic dance of energy", or the "dance of subatomic matter" with "the Dance of Shiva, the Lord of Dancers worshipped by the Hindus" (Capra 1975, pp. 11, 245); or Albert Einstein's appreciation that "the scientist is activated by a wonder and awe before the mysterious comprehensibility of the universe which is yet finally beyond his grasp" (Torrance 2002, p. 31). This phenomenon is in fact not a discontinuity in the history of science, since scientists in the past seem to have felt similar attitudes in the face of the majestic spectacle of physical nature. According to John Hedley Brooke, the attitude of Johannes Kepler toward the universe seems to have evolved from aesthetic to reverential awe, and of course the metaphor of nature as a book known clearly only to God, but nevertheless accessible to human mind, seems to have captivated Kepler as well as Galileo, Newton, and Francis Bacon (Brooke 2005, p. 168). This kind of awe can even be traced back to ancient times, where, Charles Freeman informs us, "despite his achievements as a scientist, Ptolemy remained in awe of the universe" (Freeman 2005, p. 67).

For all these scientists the fact of having unexpected access to previously unknown aspects of the laws of physics does not stop them in their tracks as a result of fearful awe, but rather their fascination acts as an impulse to curiosity and interest and as an encouragement to continue their research and make their results widely known. As Elaine Howard Ecklund puts it, the awe felt by scientists propels them toward a different kind of "engaged spirituality" that feeds back into the work they undertake as scientists (Ecklund 2010, pp. 67–68). This is similar with the prophets' or religious founders' commitment to disseminating the message of the divine being as widely as possible, being fully convinced of the far reaching positive consequences of the fact that they have made contact with previously unknown dimensions of existence. The great prophets are often depicted in the Judeo-Christian tradition as trying to escape their calling by God, but eventually accepting the task and continuing to spread the word of the revelation they witnessed until the final days of their lives, which ended usually in martyrdom (Ronald 1998, pp. 98, 105, 150). Scientists, depicted by Ecklund as "spiritual entrepreneurs", have a similar role to that of the prophets, as they "would not be motivated only by self-interest (how to make more money or achieve personal success)" (Ecklund 2010).

In spite of some contemporary views, like those of Richard Dawkins, that overtly minimize, or plainly misread the positive impact of the "awe factor" on the followers of a prophet or religious founder in comparison with the social and intellectual impact of the awe felt by the scientists (Dawkins 1993, p. 243), I argue that both scientists and prophets have spent their lives in a spirit of openheartedness, being always convinced that, after witnessing an awefull event, they have a duty to keep a record, describe their encounter, formulate in words their insight into the unknown, and even attempt at establishing or building material means to commemorate or replicate the context of the event. Inspired by Dawkins, one might reply that on this point science differs widely from religion in the fact that scientists, unlike prophets, after having lived a tremendous experience, try to look for identifiable data and present them to the critical examination of other scientists from their own community (Dawkins 1993). On this subject I would like to restate Ian Barbour's argument that "there simply is no theory-free observational language" (Barbour 1997, p. 108). Nonetheless, I believe this aspect still needs more clarification. Giving some examples from the early history of the Christian Church, I will now shift my emphasis towards the conviction of religious founders that what they were presenting as the facts of their experience had, in their time, the value of data destined to be integrated into a larger theoretical framework already accepted by their community.

First of all, it appears that the biblical writers had been highly selective in their efforts to place at the core of the Christian teaching the idea of the profound impact of Jesus's earthly existence on physical nature by miraculous events like incarnation, changing water into wine, the Transfiguration, walking on water, feeding the multitude with only a few pieces of bread and fish, and of course his Resurrection and Ascension into heaven with his transfigured body. Subsequently, up until the time of the first Ecumenical Council, it had become clear to the representatives of the Christian communities which books, out of the many that were circulating, had been retained as canonical (Lindberg 2006, p. 15). This indicates a dominant willingness of the Church doctors to establish a corpus of books that would contain an acquired set of data extracted from the witnesses of Jesus's life or from those having witnessed special revelatory events, by what today might be called an endeavor aimed at being as critical as the times would allow. Secondly, Christians had been taught by the Apostle Paul about the imperfect knowledge, communicated via human-made channels, about the current and future immersion of the physical world into the transcendent reality: "For now we see through a glass, darkly; but then face to face: now I know in part; but then shall I know even as also I am known" (1 Cor. 13: 12). That is why Paul warns those taking upon them the responsibility of becoming the experts of Christian faith: "Let a man so account of us, as of the ministers of Christ, and stewards of the mysteries of God" (1 Cor. 4:1). Thirdly, the drafters of the Nicene-Constantinopolitan creed (381) took a special approach to Christian tradition by introducing terms like *ousia*, *homoousios* and *hypostasis* which could not be found in the Scriptures (Freeman 2005, p. 179). These insertions may rather be seen as both an effort to extend the *logos*, human theoretical reasoning, at the expense of *mythos*, into the divine mystery, and as an attempt to give an innovative aspect to the tradition, in order to keep it alive, dynamic, and open to the integration of new data upon acceptance by the widest possible number of "stewards" of the divine mysteries.

This introduction of a critical and innovative spirit into the tradition sheds light on the argument I am developing about the similar religious and scientific attitudes toward an awefull experience. One of the practical advancements of this critical and innovatory spirit was the official proclamation of the veneration of icons on the occasion of the Seventh Ecumenical Council (787). From then on, icons, mosaics and stained glass windows would play a major role in the ambitious Christian project of rendering unitary a Tradition that contained many largely contrasting views about the mystery of God and its relationship with the mystery of the world. The icons were thus not meant as simple visual interpretations of myths, but their official recognition may be regarded as an attempt at rendering visible, via highly symbolical means, a reality beyond the reach of most of humanity. Against iconoclasm, the supporters of icons faced the challenge of producing concrete images of what had only been presupposed by human reason to be the reality, after analysis (by reason and faith) of the kind of data received from the divine being via revelatory channels: the awe experienced by Moses and the prophets; by Paul, who claimed to have travelled to the third heaven (2 Cor. 12:2); by all those who witnessed Jesus's miraculous actions upon the physical world; and by the saints of the history of the Universal Church.

The challenge of this effort was not only mythical, but also cosmological. Contemporary poet Tracy K. Smith, whose father worked on the Hubble telescope for many years, recounts in her poem *My God, it's Full of Stars* her awe at the sight of the first pictures composed correctly at the second attempt, after the telescope's optics had been corrected: "We saw to the edge of all there is—So brutal and alive it seemed to comprehend us back." (Smith 2011, p. 12). Imagine a similar response from somebody entering the Hagia Sophia for the first time and being visually stricken by the beauty and the arrangement of the mosaics: in the eyes of both minds, several centuries apart, grandiose representations of the universe generate similar kinds of feelings. Christian religious art can thus be seen as a prefiguration of the technological ambition of the Western mind to pierce the mystery of the world by a rational quest for meaning and knowledge of reality.

By the end of the twentieth-century, as Joseph C. Pitt writes, the technological infrastructure behind the awe felt by scientists upon the reception of data and images from the Galileo space probe traveling at high speed toward Jupiter, became highly complex: "The machinery, the programming and the capacity for mistakes is enormous. If you add the testing of scientific theories to the problem, and the interaction between the theories and the technological infrastructure, as well as among themselves, there can never again be a simple history of the ideas of science, nor should there be." (Pitt 1995, pp. 11–12). Today science avails itself of powerful new technologies, and in spite of efforts aimed at technical accuracy, scientists still gaze into the deepest layers of the images and data obtained in search of clues about what is still only vaguely known. The proto-technological project of the Judeo-Christian early tradition also appears to have been an immense coordinated global effort (global within the limits of the then-known world) to integrate and harmonize diverse "data" about the cosmic order, the divine action, and the place of humanity in that order. The goal of this joint project involving diverse communities within the Universal Church had thus been to produce a living Tradition open to creative effort in which new data and new forms of human artifacts would contribute to a better picturing of the mystery of the universe that was believed to be structured according to a theandric principle.

4. The Tension between the Two Functions of the Awesome Artifacts of Religion and Science

Overcoming the issue of iconoclasm had represented for the early Christian Church a statement of refusal to remain only in the realm of the mythological. This may seem less obvious for today's minds, where religious art is not necessarily a tool of historical and scientific knowledge. The long and complex communal process of writing, editing, and compiling what would eventually become the canonical source of Christian revealed knowledge culminated in 787 with the official recognition of the human representational effort of the divine being and the theandric universe. By officially accepting icons, the Early Church signaled once again, via a Council presented as Ecumenical, that its concerted effort across the board had always been one that transgressed mere adoration, its ultimate goal being the human cognition of the divine being and of the complexity of the universe as the Creator's work. Nevertheless, if this choice preserved the possibility of human cognitive endeavor in the *mysterium tremendum* of the divinely ordained world, this does not mean that iconoclasm was completely groundless, but that it was simply contrary to the dominant practice and cognitive expectations across the Early Church. What iconoclasm showed to be at stake were the limits of representation.

Judeo-Christian tradition manifests a profound awareness of the limits of the human representation of the divine. The special approach of the Mosaic representation of God's presence was not by the intermediary of some sculpture, but by two tablets bearing God's written words. According to Leonard Shlain, this particular way of representing God's relation to humanity appears as a major achievement in the history of the human technological development, as it stressed the importance of adoration by learning and the use of reason: "A radical new communication technology would so change cultural perceptions that the first people to utilize it would introduce the fundamental features underpinning Western civilization." (Leonard 1999, p. 79). Nevertheless, it seems that, in the immediate aftermath of God's direct revelation at Mount Sinai, the people of Israel manifested more attraction toward a representation of God via a fabulous object (a calf) made entirely of a noble metal, a choice which showed that a representation by letters, as revolutionary as it had been, simply proved unsatisfactory for the appeasement of people's passion for myth and physical form (Exodus 32:4). Several other representations followed, like that of the Ark of the Covenant, which was placed in the Tabernacle, later replaced with Solomon's Temple, which in turn fell prey on several occasions to sacking by political enemies (Magness 2012). This explains why sometimes the prophets urged the people to come to an adoration of God which was beyond representation by material objects and mythically-infused acts, but rather by acts of reason. The Prophet Isaiah claims to have had a vision where God entrusted him with the following message for the people of Israel: "To what purpose is the multitude of your sacrifices unto me? (...) Learn to do well; seek judgment, relieve the oppressed (...). Come now, and let us reason together, saith the Lord" (Isaiah 1:11, 17, 18). Jesus also showed awareness of this difficulty of representation: "God is a Spirit: and they that worship him must worship him in spirit and in truth" (John 4:24). After all, the "house of God" that Jacob talked about during his theophany was not a human-made building, but a natural place elevated to a special status, directly appropriated by God, an act only acknowledged by humans, as Eliade has argued (Eliade 1959). However, this did not deter Judaism and Christianity from representing the houses of God by huge buildings: at the inauguration of the Hagia Sophia, the emperor Justinian is believed to have exclaimed: "O Solomon, I have surpassed thee!" (Whitby 2006, p. 167).

Not only in religion, but also in science there is a perceived difficulty in doing justice, via the right means of representation, to the feelings of awe felt by established scientists. As in religion, a straightforward representation of this kind of awe in a less specialized, universally accessible language, seems less likely to impress people thirsty for the spectacular. Just as the religious community has done with icons, the scientific community presents to the general public images of the mysteries of the universe: planets, galaxies, black holes, as well as neuronal connections, cellular division, the beginning of human life, and so on, the kind of images that generate reverential awe for the amazing complexity of the universe. As Richard Dawkins puts it, "black holes are incomparably more wondrous, more romantic, than anything you read in the pseudoscientific literature, in New Age drivel, in 'the occult', in the Bible. Let's not sell science short" (Dawkins 1993). Even so, people tend to experience more awe looking at the spectacle of CGI displayed in movies about intergalactic superheroes that generally defy the laws of physics (Bell 2006, p. 71). Science nowadays thus has a similar task to the one embraced by the Judeo-Christian tradition: to deal with all the mythical popular misunderstandings of scientific achievements and create an accurate depiction of reality, using for this purpose both words (theories) and high resolution images showing its progress in inspecting either the very big or the very small. The technology is new, but the technological intention is thousands of years old, and it is not the exclusive prerogative of science.

Indeed, technology has always had an important place in the religious representation of the divine. Ignacio Götz argues that the contribution of technology in religion is so important that it may ultimately explain people's awe for religion: "The point is that, from time immemorial, technologies have been connected with the sacred probably because they, or their use, inspired awe among the people, or because its use had to be curtailed or controlled by some early, incipient capitalists: the awe the pyramids inspire is similar to the awe before a Lamborghini that sells for upwards of $100,000" (Götz 2001, p. 10). This view might resonate with the opinions of Henry Adams and Jacques Ellul with which I chose to introduce this article. All three authors tend to take as a point of departure the impression made by the latest technology and to formulate judgments about the role of the initial technology. As I have been arguing, from time immemorial, technology in its rudimentary forms has been the vehicle of religion, not only because of the social intention to disseminate widely the awe felt by privileged persons during theophanies, but also because of the human fascination for knowledge of what has been presented as mysterious and divine. The awe expressed in front of the pyramids is rather of the same nature as the awe expressed in front of medieval cathedrals, or grandiose natural landscapes due to the fact that they give the impression of being miraculous. This is largely different from the awe in front of the latest type of car, or the latest type of mobile phone, or any high-tech gadget, which is rather of the marvelous type. Indeed, what brings them closer is the exclamation: "I have surpassed thee!" In uttering these words, the emperor Justinian, like the Pharaohs of Egypt, inadvertently confused an artifact intended to induce awe for the divine with an item intended to induce the people's awe for his own personality. What the pyramids and the car have in common does not pertain to the feeling of awe, but to the feeling of pride. This explains, at least partly, the current tendency to regard political and social awe, based on pride and envy, as similar to the awe of what have been perceived as religious theophanies in the face of natural or cosmic landscapes, an awe which is based on the equal effect of fearful respect and fascination.

Being partially indebted to the Humean distinction between miraculous and marvelous (Earman 2000, p. 33), I have chosen to indicate by the term "awefull" hierophany, the event triggering both fear and fascination, whereas, in order to better characterize the limits of the artifacts meant to represent the sacred, I will choose the term "awesome", which rather reflects the contemporary amazement when faced with marvelous artifacts. I believe that my use of the term "awesome" can be contextualized within the contemporary tendency to consider all pieces of human technology from all times of equal strength in inducing a sense of sacred awe. I agree with Adams, Ellul, and Götz that all technological advances in human history have provoked great feelings of awe, and that is why I call them awesome. From this point of view, the pyramids, the Jewish temple and the Hagia Sophia have themselves been the fruit of awesome technology for their specific times, and this means they have become awesome. The fact that some of them still survive gives them a special aura, but still does not make them awefull in the absolute sense of the hierophany. From this point of view, we can accept as awefull only the lived experience "in spirit and in truth".

Both religion and science have produced special technologies to reaffirm and make present again the kind of awe that animated both religious founders and established scientists. Religious representatives and scientists have repeatedly attempted to produce representations of this awe which would bring not only a degree of truth to reason, or spirit to feelings, but the right balance between the two. When the people of Israel were thirsty in the desert, and attacked by venomous snakes, Moses devised special devices, either to obtain water in that rocky area, or to heal people by using a material object that itself resembled a snake (Numbers 20:11; 21:9). Although these devices attracted awe for the power that had been invested in Moses by God, their capacity for representation was not sufficient to induce in people an awefull attitude in truth and in spirit, since these artifacts did not impact upon people's consciences as did the general hierophany accomplished by God himself on the Mount Sinai (Exodus 19:18). Only a few days after succeeding in feeding a large number of people in the desert with just a few loaves and fishes, Jesus overtly manifests his disappointment: "You seek me, not because you saw the miracles, but because you did eat of the loaves, and were filled." (John 6:26). This clearly shows the tension, brought about by awesome artifacts and actions, between re-presenting the awefull and the practical social use of the awesome, which eventually becomes so ubiquitous that the sense of wonder is ultimately lost.

In its turn, science has also faced similar problems. The emergence of the radio communication system in the early twentieth-century, stemming from the general scientific effort of the technological application of the late-nineteenth-century discovery of Hertzian waves, gave scientists and ordinary people the feeling of having witnessed something like an awefull event. But at the same time, concomitantly with the awe felt by such a revolutionary technology, there appeared practical problems related to the economic sustainability and to the pecuniary exploitation of such a system of communication (Caselli 2014, p. 268). Today, as the radio became smaller, portable, and ultimately integrated into other communication devices, the kind of awe that animated its initial inventors has been completely forgotten. It does come back from time to time, if the radio comes in special shapes or colors, in order to trigger a limited awe, at least for a short time, as in front of a marvelous artifact. This phenomenon did not appear, for instance, in the case of a particle accelerator which, at the time of its invention in Ernest Rutherford's laboratory could be held in the hand (Brown 1986, p. 73). As time went on, the particle accelerator became ever bigger, eventually surpassing the size of the biggest medieval cathedrals. The fact that the accelerator did not become a commodity partly explains why visitors to CERN in Geneva are still affected by a sense of wonder for the mystery of matter. The emergence of other means of mass communication, like television, computers, and tablets, encouraged people to stand in awe for only a short time, before going on with their usual daily social and economic activities, now increasingly boosted by the new available technologies. Big questions, inviting to awefull attitudes about humanity's existence and relationships, have rather been superseded by questions regarding the shape, appearance and degree of technical performance of the awesome objects. In other words, people around the world, in search of *mythos*, did not "see the miracle" (John 6:26) in the awesome artifacts at their disposal, but rather perceived a marvelous way to make life more comfortable.

5. Religious, Scientific Artifacts and Anomalous Awe

Besides mentioning that the feeling of awe can be induced, recent psychological studies also refer to another two feelings that compete with awe, but never have the sense of humility that awe brings. These feeling are pride and envy (Zhang and Keltner 2016, pp. 131–32). Pride and envy can be discussed as a characteristic of a personal wish or need to compete with others, as in the case of Justinian at the political level, but this also occurs on a smaller scale, as wanting to possess better designed and more technologically advanced gadgets than other people. Pride as a political tool may indeed manipulate the feelings of awe of entire peoples. It has been the case with the personality cult around the world in many cultural and historical contexts. To give just an example, one of the gadgets of Ceauşescu, the first president of Romania, was the *People's House*, the second largest building in the world, second only to the Pentagon. Even so, in spite of the great awe inspired, this monumental architectural complex ultimately proved insufficient in keeping the leader in power. The result was an important historical event, which I mention here because it occupies a special place in the history of technology being used to induce awe: the Romanian Revolution of December 1989 was the first event ever in the history of broadcasting to be covered live by a television. Today the Romanian Television archives contain 400 h of recordings, among which 120 were broadcast live (FIAT/IFTA 2017). In spite of this wide coverage, the historical paradox is that, decades later, people are still asking for the "truth" of what happened back then, and who were the "terrorists" that shot hundreds of innocent civilians, but who simply vanished, never to be found. Some voices believe that the event was not a revolution at all, but a coup (BBC News 2009). The awe of the people was there, the spirit of revolution was also there, but the truth was absent. I call this type of induced feeling by the use of technology, rituals, powerful rhetoric, but without the right balance between the two aspects, *tremendum* and *fascinans*, an anomalous awe.

When visiting a nuclear museum in Oak Ridge, Tennessee, Arthur Molella was surprised to see the exhibits arranged in such a way as to trigger visitors' awe for the unilateral truth of the great power of military technology, making people forget about Hiroshima, Nagasaki and the great risk of total annihilation (Molella 2003, p. 211). This is another example of induced anomalous awe that rather emphasizes the so-called truth of the power of technology and a distorted spirit of patriotism. Commenting in 1952 on his limited involvement in the project leading to the first atomic bombs, Albert Einstein asserts: "I was well aware of the dreadful danger for all mankind, if these experiments would succeed [...] To kill in war time, it seems to me, is in no ways better than common murder" (Einstein 1952). This assertion may still be interpreted as a statement of the scientist's awe in front of the implications of the human capacity to make scientific discoveries with a lasting impact on the fate of the entire humanity. This kind of awe corresponds to the revelatory awe animating both the prophet and the scientist, since it reveals the *mysterium tremendum et fascinans*. The awefull character of the scientist's experience was genuine, since the fascination for knowledge of how the new discoveries of science might be used in military technology was well balanced by the trembling in front of the "dreadful danger for all mankind" in the light of the pacifist spirit, a moral value that humanity has struggled to secure over the course of its history. At the same time, the scientist was aware of the potential anomalous awe that might be generated in the eyes of some peoples by the spectacle of the destruction of others, the complete annihilation of the enemy. Only a few days before his death, Albert Einstein signed the Russel-Einstein manifesto, where he exhorted: "There lies before us, if we choose, continual progress in happiness, knowledge, and wisdom (...) If you can do so, the way lies open to a new Paradise;" (Russel 1955). This is an implicit reiteration of the fact that the artifacts used in both science and religion to induce the experience of awefull or revelatory events, can be intentionally manipulated to trigger anomalous awe. Instead, "if we choose", the awesome technologies should rather be used to achieve "continual progress", which would help bring people closer to each other and closer to a religious or secular epiphany that may move them internally toward the path of their quest for meaning.

6. Conclusions

The ideals of scientists and religious representatives are thus to move peoples, internally in their attitudes and externally in their actions, through the use of the artifacts of religious cultures and technologies, and to bring them closer to feelings of awe in front of the mystery of existence which as yet waits to be unveiled. In spite of such ideals that may encourage participatory democracies all over the world, or may initiate the postmodern renaissance of a new global culture, anomalous awe still moves peoples toward special kinds of communal pride, such as national identity, ethnical or denominational discrimination, pride in being more technologically and culturally advanced than cultures considered peripheral to their own, and sympathy for populist measures of political leaders. The internet age, thanks to social media, represents a landmark in both scientific and religious historical ideals of *mysterium tremendum et fascinans*, as it constitutes itself, as clusters of independent participatory forums of conscience in which political, ethical and social phenomena are debated. This indeed brings humanity to the verge of an emerging global conversational conscience where both the truth or the spirit are pursued in equal measure. Humanity may in fact witness a slow and quiet revolution in coming closer than ever to the religious and scientific ideals of making as many people as ever rejoice, both as individuals and as members of wider communities, the awe of being human and an observer of the universe within and without.

However, the internet age is in danger of repeating the inadvertency of which iconoclasm was aware when criticizing the upholders of the representation of God and the universe by icons. This inadvertency is linked to any human attempt at inducing awefull feelings by artifacts (e.g., temples, pyramids, cathedrals, pieces of technology): a downplaying of awefull feelings in favor of more easily graspable awe for the awesomeness of the artifacts themselves, given their practical impact on the social lives of communities or societies. It should be specified that, if this latter kind of awe resembles a second-level awe, as it is an awe in front of an artifact rather than reflecting the direct experience of the awefull event (e.g., Jacob's vision or Moses's encounter with the unburnt bush), it should not be interpreted automatically as a morally inferior awe. Indeed, this second kind of awe, for the awesomeness of the artifact itself, has been present in almost all cases of human attempts at replicating the means of achieving the experience of the awefull event lived by the prophet (ark of the covenant, Temple, Hagia Sophia), and it is responsible for cultural development around the world. An exception to the general awesome character of the artifact might be the stone used by Jacob to mark the place of his encounter with the supernatural being. It was a simple stone, modeled by nature, in which the only human intervention was its vertical lifting, as a highly symbolic gesture of humanity's witnessing of the direct consecration of the place by the divine. The more the idea of consecration has become culturally embedded, the more the human artifacts aimed at re-presenting the original awe have become complex and "awesome". As I have argued, these artifacts were destined to express both the connection with the supernatural and also social and cultural coherence.

It is not its moral character of this awe for the "awesomeness" of the artifact that makes it appear to be a second-level awe, but its controllable character. The manipulation of the artifacts, either by external authorities (e.g., authoritarian rulers or dictators), or by internal passions (such as competition or pride) of those charged with the handling of those artifacts (e.g., clergy, governments, military), may generate a distortion in the representation of an awe which is different from the original awe. If the political leader's ambition was to reorient the use of religious artifacts (cathedrals, temples or pyramids) from the worship of the divine and the miracle of the cosmic existence towards a cult of his own personality, then the re-created awe achieved by political immixture would be far from making the people approach the awe originally experienced by the prophet. Although this has been achieved many times, this awe is only awe in an anomalous way, as it does not appear as an outcome of a true balance of both truth and spirit. Indeed, history abounds with many cases of political leaders strengthening their already strong rule by means of manipulating religious artifacts or technological achievements in order to use them as a means for religious persecution, confessional dominance, destruction of declared enemies, or enslavement and colonization of peoples of less advanced regions of the world.

In contemporary times, under the influence of ideological nationalism, the truth of the human technological capacity to create a terrifying weapon of mass destruction may be praised at the expense of the moral spirit of universal peace. Likewise, the technology used for the first time in modern history to bring into the homes of millions of people the image of a humbled, once all-powerful leader in Ceaușescu, helped propagate within seconds the spirit of revolution. However this was not enough, since the awe that had been generated was only anomalous in the context of a distorted truth. Today, the contribution of the internet to intensifying human relations, and the emerging new technologies, still remain liable to the same double depreciation of the use of artifacts: firstly, a far stronger emphasis on the awesome aspects of the practical use of technological artifacts at the expense of the awe in the face of the essential questions regarding the contribution of those artifacts to the flourishing of mankind in ever-closer relationships between cultures; and secondly, the exploitation of the awesome toward generating an anomalous awe that overlooks or distorts the truth sought by human knowledge and the moral spirit of the values that have become dominant in communal relations through a long and painful historical process.

The awesome uses of the internet, that could extend to images, signs, or messages downloaded and exchanged in this virtual space, at the expense of the lived communal experience or face-to-face conversations, and the distortion of the fascination for learning more and of respect for other people's ideas, values or actions, may also lead the internet user to be subjected to manipulation toward anomalous awe nourished by individuals or institutions protected by virtual shadowy identities. Fake news, or fabricated contradictory accounts, generated by internet users themselves, by competing political powers or groups interested in implementing their own agendas; hacker attacks aiming at stealing personal data; terrorists posing as martyrs; the overall vulnerability of legal and political institutions using digital systems; the attempts by a number of governments worldwide to impose bans on websites or on users and regulate the content accessed by their citizens; all these highlight the frailty of such communication technologies. In this intricate web of public and private life brought about by the internet and new technologies, science and religion still have a major role to play, a role that goes beyond merely providing better technology and simple information, and beyond a mere hunt for identifying the witches and heretics for this new generation.

Acknowledgments: Supported by "the Fundamental Research Funds for the Central Universities", Southeast University, Nanjing, Jiangsu Province, China.

Conflicts of Interest: The author declares no conflict of interest.

References

Barbour, Ian G. 1997. *Religion and Science: Historical and Contemporary Issues*. New York: HarperCollins.

BBC News. 2009. Daring to question the Romanian Revolution. December 21. Available online: http://news.bbc.co.uk/go/pr/fr/-/2/hi/europe/8417046.stm (accessed on 23 January 2017).

Bell, David. 2006. *Science, Technology and Culture*. Maidenhead: Open University Press.

Brooke, John Hedley. 2005. Darwin, Design, and the Unification of Nature. In *Science, Religion, and the Human Experience*. Edited by James D. Proctor. Oxford: Oxford University Press.

Brown, Handbury. 1986. *The Wisdom of Science: Its Relevance to Culture and Religion*. Cambridge: Cambridge University Press.

Capra, Fritjof. 1975. *The Tao of Physics: An Exploration of the Parallels between Modern Physics and Eastern Mysticism*. Boulder: Shambhala.

Caselli, Daniela. 2014. The Gentle Art of Radio Broadcasting. In *Broadcasting in the Modernist Era*. Edited by Matthew Feldman, Erik Tonning and Henry Mead. London: Bloomsbury Academic, pp. 266–70.

Dawkins, Richard. 1993. The Awe Factor. *Skeptical Inquirer* 17: 242–43.

Earman, John. 2000. *Hume's Abject Failure: The Argument against Miracles*. Oxford: Oxford University Press.

Ecklund, Elaine Howard. 2010. *Science vs. Religion: What Scientists Really Think*. Oxford and New York: Oxford University Press.

Einstein, Albert. 1952. On My Participation in The Atom Bomb Project. Available online: http://www.atomicarchive.com/Docs/Hiroshima/EinsteinResponse.shtml (accessed on 23 January 2017).

Eliade, Mircea. 1959. *The Sacred and the Profane: The Nature of Religion*. Translated by Willard R. Trask. New York: Harcourt.

Ellul, Jacques. 1990. *The Technological Bluff*. Translated by Geoffrey W. Bromiley. Grand Rapids: Eerdmans.

FIAT/IFTA. 2017. SOS the Live Romanian Revolution. Available online: http://fiatifta.org/index.php/save-your-archive/cases/sos-the-live-romanian-revolution/ (accessed on 23 January 2017).

Freeman, Charles. 2005. *The Closing of the Western Mind: The Rise of Faith and the Fall of Reason.* New York: Vintage.

Götz, Ignacio L. 2001. *Technology and the Spirit.* New York: Praeger Publishers.

Shlain, Leonard. 1999. *The Alphabet versus the Goddess, the Conflict between Word and Image.* New York: Penguin Compass.

Lindberg, Carter. 2006. *A Brief History of Christianity.* Malden and Oxford: Blackwell Publishing.

Magness, Jodi. 2012. *The Archeology of the Holy Land: From the Destruction of Solomon's Temple to the Muslim Conquest.* Cambridge: Cambridge University Press.

Molella, Arthur. 2003. Exhibiting Atomic Culture: The View from Oak Ridge. *History and Technology* 19: 211–26. [CrossRef]

Otto, Rudolf. 1958. *The Idea of the Holy.* Translated by John W. Harvey. Oxford: Oxford University Press.

Pitt, Joseph C. 1995. Discovery, Telescopes, and Progress. In *New Directions in the Philosophy of Technology.* Edited by Joseph C. Pitt. Dordrecht: Springer Science & Business Media, pp. 1–16.

Ronald, H. Isaacs. 1998. *Messengers of God: A Jewish Prophets Who's Who.* Jerusalem and Northvale: Jason Aronson Inc.

Russel, Bertrand. 1955. The Russell-Einstein Manifesto. *Student Pugwash USA.* July 9. Available online: http://www.umich.edu/~pugwash/Manifesto.html (accessed on 21 January 2017).

Smith, Gina. 2005. *The Genomics Age: How DNA Technology is Transforming the Way We Live and Who We Are.* New York: AMACOM Books.

Smith, Tracy K. 2011. *Life on Mars: Poems.* Minneapolis: Graywolf Press.

Stanesby, Derek. 1988. *Science, Reason & Religion.* London and New York: Routledge.

Torrance, Thomas F. 2002. *Theological and Natural Science.* Eugene: Wipf and Stock Publishers.

Whitby, Mary. 2006. The St Polyeuktos Epigram (AP 1.10): A Literary Perspective. In *Greek Literature in Late Antiquity: Dynamism, Didacticism, Classicism.* Edited by Scott Fitzgerald Johnson. Aldershot: Ashgate Publishing Company, pp. 159–88.

Zhang, Jiawei, and Dacher Keltner. 2016. Awe and the Natural Environment. In *Encyclopedia of Mental Health*, 2nd ed. Edited by Howard S. Friedman. Oxford: Elsevier Academic Press, pp. 131–34.

MDPI AG

St. Alban-Anlage 66

4052 Basel, Switzerland

Tel. +41 61 683 77 34

Fax +41 61 302 89 18

http://www.mdpi.com

Religions Editorial Office

E-mail: religions@mdpi.com

http://www.mdpi.com/journal/religions